The Handbook of Set Design

Colin Winslow

THE CROWOOD PRESS

First published in 2006 by
The Crowood Press Ltd
Ramsbury, Marlborough
Wiltshire SN8 2HR

www.crowood.com

British Library Cataloguing-in-Publication Data
A catalogue record for this book is available from the British Library.

ISBN 1 86126 813 0
EAN 978 1 86126 813 6

Dedication
For Robin

Illustration Credits
Astonleigh Studio, Odiham.
Dover Books Inc.
J. Alleyne Photography, Edmonton, Canada.
Ellis Bros., Edmonton, Canada.
Fat Chance Productions, for HTV (*The Making of Mother Goose*, directed by Alison Sterling).
Barry Hamilton, Mold, North Wales.
The Sandra Faye Guberman Library, Department of Drama, University of Alberta, Canada.
Rod Staines, Chipping Norton.
The Theatre Museum, London.

All other photographs, drawings and illustrations are by the author or in his collection.
All sets and costumes were designed by the author unless otherwise stated.

Frontispiece: Setting for *The Ends of the Earth* by Morris Panych at the Timms Centre for the Arts in Edmonton, Canada. Lighting by Lee Livingstone. Costumes by David Lovett. Photo: Ellis Bros. Back cover: Nuova Opera's production of *Don Giovanni*, directed by Carol Castel, with costumes by Betty Kolodziej and lighting by Lee Livingstone. Photo: J. Alleyne Photography.

Designed and edited by Focus Publishing,
11a St Botolph's Road,
Sevenoaks
Kent TN13 3AJ

Printed and bound in Singapore by Craft Print International.

CONTENTS

INTRODUCTION

Generally speaking, people go to the theatre to see the performers. Hardly anyone will admit to going to a show to enjoy the scenery. This is why theatre posters produced specifically to attract an audience to a production will print the names of the actors in a large typeface, sometimes even bigger than the title of the show, whereas the set designer is lucky to be mentioned at all. However, it is consoling for a designer to note that, even if a play has been written by the greatest playwright who ever lived and performed by the most talented actors, audiences will always tend to remember what they *see* rather than what they *hear*. For example, anyone who saw *Miss Saigon* can describe the moment when the helicopter descended to the stage, even if he or she cannot remember a single line of the dialogue. In spite of this, they would probably not be able to tell you that the show was designed by John Napier.

The set designer should be encouraged by this, for those of us who work in theatre aim to create a rather bizarre world in which the physical laws of

A picture book set for Beauty and the Beast *at The Theatre, Chipping Norton. Directed by Johnny Worthy. Lighting by Dan Franklin.* Photo: Rod Staines

normal, everyday life become redundant and are often overthrown completely. We skip about from place to place and from time to time, for instance, and our characters rarely behave in the way we might expect in real life. For the length of the show at least we do our best to persuade our audiences to believe in the particular world we have created. However, it is hard for audiences to believe fully in Hamlet, Hedda Gabler or Gary Essendine if we remind them that a team of designers, builders, scene painters and prop makers has laboured for a long time to create the deception. We attempt to conceal the theatre's technical mysteries, so we should not complain when it appears to an audience as if it all happens by some special kind of theatrical magic that it does not fully understand.

There are times however, when, for artistic reasons, we deliberately point out to our audiences that what they are experiencing is really all mere illusion and pretence: We show them the techniques we use; we reveal the sources of our stage lighting; allow them to see the stage hands moving scenery or actors donning costumes and assuming different roles. A great exponent of this technique was, of course, Bertolt Brecht with the Berliner Ensemble, who aimed to 'alienate' his audiences by discarding most of the established stage conventions of his day. Surprisingly, the theatre magic still worked, grabbing us by the throat and often moving us to tears. The abiding memories are still visual: Mother Courage dragging her wagon around the stage, the boxing ring in *Das Kleine Mahagonny* or a glimpse of Helene Veigel standing in the breadline in *Die Tage der Commune*.

We cannot avoid accepting some theatrical conventions: Attempts at innovation often mean merely substituting one convention for another. Sometimes, like Konstantin Stanislavsky at the Moscow Art Theatre, we invent new theatrical conventions in an attempt to construct a convincing representation of real life on stage, and sometimes, like the kabuki theatre of Japan, we use theatrical devices to create a completely non-realistic, stylized world. Whatever we do, however, we cannot create Life itself, only a semblance of it. If we do it well, the audience will readily accept whatever kind of reality we offer, and consequently, the artists who have striven to create that world become an irrelevancy. The designer should accept this with some degree of humility for it is an indication of success.

A note about technical terms

All professions have their own jargon that sometimes seems deliberately calculated to befuddle outsiders, and the theatre is no exception. Some of these expressions have been heard backstage in theatres for many decades, sometimes for centuries, and they have been supplemented by more recent terminology as this has become necessary. It is useful to become familiar with these terms, so no attempt has been made to avoid them here and a glossary has been included at the end of the book.

1 THE DESIGNER'S TASK

It can sometimes be a little difficult to decide exactly what we mean by 'theatre'. It is a word that encompasses such a wide assortment of different forms, from Greek tragedy to strip shows: it includes opera, ballet, Andrew Lloyd Webber, Shakespeare, Strindberg, pantomime, Agatha Christie, musicians and magicians, ventriloquists and funambulists. It can be merely entertaining, or it can provide the most cerebral of human experiences. It can easily move us to laughter or to tears, and on some occasions has literally started riots.

'Theatre' is not merely a building containing a stage: theatre can happen in a barn, a city park, a church or a school gymnasium, in fact, it is hard to think of a location where it could not take place. One of the most exciting pieces of theatre the author has experienced personally was a production of R.C. Sherriff's *Journey's End*, a play set in the trenches of the First World War, and in this instance performed in a suburban living-room lined with sandbags and earth, and with pyrotechnic 'bombs' exploding at the bottom of the garden. The naturalistic acting style permitted by this extreme intimacy created a special kind of electricity impossible to capture on a more conventional stage.

It may help us to define the subject by considering what elements are essential to the creation of theatre. If necessary, we could manage without a script, scenery, costumes, lighting or even

OPPOSITE: **The set designer's work is complete only when combined with other artists, including lighting designers, costume designers and performers. Costume by Roger Schultz. Lighting by Kerem Çetinel.** *Photo: Ellis Bros*

RIGHT: **Richard II** *at the Redgrave Theatre, Farnham. Directed by Graham Watkins. Lighting by Mark Doubleday.** *Photo: Astonleigh Studio, Odiham*

9

a specific place to perform in. The only two absolutely essential elements are performer and audience. Theatre could consist of just one performer playing to an audience of only one. A mother telling a bedtime story to her child creates a basic form of theatre, consisting solely of that essential communication between performer and audience. It is a two-way communication: the performer can change the emotions, outlook, mood and even the opinions of the audience, and, in return, the audience's response affects the performance. The changes may often be small, but they have sometimes been big enough to cause revolutions. Theatre is a dangerous medium. This, of course, is the fundamental difference between theatre and cinema: the cinema audience can never change the performance, and the communication process is one-way only.

Peter Brook begins his formative book *The Empty Space* with, 'I can take any empty space and call it a bare stage. A man walks across this empty space while someone else is watching him, and this is all that is needed for an act of theatre to be engaged.' It appears, therefore, that the element of set design is not by any means essential to the creation of good theatre. Yet this is a book entirely devoted to just that unnecessary element. So what exactly can the set designer contribute? The designer can indicate the geographical location of a scene. The American stage designer Robert Edmond Jones, writing in 1941, said, 'The purpose of a stage setting ... is simply ... to remind the audience of where the actors are supposed to be.' This may be fundamentally true; however, scenery performing this function is a comparatively recent innovation in the lengthy history of the stage. Shakespeare, for

The Edinburgh Military Tattoo on the vast stage at Wolf Trap near Washington, DC as part of the American Bicentennial celebrations in 1976. Directed by Tom Fleming. Lighting by Robert Ornbo.

Dick Whittington sets out to walk to London on the tiny stage of The Theatre at Chipping Norton. Directed by Teddy Green. Lighting by David Norton.

example, did not find it necessary to employ a set designer to show that a scene took place in 'A wood near Athens'. He employed dialogue for this purpose, although since his plays were generally performed on an open-air 'thrust' stage, this could have been for purely practical considerations, for, at the same time, theatrical performances at court were using extremely elaborate, painted scenery and stage machinery inspired by Italian masters.

The designer can also indicate period through his designs. Nowadays we frequently adjust or completely change the period in which classic plays are set in an attempt to make them more 'relevant' to a modern audience, and the set designer can certainly assist in this respect. However, this is more frequently seen as the task of the costume designer, and the set designer may deliberately remove any specific sense of period from his work. Mood and style are always important considerations for the set designer. A play taking place in a peasant cottage, for example, will probably require a completely different type of cottage setting if it is at the cutting edge of contemporary drama than, say, a thriller, a children's fantasy or an intense, psychological think-piece.

If theatre consists of interactive communication between performer and audience, then perhaps the designer's main task is simply to assist in this process, so that the interaction may be as effective as possible. However, the use of the word 'simply' here might be misleading, for often the process is anything but simple. We sometimes need extremely elaborate settings and extravagant scenic devices to cope with the task, but, at other times, we need hardly anything at all. A good production can sometimes make its strongest impact on a virtually empty stage so that the maximum concentration can be focused upon the performances and the ideas expressed in it. There have been notable examples of very successful productions using only minimal settings. Thornton Wilder's *Our Town* is perhaps the best known, but even the triumphantly successful West End production of the musical *Chicago* used a set which merely provided a stepped, bleacher-type unit for the band, with a bare playing area in front of it.

Ideally, whatever style of setting is adopted, it should become so closely integrated with the production as a whole that it is difficult to visualize it being performed in any other set.

11

By a Company of Comedians from
The Theatres at London
at the GEORGE INN This
present Evening will be Presented
THE DEVIL to Pay in HEAVEN
Being the last time of Acting Before
Act Commences,

2 A BRIEF HISTORY OF SET DESIGN

Some form of theatre has been part of life at every period of human existence, probably even before man learned to communicate through the medium of speech. Over the centuries it has played a wide variety of roles, it has been ceremonial, religious, entertaining, didactic, philosophical, psychological, political, pornographic and many other things beside. Significantly, for an art form that many now consider primarily literary by nature, the visual element has always played a role of major importance, for a play is not complete until it has been performed and the written words brought to life by visual imagery, however basic these images may sometimes be.

PRE-HISTORY

Theatre existed long before it became related to drama. In primitive societies the acquisition of a food supply is crucial to survival, and the palaeolithic cave paintings at places such as Lascaux in south-western France, dating from as long ago as 15,000BC, show mainly animals that were hunted for food. Occasionally the paintings include the hunters too. The pictures appear to have had some kind of magical significance, possibly created to bring good fortune in the life and death activity of the hunt.

But the creation of a painting is a relatively

*OPPOSITE: **This engraving of Strolling Actresses in a Barn** by William Hogarth (1738) includes a variety of scenic pieces, props and stage effects, including a classical portico with garlands, tree wings, wave machines, a flying dragon and chariot, and footlight candles set in lumps of clay.*

*RIGHT: **Part of a palaeolithic cave painting at Lascaux in the Vézère Valley, near Montignac, south-western France.** Photo: The Sandra Faye Guberman Library*

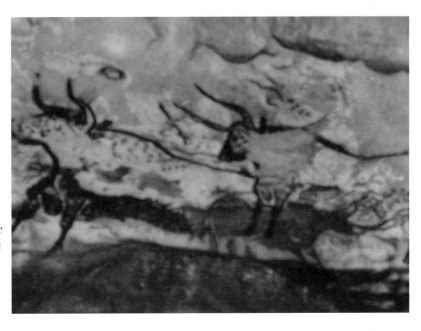

sophisticated artistic activity. Theatre can happen more spontaneously, without the need for paint or drawing materials. It seems likely, therefore, that some form of magical or ceremonial dramatic activity preceded even these ancient paintings. It also seems entirely probable that the thrilling adventure of a hunt would be re-enacted around the cooking-fire at night, incorporating the excitement of drama, the mystique of ceremony and as a way to instruct the youngsters. The discarded animal skin, saved for clothing, could provide a costume for the actor performing the role of the prey and enhancing the visual aspect of the performance. The tribesman who first adjusted a piece of fur around a performer's neck was the first costume designer. However, it would be a long time before the first set designer appeared.

GREECE

The theatre of the spoken word originated in ancient Greece, probably during the sixth century BC, but the plays of dramatists such as Aeschylus, Sophocles, Euripides and Aristophanes, from which the entire western dramatic tradition has developed, date from the fifth and the fourth century BC, the great Golden Age of Athenian drama.

The dramatic performances of this period were rooted in religion and specifically the worship of Dionysus, the god of fertility, wine and ecstasy. Indeed, the stages had an altar (or *thymele*) to Dionysus at the centre of the acting area. The festivities included processions, sacred rites and dramatic presentations, both serious and farcical. These rites bore little semblance to the religious ceremonies of today and inevitably resulted in a literal orgy of intoxicated sexual abandon in which everyone participated in honour of the god.

The theatres were huge, usually built into a natural amphitheatre that could contain the entire population of the locality, for everyone was expected to attend. The ruined remains of many Greek amphitheatres still exist and may be visited to this day. However, nothing at all remains of the theatres of the Golden Age for those were built of wood and have decayed completely. By the time the

stone amphitheatres were built the period of this remarkable flowering in art of all kinds was already in decline.

The stages were constructed around a circular dancing area called the *orkestra*, about 24m (about 78ft) in diameter. Audience seating surrounded the greater part of the *orkestra* and was called the *theatron* or 'seeing place'. (Interestingly, the very name of the building that still houses our drama today refers to 'seeing' rather than 'listening'.) Later theatres had an elevated stage at the rear of the performance area, backed by a structure known as the *skene* that provided an off-stage area but also offered a versatile scenic background to the drama that could suggest a temple, city gates or the entrance to a palace. It is supposed that *periaktoi* (see Chapter 8) were used at the traditional three entrances in the *skene*.

Later stages probably contained some machinery for special effects. We are familiar with the term *deus ex machina*, referring to a mechanical device to lower a god to the stage, and this certainly appears to have been employed in the theatres of ancient Greece. No one really knows exactly what form this machinery took, it may possibly have been some kind of crane situated on or behind the *skene*, although this conjures up an unfortunate image of a hapless actor dangling from a wooden hoist rather than a magical descent from the clouds.

The *ekkyklema* seems to have been an ancient form of what we now refer to as a *truck*. It was a method of revealing a group of actors or of bringing them on to the stage by means of a travelling or pivoting platform. Again, there is little evidence of exactly what it looked like or how it worked; it might simply refer to the opening of doors in the façade of the *skene*.

Rather oddly, to our modern sensibilities, the drama of ancient Greece was competitive. In fact, the first recorded production of a play with dramatic dialogue was at a dramatic contest in Athens in 534BC. It was won by Thespis, a poet, playwright and actor who, although none of his works have survived, is remembered in the term 'thespian', referring to an actor. A surprising number of present-day theatrical traditions date

Theatre at Epidaurus in Greece, designed by Polyclitus the Younger in 350BC.
Photo: The Sandra Faye Guberman Library

back to the theatres of this time: issuing tickets for reserved seats and the habit of clapping performers to show approval, for example. The dramatic convention of the time that forbade violent actions to be shown on the stage, forcing them to be suggested as taking place out of sight behind the *skene*, gives us the word 'obscene' for anything considered unfit to be seen.

ROME

The Romans admired everything Greek; they adopted Greek fashions in clothing, architecture, art and, naturally, in drama. However, as with all the other aspects of Greek culture adopted by the Romans, the drama was 'improved' and adapted to Roman taste. The Romans removed the religious element from dramatic productions and the altar vanished from the *orkestra*, which became semicircular rather than completely round. The Greek *skene* was elaborately developed in the same grandiose architectural style seen in the Roman civic buildings. These freestanding structures were inevitably smaller in plan than the huge Greek amphitheatres but provided much greater opportunities for scenic effects. The theatres were

still open to the sky, but the more solidly constructed architectural background to the stage, now called the *frons scenae*, meant that gods could descend with more grace than from the open spaces above the Greek *skene*, and some painted scenery was probably incorporated, appropriate to the specific performance. As the *frons scenae* was built only about 3m (10ft) from the front edge of the platform, the raised acting area was restricted to a long, narrow strip. It is hardly surprising therefore that almost all Roman plays took place in a street setting of some kind.

The human proportions of actors' bodies must have appeared somewhat inadequate by contrast to these impressive edifices and some efforts were made to correct this by the use of costume devices calculated to make the actors appear bigger: a greatly built up shoe called the *cothurnus* was worn, and a huge, grotesque mask enlarged the performer's head. However, the most refined dramatic performances took place not in the theatres but in the more intimate surroundings of private villas, where long, dramatic narratives became sophisticated after-dinner entertainment. The plays were inevitably Latin translations from the Greek. Indeed, not a single truly Roman play

The Odeum of Herodes Atticus erected in the second century AD. Photo: *The Sandra Faye Guberman Library*

has survived. By contrast, the really popular theatre of ancient Rome took place in the spacious amphitheatres built for sports and spectacle. They were scattered throughout the Roman Empire, built to massive proportions and with as much elaboration and ingenuity as possible. The largest could seat as many as 50,000 spectators on marble seats, protected from the heat of the sun by the *velarium*, a huge awning, ingeniously rigged to be drawn over the spectators. The spectacles that took place in these arenas were state-organized and state-subsidized. There was an official policy of 'bread and circuses' aimed at currying favour for the civic authorities and the emperor-god in particular.

This was the theatre of spectacle, and many of the amphitheatres held elaborate built-in devices for special effects: trapdoors were used, often incorporating machinery to enable performers, animals and large scenic elements to be raised through the floor. Sometimes it was possible to flood the whole arena to stage a realistic sea battle with real ships. The theatre had now become more of a spectator sport than a religious ceremony. With the First Punic War in 264BC life and death gladiatorial combats were introduced, and the popularity of the bloody spectacle of men and women being hacked to death meant that this kind of brutality became incorporated into the dramatic

interludes that traditionally interspersed the gladiatorial combats. Thousands of exotic and ferocious wild animals were imported to contribute to the slaughter by killing and being killed. Mythological scenes incorporating animals were grotesquely re-enacted, with, for instance, a woman strapped to the back of a bull representing Europa and a condemned criminal as Orpheus being literally torn to pieces by bears amid decorative artificial woods.

These bloody thrills were contrasted with interludes by *mimus*, a popular bawdy and lascivious clown, often displaying nudity, gross sexuality and real executions. With the advent of Christianity, this type of performance was considered unacceptable and the performers were excommunicated by the Church in the fifth century.

MEDIEVAL EUROPE

In Britain and Europe also drama had its roots in religious ceremonial. This is hardly surprising, for at that time all public art was seen to have the sole purpose of instructing a generally illiterate population in the ways of Christianity and to warn of the horrors of Damnation. The stories of the Bible were told in painting, sculpture, music, poetry and stained glass. The Mass itself is, quite literally, a form of dramatic presentation: a physical re-enactment of the Last Supper, with performers elaborately vested in heavily symbolic costumes. Further re-enactments took place at special festivals: the Passion of Christ at Easter and the Nativity story at Christmas. Originally intended to be solely didactic, these simple performances took place about the altar, but, as with any dramatic presentation, as actors developed their roles with each annual repetition, the performances became extended and more elaborate, and an element of crude knockabout farce began to intrude. Over the years, the Church realized that these theatrical interludes were developing into something quite different from what was originally intended, and, in the thirteenth century, the clergy were forbidden to take part and dramatic performances were removed from the Sanctuary and permitted only outside the church. However, the performances still took place in the shadow of the church, where the great West Door could form an ecclesiastical background to the action and permit a climactic *coup de théâtre* when the doors could be swung open to reveal a candlelit altar at the far end of the church, suggesting the celestial reward in store for those who followed the Church's teachings and led a good life. Many English cities developed their own lengthy cycles of Mystery Plays that attempted to encompass the entire Biblical story, some of which survive and are still performed. The term 'Mystery' is not used in its modern sense here but derives from the Old English *misteri* meaning a craft or trade, referring to the guilds that mounted the plays, the members performing a section appropriate to their trade. Thus the carpenters might perform the building of Noah's ark and the fishmongers perform the miraculous draft of fishes. It is easy to imagine an element of competition now entering into the performances, encouraging ever more elaborate scenic effects.

Severed from the restrictions of the Church, methods of staging were developed to meet popular demands. More people could see the presentations if the performing area were raised, and the obvious way to do this in a primarily agricultural society was simply to wheel out a flat-topped farm wagon to serve as a stage. The size was limited, of course, but several wagons could be grouped together or used for a logical sequence of scenes, each wagon presenting a different location. The wagons were known as 'pageants' and could be used in a variety of ways – they could be grouped in a circle, with the audience standing in the middle, arranged in a line or semicircle, or even moved from location to location, presenting different scenes from the drama at each stop. The pageants were often elaborately decorated, probably carrying some kind of painted background, and sometimes with a structure permitting angels to be lowered from above, or devils to appear from a yawning 'Hell Mouth'. However, for the first time scenic elements were now introduced to suggest specific locations rather than just for special dramatic effects.

The final scene of the Passion Play at Valenciennes in northern France from an illuminated manuscript of 1547, showing Hell Mouth at stage left. Photo: The Sandra Faye Guberman Library

A further result of separation from the Church's restrictions was the now unhampered development of the cruder and more popular elements of the production, and, since evil has always been more attractive than good, the role of the Devil must have been greatly coveted for its opportunities for broad comic invention, involving bawdy business with his pitchfork and the tossing about of fireworks. The Devil also had the most spectacular pageant wagon, containing Hell itself, and logically appearing at the climactic finale of the presentation.

The Mystery Plays, more popular than ever when divorced from their liturgical context and now sited on movable pageant wagons, were easily transportable, not only from one part of a town to another, but also from city to city. The touring players had arisen. However, these early professional actors must have soon discovered the besetting problem of all street performers even to this day: it is far too easy for an audience to walk away when the hat is sent round to collect contributions. A solution was provided by the wayside inns: these existed to provide overnight accommodation for travellers, together with food, drink and safe stabling for horses. They were usually built around a central courtyard with wide, lockable doors opening to the road. The stables surrounded the yard and accommodation was in rooms above the stables, usually linked by a covered gallery or galleries running all round the yard. This, of course, was an ideal situation for performance: a wagon stage could be erected at one side of the yard, the rooms behind providing an off-stage area and the audience was literally captive; unable to disperse easily when a collection was taken. The players now had a workable theatre where good profits could be made. For the first time, commercialism reared its gilded head.

London, still a Mecca for theatre people, already provided a wide variety of popular entertainments for its inhabitants. The City of London enforced strict regulations to maintain law and order within its walls, but beyond these, south of the river, where the City's laws did not apply, dock workers and disembarking sailors after a lengthy time at sea found that everything they desired was provided for ready cash. Here there were inns, brothels (called 'stews'), gambling, cockfighting and bear baiting. The bear pits were circular, the diameter established by the length of the bear's chain when tethered to a pole at the centre. The seats were stacked in galleries one above the other so that spectators were protected from the beasts but still close enough to enjoy the spectacle.

Travelling players must have immediately recognized the excellent facilities and commercial opportunities provided by these arenas. The stage could be erected to one side, just as in the inn yards, the galleries at the back of the stage could be used for dressing rooms and a backstage area, and the audience could be charged for admission. It is hardly surprising that the first permanent commercial theatre building was constructed along the same lines. It was called 'The Theatre', and built by the actor James Burbage in Shoreditch just outside the City limits in 1576. Very little scenery was used, although there may have been a curtain hung across the galleries at the back of the stage to provide a useful inner-stage area. The programme was considerably more varied than that offered by any theatre today: audiences could enjoy sporting activities such as fencing and athletics, bear baiting and cock fighting, or, on one afternoon, the first production of *Hamlet*.

The very successful theatre in Shoreditch ran into serious trouble when its lease expired in 1597: a new lease was denied by the landlord and so, on a dark winter's night in 1598, as much as possible of The Theatre was dismantled, the timbers transported across the Thames to the south bank and used to build a new theatre just across the street from a playhouse called The Rose. It was to be the largest playhouse built in England to that date and was named The Globe.

THE PLAYHOUSES

The greatest flourishing of English drama took place in London at this period and its audiences were not the aristocracy nor intellectuals, but ordinary Londoners who crossed the river by London Bridge or by ferry to enjoy an afternoon off work. The Globe could cram in an audience of nearly 4,000 and it has been estimated that about one-eighth of the population of London visited the theatre at least once a week.

The public theatres of Shakespeare's day used virtually no representational scenery. In any case, no real scenic illusion was possible on these open-air, 'thrust' stages lit solely by daylight (performances usually began at 2.00pm). If it was necessary to suggest a change of location or a scene taking place in a storm or at night, then the dialogue would make this clear. Hardly any pictures exist showing the structure of stages at this most important period in the development of English drama for this was merely popular entertainment for working people. However, much can be deduced from written sources such as theatre inventories, letters and internal evidence in the plays. The architecture of the playhouse provided a useful range of facilities such as a backstage area, an inner stage and one or two galleries above the stage that could be utilized for Juliet's balcony, the walls of a castle or used as a musicians' gallery. The pillars supporting a roof over the acting area could become the pillars of a royal palace or trees in the Forest of Arden. The audience's imagination supplied the rest, apart from the special effects. Several devices were available to lower gods from the painted ceiling or to enable devils to rise through a trapdoor from of a sub-stage Hell. Props included not only furniture but also some artificial rocks and trees, and trick props for a variety of effects such as a beheading or a disappearing banquet. Much attention was paid to music and sound effects, with musicians in the gallery above the stage, and cannons fired from the roof for battle noises or thunder. The last effect proved disastrous on 29 June 1613, when a spark from a cannon during a performance of *Henry VIII* set fire to the thatched roof and burned the theatre to the ground. It was speedily rebuilt, larger, much improved, more elaborately decorated and with a tiled roof.

It would be satisfactory to be able to show a direct linear development from the Elizabethan playhouses, with their vestigial scenic elements, to the theatres of today, where scenery is accepted as an important part of the theatrical experience.

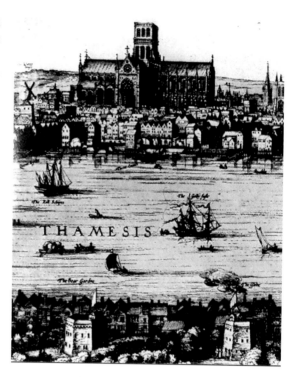

View of London from the south bank of the Thames in 1616 showing the Bear Garden and the Globe Theatre. Photo: The Sandra Faye Guberman Library

However, this is not possible because eventually, in 1642, the long, historical love–hate relationship between the theatre and the Church resulted in the closure of all public playhouses by the Puritans, and the line was abruptly curtailed.

MASQUES AND THE COURT THEATRES

At the same time as the public playhouses on the south bank of the Thames were providing popular entertainment for the masses, the courts and palaces of Europe housed private entertainments of a much more scenically spectacular kind. The trappings of the great hall or long gallery, with windows, panelling, family portraits and domestic ornaments, must have provided an uncomfortably obtrusive background for dramatic performance.

However, aristocratic households could engage an artist to supply paintings to conceal the usual features and offer a pictorial background more suited to the dramatic performance on hand. The painter would use familiar techniques, stretching canvas on wooden frames just as he had done with any other picture. The size would be limited by the dimensions of the doorways, necessitating the use of several paintings set side by side to cover a wide area. It must have taken only a small step to realize that the painted backgrounds could be easily changed by sliding the painted panels to either side by hand, to reveal other painted panels set behind them. The problem of providing off-stage areas from which performers might enter the scene could be solved by setting additional painted panels at the sides of the acting area, masking the ends of the painted background and extending the stage picture forwards, so creating the convention of painted background and wings that we still frequently encounter in some form today.

The early court masques were comparatively simple affairs, designed specifically to honour some important guest and consisted mainly of music and formal dance. However, travellers returning from the Continent brought reports of spectacular entertainments seen at the courts of Italy and France, and in 1604 James I of England, encouraged by his queen Anne of Denmark, engaged the architect and artist Inigo Jones (1573–1652) to devise courtly entertainments to rival those of Europe. In 1605 Ben Jonson, the court poet, collaborated with Jones to produce *The Masque of Blacknesse*, which, replete with wave machines, sea monsters and many magical transformations, brought to England a new and spectacular type of theatrical production such as had never been seen before. Subsequent productions became ever more spectacular and costly, until the unfortunate King James faced near financial ruin.

BAROQUE

Whatever efforts were made in England, it had to be admitted that the Italians led the field in the new illusionist theatre. Here, the drama took second place to scenic effects and the spoken word was almost completely abandoned in favour of operas and ballets that could better exploit the new techniques. Luxurious theatres were built to house the performances, and the 'horseshoe' style of auditorium, with seats in 'boxes' stacked in tiers around the perimeter and decorated in a palatial

A scena per angolo design by Giuseppe Bibiena, bringing a startling new realism to painted perspective scenery. Photo: Dover Books

gilded style, became established as the most suitable form for this type of presentation.

Among the many artists who produced scenery for these lavish Italian theatres, the Bibiena family was most notable for providing a whole dynasty of theatre designers and architects. The dynasty began with Giovanni Maria Galli (1625–65), whose son Fernando (1657–1743) caused a scenic revolution by introducing the *scena per angolo* or 'angled scene' to the stage. Up to this time, all perspective scenery had been dependent upon a single vanishing point to create painted scenes that appeared to recede dramatically straight into the distance, but Fernando used two vanishing points to produce much more realistic views that appeared to recede away from the spectator at an angle to the stage, and in two directions at once. Fernando's brother Francesco (1659–1737), his sons Alessandro (1687–1769), Giuseppe (1696–1757) and Antonio (1697–c.1774), together with Giuseppe's son Carlo (1728–87), all worked as theatre architects and scenery designers and were together responsible for many remarkable theatrical innovations.

THE RESTORATION AND THE ADVENT OF ROMANTICISM

In England, the public theatres had been closed by the Puritanical Commonwealth, and only private theatrical performances were permitted. However, the Restoration of Charles II ushered in a new age of scenic innovation that now included stage lighting. Early indoor performances were lit by candles, in whatever chandeliers happened to be available in the rooms where the performances took place. However, before long these were supplemented by additional lighting directed specifically towards the stage, first by rows of candles and then by wicks floating in containers of oil set along the front edge of the stage, with metal shields hiding the glare from the audience. Candles on stands were also concealed behind wing flats. Scene changes took place in view of the audience, flats sliding along specially placed grooves controlled by an elaborate system of ropes, pulleys, winches and hoists that allowed all the pieces to move simultaneously. The scene changes were viewed as an important part of the entertainment and were carefully designed for maximum effect.

A desire for more realism in stage settings eventually produced a reaction against the baroque style and the fantastically elaborate, painted palaces gave way to a more realistic style of scene, often featuring landscapes with highly ingenious weather effects.

In 1771 the great actor-manager David Garrick, engaged the painter Philip James de Loutherbourg (1740–1810), at great expense, to revolutionize the scenic style at his theatre in Drury Lane in London. De Loutherbourg might be considered to be the first stage designer since he provided coloured renderings and scale models for scene painters, instead of painting the scenery himself, which was normal practice at the time. Under his guidance, the chandeliers were banished and all light sources were hidden. This enabled the effective use of gauzes, cut-cloths and transparencies, with impressive, changeable lighting effects created by the ingenious use of coloured silk filters and various shuttering devices for dimming or brightening the light. Audiences could now delight in plays that included effects such as moonlight, firelight, fogs, mists, lightning and volcanoes. They could also see recognizable views of actual places such as London or the Lake District.

This was the age of the scene painter. Indeed, playbills of the period contained descriptions of each scene in the play, together with the name of the painter who created it. Huge teams of painters were engaged for major productions, and classic plays by dramatists such as Shakespeare were produced with a succession of realistically painted scenes, sometimes so elaborate that the front curtain had to be used to hide the lengthy scene changes, and often special 'carpenter's scenes' or painted 'frontcloth scenes' were used so that the action could continue while an elaborate set was built behind it in the traditional pantomime style still used today.

The painted scenery was much enhanced by the introduction of gas lighting. It was first used to light front of house areas, but in September 1817

This engraving of a scene from **The Maid of the Mill** *by John Inigo Richards in 1765 shows some notable innovations: windows and doors are practical, and there is even an actress sitting at a first floor window; the mill upstage centre has a practical bridge and working mill wheel.*

the Lyceum theatre in London announced that gas lighting was used to light the stage 'with complete success'. The flicker of candlelight gave way to the brighter, but soft, steady and, above all, controllable glow of gaslight. For the first time the auditorium lighting could be lowered during the performance, providing a dramatic focus upon the stage.

Sets were still mainly designed in a basic 'backcloth, cut-cloth and wings' style. Built pieces were often introduced for special scenes, but, no matter how ingenious, scenery was still mostly painted and two-dimensional.

NATURALISM

It was the remarkable and often underrated Madame Vestris (1797–1856) who, with her scene painter Charles Tomkins, was probably responsible for the first 'box set' on the English stage in 1832. She was a singer and actress who, at the age of 16, dressed in tights as the first principal boy in English pantomime, attracted the attention a French dancer named Armand Vestris. They married, but in 1830, deserted by her husband, she became the first British woman to manage a theatre when she took over the Olympic Theatre in London. The wings and backcloth style of scenery that had been in use for so long was not really suitable for the more domestic type of drama that was now being written by a new generation of playwrights. In order to suggest a more realistic room on stage she had the wing flats turned at right angles to the front of the stage to suggest side walls and a framed canvas ceiling lowered on top. Functioning doors and windows were incorporated, and Madame expended a large sum of money buying furniture, carpets, pictures and other dressings, which were usually painted on to the scenery direct. The careful attention she paid to every detail of set and costuming established her as an innovator of taste and refinement, but contributed to her bankruptcy in 1837. She later remarried and took over the management of Covent Garden in 1839. Here she championed the work of the Irish emigré American playwright Dion Boucicault (1822–90), who not only wrote plays concerning important social issues of the day, such as slavery and the plight of the poor, but also strongly influenced scenic design by introducing melodramatic spectacles that became known as 'Sensation Scenes'. The popularity of these scenes pushed designers to the extremes of extravagance in order to stage elaborate scenes of shipwrecks, horse races, balloon journeys and the like, all depicted with as much realism and ingenuity as possible. It is small wonder that Madame Vestris once more found herself bankrupt and her husband in prison. However, they later took over the Lyceum, where even more elaborate productions were mounted, exploiting the adaptability of gas lighting to include startling transparency effects. Yet again, bankruptcy was the unfortunate but inevitable result. Later, in 1871, the Lyceum Theatre became home to the young Henry Irving, whose lavish productions made it London's most prestigious venue for many years.

The last great exponent of the Sensation Scene was the scene painter and designer Bruce Smith, who was so successful in this genre that he became known as 'Sensation' Smith. He devised ever more elaborate scenic effects, until in 1909 he attained the apogee of sensation with the production of *The Whip* at Drury Lane. This play, about a defeated attempt to nobble a racehorse, involved an on-stage horse race run on a treadmill and a train complete with engine, passenger carriages and horse box that was seen to set out from a London station and later to crash spectacularly, the engine turning over in clouds of steam while the racehorse was saved by the hero uncoupling the horse box in the nick of time. However, like the train, the Sensation Scene had reached the end of the line, for by now this type of plot could be enjoyed with a good deal more genuine realism in the cinema. A different type of spectacle was required in the theatre.

THE MODERN AGE

It was not until after the Second World War that theatre programmes began to credit a 'designer'. The scene painters were still the major artistic force in the theatre during the first half of the twentieth century, with the paint shops in the back streets around Covent Garden turning out pictorial wonders under the supervision of artists such as Hawes Craven, William Telbin, Walter Hann,

Sir Henry Irving and Ellen Terry in the vault scene from **Romeo and Juliet** *at the Lyceum Theatre in 1882. Designed and painted by William Teblin.* Photo: The Sandra Faye Guberman Library

23

Gordon and Joseph Harker. However, a new movement began to rebel against scenery that was still basically little more than a painted background to the dramatic action.

Up to the turn of the century, productions were traditionally rehearsed by the stage manager and the scenery was a combination of new pieces commissioned from scene painters and old ones pulled from stock. The stylish productions of the great actor-managers such as Irving, Kean and Beerbohm Tree were the exceptions rather than the rule. However, at the Moscow Art Theatre Konstantin Stanislavsky (1863–1930) brought a fresh approach to the presentation of the new naturalistic dramas by playwrights such as Chekhov and Gorki; but it was the increased flexibility of electric stage lighting developed in the later years of the nineteenth century that enabled one or two remarkable innovators to revolutionize the art of scenic design.

Edward Gordon Craig (1872–1966), the son of Sir Henry Irving's leading lady Ellen Terry and the architect E.W. Godwin, became an actor with Irving's company at the Lyceum Theatre at the age of 16. In 1900 Craig began to direct and design his own productions. His work did not depend upon the skill of scene painters, instead he developed a sculptural approach, designing comparatively

simple sets in which plays could be presented without the encumbrance of lengthy scene changes and in which stage lighting was not merely an adjunct to illuminate scenery and actors but an integral part of the performance. Naturalism played no part in Craig's designs; his work was suggestive rather than a detailed statement. He proposed a new kind of 'total theatre' in which the actor would no longer be merely the servant of the playwright, but, instead, would become part of a completely integrated theatrical experience. In fact, he argued, the ideal actor would be an *Übermarionette* or 'super-puppet'.

The Swiss designer Adolphe Appia (1862–1928) had also seized the new opportunities offered by electric lighting to bring about an original approach to staging the monumental operas of Richard Wagner. Dismayed by Wagner's insistence upon painted realism for his heavily symbolic works at Bayreuth, Appia, like Craig, worked with solid sculptural forms lit by shifting, coloured lighting to bring an epic quality to his settings. Craig and Appia, the two great formative designers their age, independently produced ideas that influence the work of stage designers to this day. They met only once in 1914, at an international exhibition of scene design in Zurich. Craig, embittered by what he perceived as the

The train crashes and the racehorse is rescued in the nick of time in The Whip. *Another triumph for 'Sensation' Smith of Drury Lane. Photo: The Theatre Museum*

Scene design by Edward Gordon Craig.

Design for Gluck's Orfeo ed Euridice *by Adolphe Appia, 1926.*
Photo: The Sandra Faye Guberman Library

general rejection of his work, moved to the south of France in 1929. In 1955, in recognition of his contributions to the theatre, he was made a Companion of Honour but said he could not afford to travel to London to receive the award.

From the early years of the twentieth century to the present day, depending on your point of view, the work of stage designers may be seen as either a hopeless mish-mash of conflicting ideas or an exciting, stimulating mixture incorporating a wide range of styles. Certainly no particular style seems to be predominant. Elegant box sets, such as those designed by J. Hutchinson Scott in the 1950s, can still be found in London's West End, side by side with some of the most innovative examples of modern design. As late as the 1960s the romantic painted scenery of Oliver Messel entranced audiences at the Royal Opera House in Covent Garden, while a few yards away the monumental machines designed by Sean Kenny for shows such as *Oliver!* and *Blitz* were stunning in a completely different way.

The demise of the provincial repertory system, which survived for a good many years mainly by producing reworkings of recent West End successes, means that theatre designers no longer think in terms of box sets and stage flats but extend their imaginations to create settings in an extensive variety of different styles. Theatres such as the Citizen's Theatre in Glasgow, the Library Theatre in Manchester and Stephen Joseph's Theatre-in-the-Round at Scarborough have encouraged designers to rethink their approach to their craft, and theatre design courses in our drama schools and universities encourage innovation, the development of new techniques and the use of new materials.

In recent years, set design has become closely integrated with lighting design and the dividing line between them has become more and more blurred. Indeed, many stage design courses now incorporate set, lighting and costume design, and designers are frequently competent in more than one discipline.

3 THE THEATRE BUILDING

A VISIT BACKSTAGE

Actors sometimes refer to the theatre as the 'fun factory', and some parts of it can, in fact, be compared to a factory. Like a factory, a theatre is a workplace and contains hazards; accidents can easily happen and stringent efforts should always be made to reduce risks. To the uninitiated, a theatre can seem a strange, bewildering place, inhabited by people with peculiar jobs that are not clearly understood, and who speak in a confusing jargon that is often difficult to interpret.

The stage door leads into a world that immediately strikes us as having none of the glamour we would normally associate with a visit to a theatre, and actors' dressing rooms often have more of the qualities of military barracks than retiring rooms for the stars.

The stage, seen under working lights, seems gloomy and dusty, and contains a confusing array of technical equipment. Looking up, we are sometimes surprised to see that, above the stage, is a high tower filled with cables, ropes and metal bars. This is the fly tower, housing the flying system. Scenery and lighting equipment can be attached to the bars and raised or lowered as required. The great height is needed to fly large scenic pieces such as backcloths out of view of the audience. The bars hang on cables or ropes that pass over pulleys in a sturdy framework set high up near the roof called the grid, they pass over more pulleys to one side of the stage where they can be

OPPOSITE: *Between productions, the stage is a dark and gloomy space, waiting to be brought to life by the presence of actors, designers, technicians and audiences.*

operated from a platform called the fly gallery set against a side wall of the stage. Nowadays, these sets of flying lines are usually counterweighted, and another, higher gallery is required to load and remove the heavy weights needed to balance the weight of the scenery or lighting equipment (usually referred to as 'lanterns' or 'luminaires'). Some sets of fly lines are designated specially for lighting, and these are usually raised or lowered by means of winches to avoid the necessity of continually having to adjust counterweights as lanterns are added or removed. The bars mentioned above are often conveniently internally wired to avoid a tangle of drooping cables.

If the stage is well designed there will be a considerable amount of wing space beyond the limits of the proscenium opening and usually out of sight of the audience during a performance, but essential for technicians to carry out their offstage tasks.

The best stage floors are not the beautifully finished, concert-hall type but the kind that is covered with a temporary surface of plywood or hardboard so that it can be painted or textured as required and replaced when it becomes necessary. Sometimes the stage floor contains removable sections called 'traps', and sometimes there is an extension to the front of the stage (an 'apron' or 'forestage') that, in some cases, can be raised or lowered to provide an orchestra pit for musical shows if needed. Rows of small trap doors in the floor at the sides of the stage ('dips') give access to electric sockets.

Most public theatres above a certain seating capacity are legally required to install a special safety curtain to isolate the stage from the auditorium in an emergency. This is not really a curtain at all but a heavy, fireproof wall just behind

27

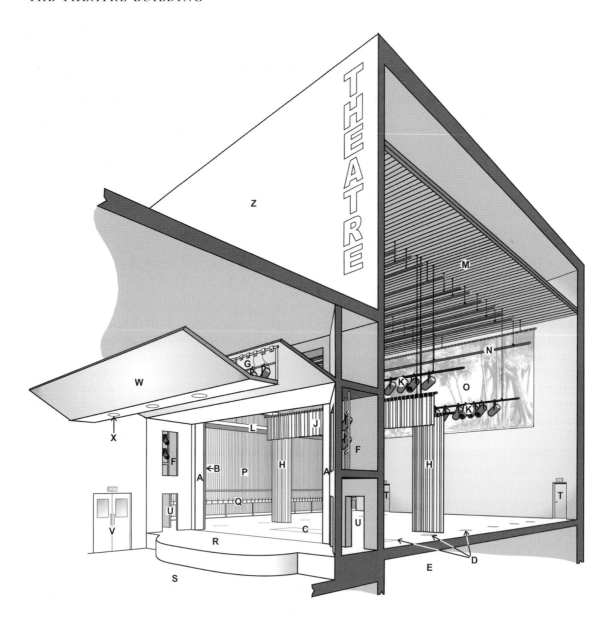

A	Proscenium	K	Lighting bars with lanterns	S	Auditorium (seats omitted)

A   Proscenium
B   Guide for safety curtain
C   Trap
D   Dips
E   Trap room (under stage)
F   Slots with light booms
G   Auditorium lighting position
H   Legs
J   Border

K   Lighting bars with lanterns
L   Fly floor
M   Grid
N   Unused bar
O   Painted backcloth
P   Counterweight operating lines
Q   Pin rail with brakes for flying lines
R   Apron or forestage lift

S   Auditorium (seats omitted)
T   Access doors from dressing rooms
U   Access to forestage
V   Public access doors to auditorium
W   Auditorium ceiling
X   Auditorium light fixtures
Z   Fly tower (exterior)

Typical proscenium stage with fly tower.

the proscenium capable of being rapidly lowered if this becomes necessary. In the event of a fire breaking out, the high fly tower will act as a chimney, converting the whole theatre into a giant fireplace that can increase the danger dramatically. Therefore the safety curtain must always be kept in good working order and nothing must ever be allowed to obstruct it. This is often a source of extreme annoyance to the set designer who would like to extend his set on to the forestage underneath the safety curtain. There are usually some large, normal curtains hanging just behind the safety curtain, always referred to (as are all stage curtains) as 'tabs', an abbreviation of tableaux curtains. The big curtains nearest to the front of the stage and intended for use at the beginning and end of each act are the 'house tabs'.

The stage manager and the lighting and sound operators are usually housed in control rooms at the rear of the auditorium, observing the performance through a glass panel and keeping in touch with the several areas of the stage by means of microphone and headphones ('cans') and a system of coloured cue lights: red for 'stand by' and green for 'go'.

If the theatre is a producing house, that is, one that mounts its own productions instead of

The mysterious world of the fly gallery high above the stage.

importing them from elsewhere, it will usually contain workshops for constructing and painting the scenery and props and a wardrobe department for making and maintaining the costumes. There are probably also some areas intended for storage, but, inevitably, never enough. A storage area where everything is so tightly packed in that it becomes impossible to see what it contains is almost useless.

A well-appointed theatre workshop at the Timms Centre for the Arts in Edmonton, Canada, with the artificially lit paint shop beyond.

TYPES OF STAGE

Theatres exist in a wide variety of configurations, generally classified by the audience's relationship to the performing space. Below are brief descriptions of some of the most frequently encountered forms.

The Proscenium Stage

Still the most popular format, usually comprising a raised platform with the audience all seated at one side, and some form of physical separation in the form of a proscenium or picture frame between the audience and the performing area. Sometimes an apron or forestage juts out through the proscenium into the audience. This type of theatre usually contains some facilities for rigging scenery, stage lighting and effects, ranging from the merely basic to the extremely elaborate. This is the theatre designed for scenic illusion, in which it is easier to control exactly what an audience sees than in any other form. However, the proscenium is both a physical and psychological barrier between performer and audience, emphasizing the two separate worlds they inhabit. This rather alienating sense of separation can sometimes be mitigated by the design of the set.

The Thrust Stage

Here the stage juts out into the auditorium rather like an extended apron. The audience usually sits on three sides of the stage, the other one being occupied by a rear-stage area where there is some possibility for scenic effect. The main advantage is a sense of intimacy caused by stripping away the proscenium barrier, but more than half the audience is generally looking across the stage towards the audience at the opposite side and this can create a sense of disadvantage when compared with the view of those sitting at the front.

Theatre-in-the-Round or Arena Stage

Any form of staging with the audience completely surrounding an acting area of virtually any shape or size. The barrier of the proscenium is removed completely and more intimacy with the audience is possible, but the audience is generally conscious of the audience on the opposite side of the stage and the performer often has difficulty communicating to those parts of the audience seated behind him. No complete scenic illusion is possible here.

The Traverse or Alley Stage

The audience sits at both sides of a longish performing area, with offstage areas at either end that may be used for actors' entrances and for minimal scenic effects. Again, there is a sense of intimacy with the performers, but the same restrictions apply as with theatre-in-the-round and the thrust stage.

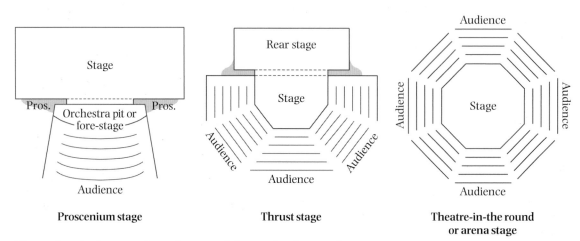

Plans of typical proscenium, thrust and theatre-in-the round or arena stages.

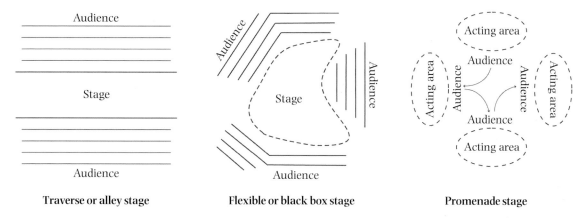

Traverse or alley stage   **Flexible or black box stage**   **Promenade stage**

Plans of typical traverse or alley, flexible or black box and promenade stages.

The Flexible or Black Box Stage

Currently popular in schools and colleges because of its versatility, this is actually an empty space in which the audience's and the performance areas may be configured to suit the needs of each individual production. In it simplest form it may be merely an empty room, but this type of stage may be fully equipped with versatile seating units, counterweighted flying facilities and complete lighting and sound systems, making it an excellent type of venue for experimental staging.

Promenade Staging

Here the audience moves physically from one area to another during the performance, often in the open air. This form can be effective when used with skill, but not all plays lend themselves to this type of staging. Its effectiveness generally depends more upon the skill of the director than that of the set designer.

Site-specific Staging

This is theatre performed in some specifically selected space other than a theatre. It may be virtually anywhere: a derelict warehouse, a disused factory, a wood or a railway station. It is a form of theatre for which it is impossible to formulate any rules. It may contain no scenic element whatsoever or it may contain a vast amount of elaborate scenic and lighting effects.

Plays have been performed in barns, tents, on lakes, in telephone boxes and in domestic kitchens. There is no perfect stage. It will be seen that any form of staging has both advantages and disadvantages, and the designer need to analyse these carefully to decide upon the most appropriate approach to the work in hand.

STAGE DIRECTIONS

These are now used in a more or less standardized format. In Britain and North America *stage right* (SR) and *stage left* (SL) are always used from an actor's point of view as he faces the audience.

Old stages were usually built with a raked floor

	USR (Up-stage right)	USC (Up-stage centre)	USL (Up-stage left)	
Off-stage right	RC (Right centre)	C (Centre)	LC (Left centre)	Off-stage left
	DSR (Down-stage right)	DSC (Down-stage centre)	DSL (Down-stage left)	

Pros.   Pros.

Stage directions.

to aid perspective scenery. It was higher at the back than the front. Thus *upstage* (US) is used to indicate the back of the stage and *downstage* (DS) indicates the part nearer to the audience – so any part of the stage may be indicated by the use of a combination of two or three letters (see diagram). These terms are in general use, in both their spoken and written form.

For black box or arena stages modified compass directions are usually adopted. In these cases *North* should be indicated on the stage plan as on a conventional map.

SIGHTLINES

A sightline is simply a line of vision towards the stage from a particular location in the auditorium. Whatever form of staging is to be employed the designer should always make a careful study of the sightlines in that specific situation, that is, simply consider which part of the acting area is in full view of the entire audience and which parts of that area are most favourable to the performer. They

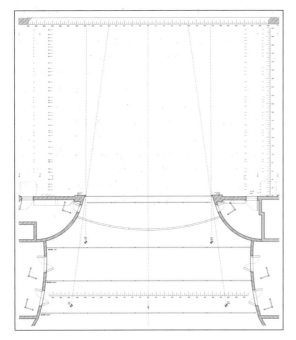

Plan of stage and auditorium.

will vary considerably from stage to stage, even on stages of approximately the same size and format. This often causes problems when a show is to tour to several different venues; it is not just a question of 'Will the scenery fit?'

It is useful to visit the actual stage where the performance incorporating your design is to take place, and you should always try to do this before starting work. Stand on the stage and face the auditorium in a position where you can see every seat in the house with the minimum amount of head movement. This is a 'point of power', that is, a position where every member of the audience can clearly see the actor's face. This special place will be somewhere near the front of the stage in a conventional theatre, but probably not right at the front. In a conference, or even at an informal meeting, the participants will be able to communicate with far greater ease if the seating arrangement is sympathetic, and this means ease of eye contact even more than physical closeness. The same situation occurs in the actor–audience relationship. Note that any stage usually has areas from which it is remarkably inappropriate to communicate with the audience, such as near the back wall or at the extreme sides. This does not mean that these are wasted areas. We shall see later that, without them, the designer's task becomes a much more difficult one. Do not feel that your setting has to occupy every square centimetre of a large stage. As far as possible, concentrate the action of the play on that part of the stage where an actor can relate to his audience with the greatest ease.

Every theatre should have scale drawings of the stage and auditorium available and you should make sure that you have copies of these. A detailed and accurate stage plan is essential, but a stage section and elevation are also usually needed. Technical drawings will be discussed in much more detail in a later chapter, but, for now, let us use a stage plan to examine the important question of sightlines.

The plan should include the entire stage area and at least the front part of the auditorium, showing the positions of the end seats of the front row, and the positions of the worst seats in the house. Note that the worst seats may well be at the ends of the front row or they may be end seats of a row much further back in the auditorium. Imagine that you are sitting in one of these seats and work out how much of the stage you will be able to see, and what would prevent your seeing the other parts (usually, the proscenium). You will find that anyone in an end seat of the front row will be able to see a large part of the opposite side of the stage, but the proscenium will prevent his seeing much of the stage at the side on which he is sitting. We can draw then lines on the plan indicating the limits of his field of vision; these are referred to as the sightlines.

You will see from the diagram that a spectator sitting at the right-hand end of the front row can see everything between sightlines A–A, whereas the spectator at the other end of the front row can see everything between sightlines B–B. Sightlines are also indicated from the worst seats in the house (C–C and D–D). Thus the shaded area is the only part of the stage that can be seen from *every* seat in the house. This does not mean that everything on stage should be situated only in the area between the sightlines, but any feature that must be clearly seen by every member of the audience, for example, the doors through which Oedipus is to enter after blinding himself or Richard III's throne, may be set in this area only, and other scenic elements must be organized to accommodate this.

The method of determining sightlines described above refers to a typical proscenium stage, but the sightlines can be worked out in a similar fashion for almost any type of stage, with or without a proscenium. In some flexible forms of staging the designer may be presented with the opportunity to design the particular arrangement of audience

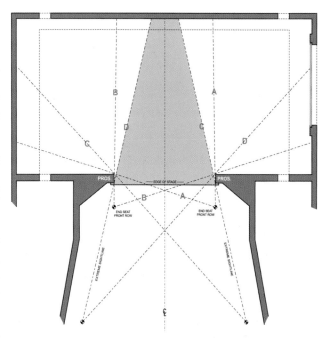

Stage plan with sightlines.

seating and then, of course, the consideration of sightlines becomes even more important. This purely technical matter of sightlines is deliberately placed right at the start of our consideration of the design process because good stage design is attained by combining the creative imagination with a good working knowledge of the technicalities involved. In many ways the stage designer may considered to be more artisan than artist. But this is not an ignoble calling, for Michelangelo, who not only designed and painted the ceiling of the Sistine Chapel but plastered it too, also referred to himself as an artisan.

4 THE DESIGN PROCESS

READING THE SCRIPT

The design process usually starts with a text. This may be for a new work or one already produced. It may be a classic that has been produced many, many times. In each case the designer should try to read it as if it were completely new and fresh to him. In fact, read it several times. It is a good idea to read it straight through at a sitting for the first time, to get the general feel of the piece and see what impressions it produces. At a second reading have a notebook beside you and make notes and rough sketches as you read. Make a careful note of any specific physical requirements that may be necessary, items that it would be impossible to do the play without. These are generally few: in *Romeo and Juliet*, for example, you may note that a balcony is essential, or at least an upper level which can *suggest* a balcony. In a thriller it may be a large chest to contain a dead body. In a farce it may be the door to a room where some unfortunate character is trapped without his trousers. A second list may contain physical items it may be desirable to include but which are not really essential to the production, a samovar or an icon, for example, to give a sense of Imperial Russia in a Chekhov play.

Make sketches of any images that occur to you as you read the text. At this stage do not attempt the drawings of a complete set but small sketches of specific moments: Juliet on the balcony with Romeo below, a character sitting on a chest, not knowing that it contains a dead body, or the

OPPOSITE: A small, but detailed set model for a schools tour has just been completed by the designer.

positions of actors in a farce when the door opens revealing the actor who has lost his trousers. You can choose specific moments throughout the play and gradually build up a storyboard, not necessarily one that is entirely logical but a series of speedy sketches to get the creative imagination working.

MEETING THE DIRECTOR

Arrange to meet the director at the earliest possible opportunity after reading the script. The working relationship between director and designer is crucial, and you must find a common method of approach. If you are thinking of, say, *Romeo and Juliet*, as a romantic tale of star-crossed lovers and he sees it as a hard-edged, political polemic, then one of you will have to change or at the very least severely modify your point of view.

You may prefer the first meeting with a director to be an informal one, perhaps over a coffee or a drink, maybe in your own home. You need a chance to get to know each other at this stage, to examine each other's views on the theatre and life generally and discover the best way to work together. No two directors will have the same approach, sometimes a director will come to you with specific requirements, and sometimes he will appear to have few opinions at all. Do not be too concerned if the director's views conflict somewhat with yours. If you can develop a mutual respect for each other's work, then the results will be better than either of you could produce individually. The worst kind of director to work with will sometimes make a remark such as, 'I'm sure you are a very talented designer, so why don't you just show me your ideas and I'll be perfectly happy to go along with them.' This flattering, though ultimately depressing statement completely rules out any form of cooperative artistic creation and the work of both of you will be diminished.

At this meeting it will be difficult to resist scribbling some ideas on paper. These may be very rough indeed, frequently on a paper napkin or the back of a beer-mat, and having very little meaning for anyone not present at the discussion. Do not throw them away, for they can sometimes be a valuable source of inspiration at a later stage in the design process. Keep a special folder for each show you work on in which you place anything of

---

The Designer and the Director

The relationship between designer and director is a crucial one. If the right creative partnership develops, not only will the set be better, but the production as a whole will benefit too. When the relationship is really successful, design and production become so closely fused together that it becomes impossible to separate them. For example, it is now difficult for us to think of a play by Bertolt Brecht without the distinctive style of the Berliner Ensemble and Caspar Neher's innovative design work immediately springing to mind. The relationship may not always be a cosy one, but, provided that there is a mutual respect for each other's work, even the friction of opposing views can often be productive. When a good working relationship is established you will find that you are able to make suggestions to the director about his production in the same way as he will make suggestions to you about the set. Always be tactful when doing this, however, for some directors may strongly resent it. When you find a director with whom you can produce really good work you will probably find that you will be invited to work together again on other shows. This will give you both the opportunity to build upon previous experience and may often prove to be a very productive, creative and long-lasting working relationship.

---

relevance to the design process. These hasty scribbles may be added to the written notes you made on first reading the play.

DEADLINES

In spite of the fact that theatre is a communal activity resulting from the collaborative work of a creative team of specialists, the set designer will usually spend many hours in solitary activity, drawing and making models. This will require a certain amount of self-discipline for the deadline is precisely fixed, and, at a specific time on a certain day, the first performance will begin. All your design work must, of course, be completed long before then. The production manager will give you deadlines for several stages of the design work, such as when drawings are required for costing, when the build period will begin and when the model should be available. An important date to note is the first rehearsal, when you will usually be expected to present your designs to the acting company. You will probably find it helpful to make out a personal schedule for yourself, showing what stage in the process you intend to reach by a specific date. Deadlines have a way of creeping up unexpectedly.

RESEARCH

You will probably need to do some form of research for almost any show you design, and it can be a valuable source of inspiration. The form it takes will, of course, depend upon the nature of the production and your own particular interests. A period play will probably involve searching through books for pictures of period rooms and details of period decoration and style; here the Internet may also be a valuable research tool.

Go to original sources whenever this is possible. Looking at paintings or period objects in an art gallery or museum can often stimulate a creative excitement that is absent from photographs of the same objects. When designing a production of Shaw's *Pygmalion* the director and I went in search of the actual plinth under the portico of St Paul's

Storyboard for J.M. Synge's **Riders to the Sea.**

Church in Covent Garden where Eliza Doolittle sat with her basket of violets, and we later visited Wimpole Street to look for Professor Higgins's house, and Cheyne Walk for Mrs Higgins's house. During this time we spent several hours discussing the production and bringing our creative attitudes into line with each other. The final production was considerably improved in several aspects as a result of the expedition.

Do not ignore the value of serendipity during research, it can sometimes produce unexpectedly rich results. Pictures or objects that do not immediately appear to be relevant can often turn out to be a source of inspiration. Apart from the fact that it is an enjoyable activity, it is probably not a good idea to ask an assistant to carry out research for you since a search concentrated solely on specific items would mean that potentially valuable peripheral material may be ignored. Make a collection of pictures from magazines and newspapers in a large box file, selecting not just those which have an obvious research value but any pictures which have some kind of appeal to you personally. Your collection can become a treasure trove of inspiration. It is not necessary to organize the pictures systematically since looking through them to find a specific item means that a large amount of other visual material must be sorted through along the way and frequently it is the randomly discovered pictures that prove to be the most valuable sources of inspiration.

The research period for a show can often prove to be so enjoyable that it is easy to forget that there are deadlines to meet. You may find it useful to set a predetermined date on your work schedule for the completion of this initial research.

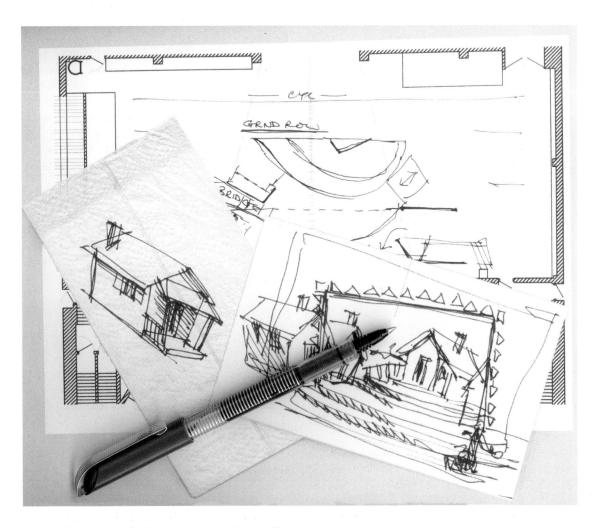

Rough sketches made after a meeting with the director.

BEGINNING WORK

Having read the play, made out a number of lists, met the director, pinned up schedules, assembled the research material and sharpened your pencils, it is now time to start the actual design. This first step is one we often find difficult to take. Try beginning with a review of the collection of sketches in your folder; some of these may represent an idea in plan form, while others may be rough perspective sketches. Bear in mind that the theatre is a three-dimensional space and the stage layout needs to be planned at the same time as the pictorial composition of the set. For this reason, now develop your most promising sketches a little further, drawing a small, rough plan and perspective view, one above the other on the same page. This technique will force you to consider your set as a series of inter-relating spaces and not as just a two-dimensional stage picture.

At this stage it is often helpful to cut out pieces of paper or thin card to represent various elements of the set, especially if parts of it are to move from scene to scene.

FURNITURE

Most sets require furniture of some kind and this must be an important consideration for the set designer. You may find that you need a completely furnished, Edwardian drawing room or a junk-filled basement. On the other hand, you may need nothing more than a single throne. If you are designing an exterior scene, the furniture might include objects that we do not normally consider to be furniture – a low wall for sitting on, a large stone, a wooden bench or some old boxes. Even in a completely abstract setting there may be objects designed specifically for an actor to sit or recline upon. These all count as furniture in theatrical terms.

In a normal room the distribution of furniture is governed by the dimensions of the room and the activities that usually take place in it. No consideration is given to the possibility of unusual or unexpected events. On stage, however, the arrangement of furniture is based upon slightly different considerations: how many need to sit down at the same time? Do they need to sit close to each other? Does the seating arrangement allow them to converse with each other and communicate with the audience at the same time? The set designer knows in advance, for example, whether a murder or a seduction will take place on his set and will arrange the stage so that this can take place effectively in theatrical terms.

On stage, the dimensions of a room can be adjusted to accommodate the furniture it is to contain. However, although an apparently random arrangement of furniture across the acting area may sometimes be convenient from a theatrical point of view, it can never be convincing without some degree of logic behind the arrangement. In everyday life furniture is usually arranged around a focal point such as a fireplace, a television set or some kind of table, try to emulate this on stage.

Carefully estimate the size of the pieces of furniture you require. Measuring your own can help, even if is not exactly like the furniture you will eventually use. Draw plans of chairs, tables and so on to scale and cut them out of paper or thin card so that you can move them about on your plan. You can thus gradually build up a small library of these scale furniture plans and keep them for reuse. A collection of scale plans of standard piano shapes and sizes is invaluable when designing a set that needs to contain one.

ROSTRA

The actual floor of the stage is inevitably flat. However, you can often create a more exciting set by incorporating variations in the level of the floor. Temporary platforms used on stage are referred to as 'rostrums' or 'rostra'. Check to see whether any stock rostra are available and find out their dimensions. They may be built either as solid units or collapsible for easy storage. Irregular shapes and heights will need to be specially built, but you can economize by using stock units where this is possible. Remember that an actor will feel insecure performing on a high level with no handrail, so plan for these where necessary. Remember too that

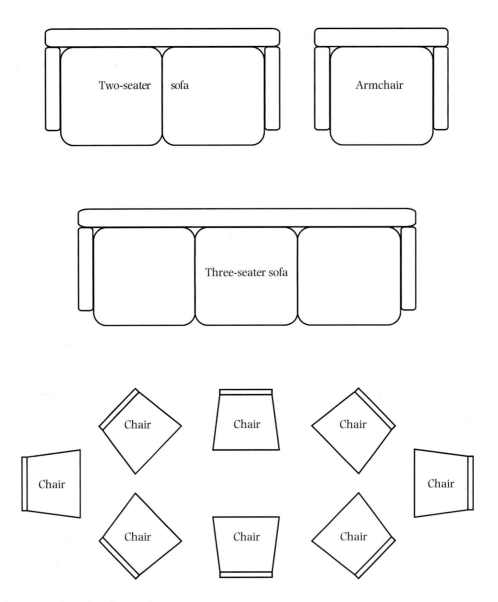

Scale furniture plans (scale: 1:25).

a rostrum running into the wings will need steps for actors to get access to it, placed out of sight on the off-stage side. These access steps are usually referred to as 'get off steps'.

Sometimes you will need a platform that is high enough for actors to walk underneath it. A domestic doorway is about 2m (6ft 6in) high, so you should not consider anything lower than this.

Remember as well that the upper level will require some thickness to support an actor's weight and so you should probably allow another 15cm (6in), making the lowest height of a rostrum designed to be walked beneath about 2.15m (7ft). Check with the costume designer: if an actor is to wear a top hat or a tall headdress you may have to make it higher.

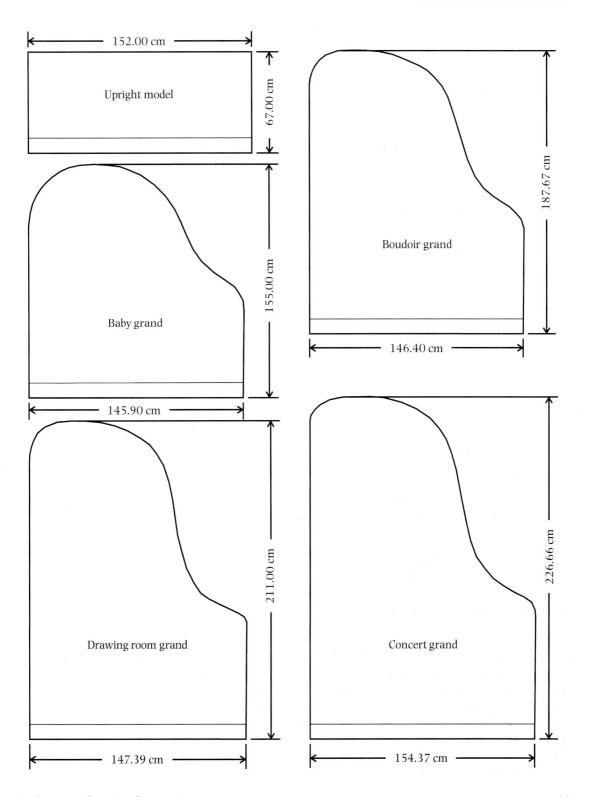

152.00 cm

Upright model

67.00 cm

155.00 cm

Baby grand

187.67 cm

Boudoir grand

146.40 cm

145.90 cm

211.00 cm

Drawing room grand

147.39 cm

226.66 cm

Concert grand

154.37 cm

Scale piano plans (scale: 1:25).

STEPS AND STAIRS

Any rostrum higher than about 25cm (9in) will usually need a step or steps to provide easy access to it. Steps should be designed so that the actor can negotiate them with ease. The number of steps will, of course, depend upon the height of the upper level. The vertical piece between each step is referred to as the 'riser' and the part you step on is called the 'tread'.

The risers and treads in domestic stairs vary considerably in size: the riser may be anything from around 15cm (6in) to 18cm (8in) in height, and the depth of tread has an even wider variation. On stage, an actor needs to negotiate steps with greater ease than in real life. He needs to be able to speak distinctly as he walks up the stairs without having to catch his breath, and sometimes needs to stop at a particular step to play a short scene, which is difficult if the risers are high and the treads are narrow. He should never have to be concerned about avoiding a stumble. As designers, we can help him by designing a staircase that can

be easily negotiated and without the need for him to look down at every step. Examine the steps you encounter in your daily life: which are the easy ones? Which take the most effort when you walk up and down them? Measure the height of the risers and the depth of the treads and make a note of those that work best. Do you find that there is an ideal ratio of riser to tread?

If the set is to contain a rostrum that is, say, 90cm (3ft) high, you should decide at an early stage how many steps you will require to reach this height. A riser of 15cm (6in) is fairly low and has the added advantage that it will divide equally into the height of the platform: You will need five steps, not six. The rostrum itself can form the top step.

You now need to decide upon the depth of the tread so that you can work out the total length of the steps for which you will need to allow space on the plan. Let us be generous and construct a comfortable flight of steps with each tread 30cm (1ft) deep. Still working with our 90cm-high rostrum, the stairs will need to be 1.5m (5ft) in total length. Check that you have sufficient space

An elegant staircase with passageway underneath, designed by Lisa Hancharek for The Beaux' Stratagem, *receives its finishing touches in the workshop of the Timms Centre for the Arts in Edmonton, Alberta. The well-proportioned treads and risers make the staircase easy to negotiate. The banisters and handrail provide necessary support for the actors, but also emphasize its sweeping curve.*

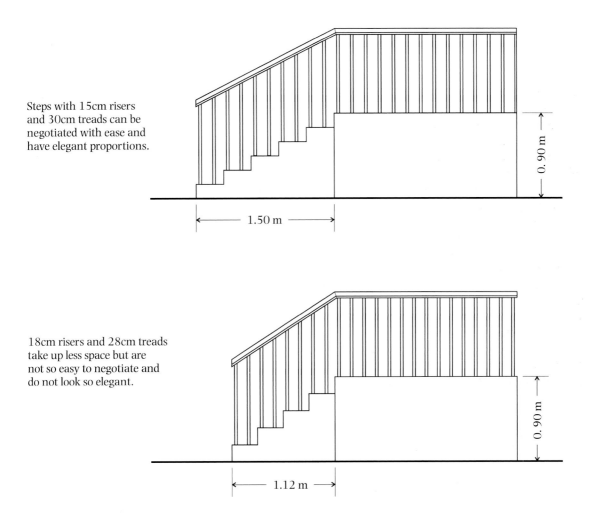

Steps with 15cm risers and 30cm treads can be negotiated with ease and have elegant proportions.

0.90 m

1.50 m

18cm risers and 28cm treads take up less space but are not so easy to negotiate and do not look so elegant.

0.90 m

1.12 m

Dimensions of steps.

at an early stage in the design process because you may have to adjust by lowering the height of the rostrum, which will also, of course, shorten the run of steps. Alternatively, you could slightly shorten each tread, with a corresponding loss in comfort for the performer. Remember to incorporate handrails or banisters where these are needed.

I have chosen a relatively low rostrum in this case, but these considerations become really crucial when the rostrum is considerably higher. Occasionally a rostrum will need to be so high that to fit in sufficient steps to reach the top in the space available can be problematic. Remember, however,

that stairs can negotiate angles or curves and contain intermediate levels. Designing steps to fit an available space need not be detrimental to your design. In fact, these technical considerations can often be a source of creative inspiration. If you are considering the incorporation of rostra, slopes or stairs into your set, start designing these elements at an early stage.

RAKES, RAMPS AND SLOPES

Our older theatres were often built with sloping stage floors to assist the sightlines and enhance

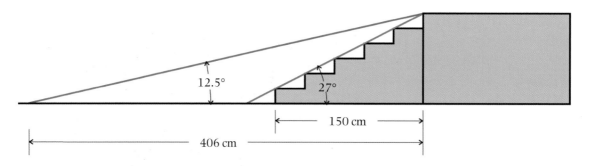

Estimating the dimensions of a ramp.

perspective scenery. Most modern theatres have flat stage floors, but sometimes the designer will wish to incorporate a ramp or a raked stage into his set as a design feature. A raked stage can have the effect of presenting the performers to the audience in a dramatic and forceful way. However, there are inherent dangers: read the play again, imagining it taking place upon a slope. Are there any essential wheeled objects that may cause a problem, a wheelchair or a pram for instance? Is anything dropped on to the floor during the play that may roll? Stage fights can sometimes be difficult on a rake. Discuss it with your director at an early stage and give a great deal of attention to the precise degree of slope, an angle of 7.5 degrees is generally considered safe, but one between this and about 20 degrees may be considered accident-prone. No definitive guidelines can be given here since many factors need to be taken into account, such as the type of surface, the action that is to take place upon it, the type of footwear to be worn and the style of the production. It is a good idea to ask your builder to make a mock-up of the slope so that you can try it out for yourself and demonstrate it to the director, and the performers too, if possible, to gain their approval before work begins on the actual construction.

Do not make the mistake of thinking that you can substitute a ramp for a run of steps and expect it to occupy the same amount of floor space. The ramp will always need to be considerably longer than a flight of steps leading to the same height or it will be too steep to be practicable.

DEVELOPING THE ROUGH SKETCHES

How you proceed from this stage depends much upon the type of set and your own preferences. You may like to develop the stage plan in greater detail, working accurately to scale, or you may prefer to branch out into the third dimension by making a rapid sketch model. This may be quickly done by cutting out the main pieces of the set from cartridge paper, sticking them together with Sellotape and drawing on features such as doors or windows with a felt-tip pen.

It is not a good idea to begin making the final model until all the preparatory work is complete. Model making is a lengthy process and you will not want to waste a great deal of time building features that will eventually have to be changed. You may find it helpful to complete all the plans and working drawings before beginning the model. This method of working has many advantages: costs can be estimated from the drawings and, if possible, the construction of the set can begin without the need for the model to be completed; by building the model from the working drawings you may be able to detect any errors before the build and possibly avoid expensive alterations at the construction stage. Whichever working method you choose, you should arrange frequent meetings with the director throughout the process so that you may benefit from his creative input and he may become familiar with the opportunities offered to him by your design.

RIGHT: Developing the rough sketches for a production of We Won't Pay! We Won't Pay! *(see following pages).*

LEFT: Rapidly constructed, rough set model for a black-box production Courage to Kill *with cut-out figure to give scale.*

45

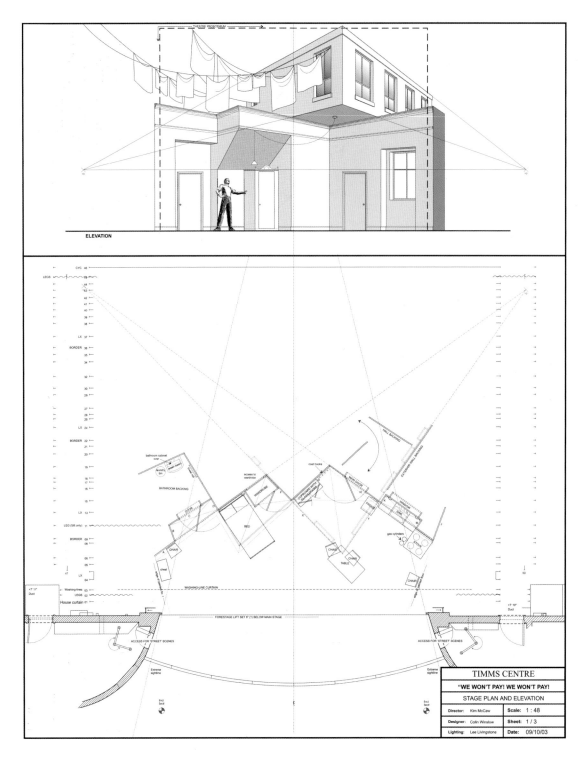

Stage plan and elevation.

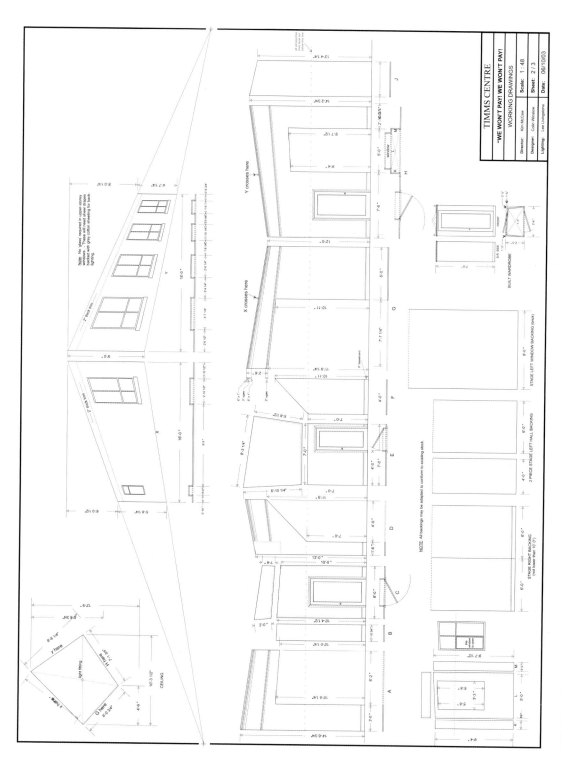

Working drawings.

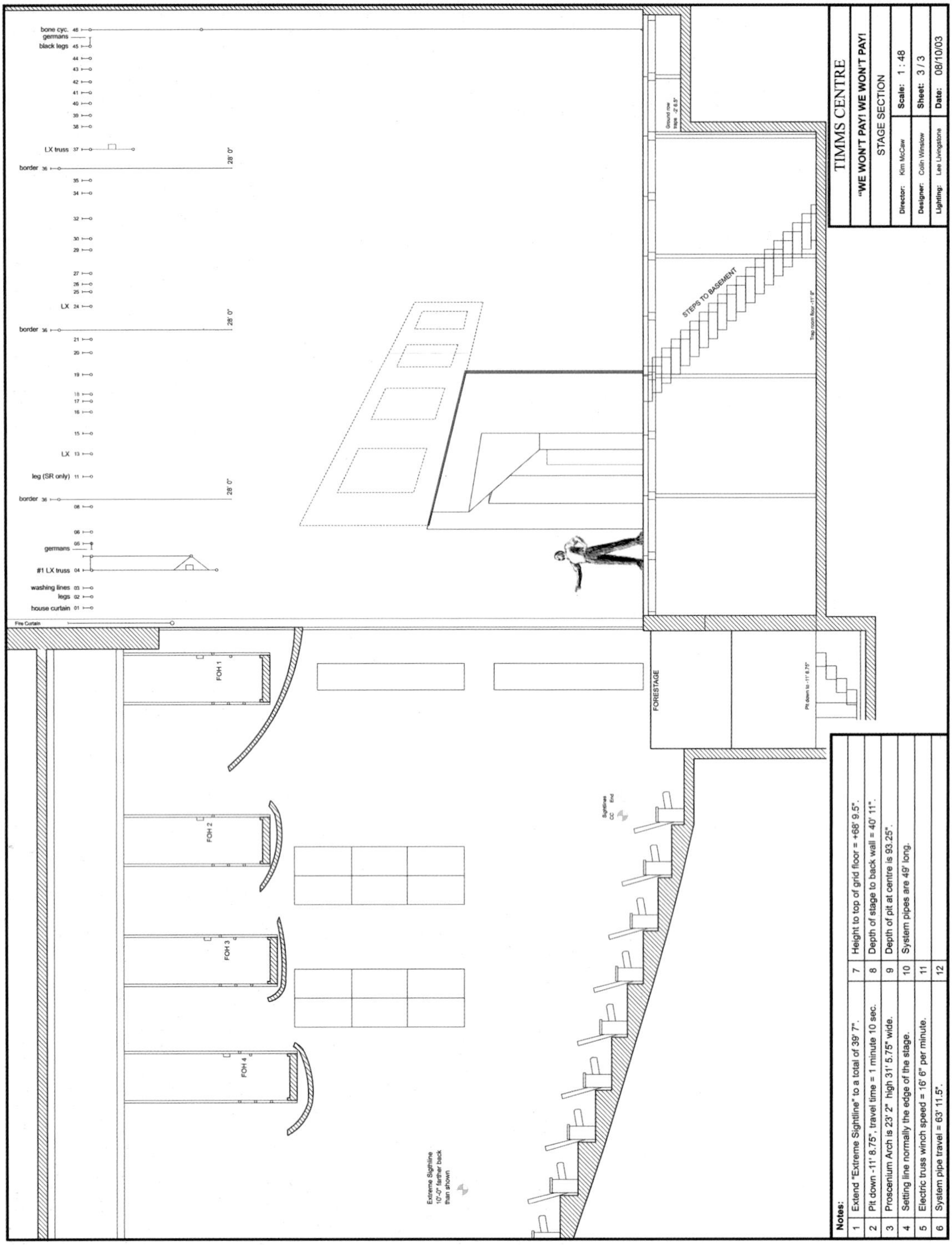
TIMMS CENTRE
"WE WON'T PAY! WE WON'T PAY!
STAGE SECTION
Director: Kim McCaw
Scale: 1 : 48
Designer: Colin Winslow
Sheet: 3 / 3
Lighting: Lee Livingstone
Date: 08/10/03
Notes:
1 Extend "Extreme Sightline" to a total of 39' 7".
2 Pit down -11' 8.75", travel time = 1 minute 10 sec.
3 Proscenium Arch is 23' 2" high 31' 5.75" wide.
4 Setting line normally the edge of the stage.
5 Electric truss winch speed = 16' 6" per minute.
6 System pipe travel = 63' 11.5".
7 Height to top of grid floor = +68' 9.5".
8 Depth of stage to back wall = 40' 11".
9 Depth of pit at centre is 93.25".
10 System pipes are 49' long.
11
12
FOH 1
FOH 2
FOH 3
FOH 4
FORESTAGE
STEPS TO BASEMENT
bone cyc.
germans
black legs
LX truss
border
LX
leg (SR only)
#1 LX truss
washing lines
legs
house curtain
28' 0"

Stage section.

ABOVE: Set for Dario Fo's We Won't Pay! We Won't Pay! *at the Timms Centre for the Arts. Directed by Kim McCaw. Lighting by Lee Livingstone.*
Photo: Ellis Bros

RIGHT: Set for Dario Fo's We Won't Pay! We Won't Pay! *Short scenes outside the apartment were played before a tangle of washing lines, streaked with gobos by lighting designer Lee Livingstone.*
Photo: Ellis Bros

PLANS AND WORKING DRAWINGS

The stage plan is probably the most important drawing you will produce and there are several people who will need to have a copy of it: the director, the lighting designer, set builders, the production manager, the stage manager and possibly the props department and the scene painters. Some may require more than one copy and you will probably need two copies for yourself. Not quite so many people will need copies of the other drawings, but you will need some of each sheet. Copying the drawings may be expensive, especially on an elaborate show that runs into many sheets; ten to twenty sheets for one show are not unusual.

If you can produce your sheets of drawings to the standard 'A' (metric) international paper sizes you can save a considerable amount of expense in duplicating costs; for example: an A1 size sheet is 59.4cm × 84.1cm. If your drawing is just a centimetre or two bigger in either direction you will be charged for copying the next size up (A0, or 84.1cm × 118.9cm) and the cost will be considerably more for much wasted space. You can legitimately ask for copying costs to be paid out of the production budget, but this, of course, means that you will probably have a little less to spend on your set.

You will find a more detailed discussion of technical drawings in Chapter 5.

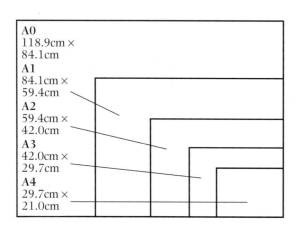

A0
118.9cm ×
84.1cm
A1
84.1cm ×
59.4cm
A2
59.4cm ×
42.0cm
A3
42.0cm ×
29.7cm
A4
29.7cm ×
21.0cm

International paper sizes.

THE SET MODEL

The set model may be viewed as a three-dimensional scale drawing, with colour and texture applied. Most of us have been drawn to miniatures from early childhood in the form of a dolls' house or a model railway layout, and a beautifully made set model can be an attractive and desirable object in its own right. However, the set model, although attractive, plays an important function in the development of the final design. It is not a toy. If you have already looked at some of the technical drawings in this book you may find them a little difficult to grasp immediately. Interpretive skills and the time to compare several drawings are needed to appreciate the set they describe fully. With the model, however, no special skill is needed. Anyone can instantly gain a good impression of the designer's intentions, in all three dimensions, and from any angle.

The set model is built to scale, usually the same scale as the stage plan, and should be as accurate as possible. You will also find a more detailed discussion of the technicalities involved in model building in Chapter 5. A word of warning: a good set model takes a long time to produce, take care not to underestimate this when scheduling your work; when you have carefully estimated the length of time you will need to build a model, *multiply it by three*. This will give you a more accurate estimate of the actual time involved.

PRESENTING YOUR WORK

After weeks of solitary work researching, drawing, preparing technical drawings and constructing the model, the day will arrive, usually all too soon, when you will attend the first rehearsal to meet the cast and the technicians and to present your designs. This may sometimes be a rather unnerving experience, which will be more enjoyable for all involved if you make a few simple preparations:

• make sure that your model is really solidly constructed with as much of it as possible firmly fixed in place so that there is no chance of parts coming adrift or breaking off;

RIGHT: *Painted and furnished presentation model for* Courage to Kill *in the studio theatre at Theatr Clwyd. Directed by George Roman.*

BELOW: *Demonstrating a scene change to the cast at the first rehearsal.* Photo: Fat Chance Productions

- decide on a good place to set up the model so that everyone can see it as clearly as possible; place the model on a stand of some kind so that it can be viewed at eye level, as if from the audience's point of view;
- any model will be greatly enhanced by positioning a light or lights above it; small, adjustable halogen desk lights are useful here;
- be prepared to demonstrate any scene changes or scenic effects with as little fiddling as possible; rehearse them beforehand, a small laser pointer can sometimes help when presenting a set model to a large group of people.

You will probably be expected to speak briefly about your design, so be ready to do this. It is not necessary to prepare a formal address, but you may find that it helps to decide upon your opening sentence and learn this by heart. Once you are over this hurdle, you will probably find that you will be able to continue with little effort. Keep it short and concise.

THE REHEARSAL PERIOD

The set designer is not usually expected to attend rehearsals, but it is a good idea to make an effort to keep in close touch with developments. The stage management will have marked out your set on the floor, so you now have an opportunity to begin to assess the implications of the actual dimensions of the set you have designed. You should get regular notes from the stage management about any concerns arising from rehearsals, always check these carefully and discuss them with the director if necessary.

During this period you will be expected to make regular visits to the workshops to monitor the progress of set construction and painting. You will also be needed to assist in the selection of furniture and dressings, and any soft goods required, such as curtains and upholstery fabrics, must be chosen. Do not buy anything yourself for a show unless you have already cleared the purchase with the production manager or whoever may be

Discussing progress with Jane Cooke, Head Scenic Artist at Bristol Old Vic. Note the slot in the paint shop floor that allows the paint-frame to be winched down to provide access to the top of scenery attached to it.
Photo: Fat Chance Productions

A well-organized storage area for small props and set dressings is a great asset.

responsible for handling budgets. You will, of course, keep all your receipts for reimbursement, including any travelling expenses involved.

If you are lucky, the theatre will have its own props room stocked with furniture and props from previous productions that can be recycled as needed, but you may have to spend a long time scouring markets and second-hand shops for just the right pieces of furniture and dressings you need for your set. There are some excellent specialist hire firms which will be able to produce almost anything you could imagine, but these tend to be expensive. Remember that the hire charge is usually calculated on a percentage of the value of the goods hired and the length of time for which they are needed. For a modern play it may be cheaper to buy

new furniture from a firm such as Ikea rather than hire it. If your theatre has its own props department you can ask for special items to be made to your designs; give it detailed drawings and copies of any reference material you may have found.

The hunt for props may sometimes be depressing. It is often impossible to find exactly what you have in mind so compromises have to be made. Since the production is being developed in rehearsal at the same time, you will get notes from the stage management of the changes required that will often conflict with choices you have already made. Props are also frequently cut in rehearsal and these inevitably are the ones upon which the most time and effort has already been expended.

Visit rehearsals whenever you can and note how

A store of furniture from previous productions available for reuse.

the actors are using the rehearsal furniture. How many people are sitting on the sofa at the same time? Is anyone sitting on the arms or the back? Actors frequently use furniture on stage in ways that it was never intended to be used in real life: chair backs are often sat upon and tables stood upon. Make sure that the furniture you select will be suitable for the planned action, and strong enough to withstand the kind of treatment it will receive.

During this stage you may have to make some adjustments to your set design. They should be minor ones, but, from time to time, unexpected problems occur or some changes are needed that require major alterations. This can be disheartening for the designer, but do not automatically reject suggestions without giving them due consideration. The production is still at a formative stage. Do not lose sight of your original intentions, but try to retain a degree of mental flexibility at the same time. Good theatre is always the result of teamwork and

the process of mounting a production is organic by nature. Your baby must be allowed to develop into a healthy youngster.

ON STAGE

Before the set up begins on stage, the lighting technicians will need to hang their lanterns in the positions required by the lighting designer, unless a standard fixed rig is to be used. In any case, some areas may become difficult to gain access to when the set has been built in position, so any lighting or sound equipment in these areas needs to be rigged before construction begins on stage.

Eventually the day will come when your set will be erected on stage. This is an anxious time for the designer, but, if you are not actually working on the construction, try not to hamper the team who are probably working under considerable pressure at this time. Bring up any serious concerns you may have, but keep petty considerations until the immediate pressure has been relieved. Much work will inevitably need to be carried out on stage when the set has been built. Furniture needs to be set in position and marked so that it can be replaced in precisely the same place, set dressings need to be arranged and some touching up and finishing off will almost certainly be needed. The production manager should schedule a time when this can be carried out. If your floor is to be painted *in situ* then make sure that time is scheduled for this when no other work is happening on stage and also that sufficient time is allowed for it to dry completely and be glazed or varnished, if this is required.

The lighting designer will have special sessions scheduled to light the play and will, of course, need the completed set to do this. If you wish to carry out any work on the set at the same time, such as arranging dressings or touching up paintwork, you should ask the lighting designer if he is happy for you to do this, but bear in mind that this time is intended primarily for lighting and you should not complain if you find yourself working under very low light levels and plunged into total darkness every few minutes.

The first rehearsal on the set is usually the technical rehearsal (or 'tech'). As its name suggests, it is primarily to rehearse all the technical aspects of a production with the actors, and there will be frequent stops and long tedious waits while various details are adjusted. No one cares much about the acting at this point and so long runs of dialogue without any technical events will often be cut to save time. This type of rehearsal is often called a 'cue to cue'. The precise choreography of any scene changes will be worked out at this rehearsal, so a complicated show such as a musical may have a technical rehearsal scheduled to last for several days. Be prepared for a long and frustrating time, remain calm whatever happens and take careful notes of anything related to the set that still needs work or adjustment. Do not help with scene changes or other technical operations unless you are going to be doing this at every performance, the stage crew needs to practise coping without your help.

The technical rehearsals will inevitably be somewhat shaky affairs, with much potential for things to go wrong, so do not be unduly dismayed if all is not perfect at this stage, this a time for correcting errors and making important final adjustments.

DRESS REHEARSALS

All the elements of the show are brought together for the first time at the dress rehearsal. As the first rehearsals in the set are primarily for the benefit of the technicians, the actors will probably save their energy and not attempt to give a full performance. Only in the final dress rehearsals will the actors attempt to give the kind of performance they will eventually present to an audience. At dress rehearsals the designer's place is in the auditorium; move around discreetly, checking sightlines from the end seats of the front and the back row, including the upper levels if you have any balcony seating. Can you see anything you are not intended to see? Do not interrupt the rehearsal, let the actors and technicians work unhampered by your particular concerns, but take careful note of anything you find unsatisfactory or wish to adjust and you should have an opportunity to have your say later, usually immediately following the rehearsal, when the director will assemble the company for notes. The final dress rehearsal should be as close to an actual performance as possible. This rehearsal should run without any stops unless something really serious has gone wrong.

THE FIRST NIGHT

Your job is done. Do not suggest any changes unless you feel that they are desperately important. All you have to do now is graciously accept compliments on your work and the plaudits of colleagues and friends.

A production desk has been set up in the centre of the auditorium for the use of the production team during technical rehearsals. here the lighting designer, checking his monitors, is setting cues with the stage manager beside him. A couple of rows behind, the sound designer is setting levels with his board operator.

5 TOOLS AND TECHNIQUES

DRAWINGS AND SKETCHES

There is no doubt about it: the designer's main tool is his pencil, and it is a tool that he needs to be able to use proficiently. It is hardly possible to have a discussion about the set with a director or technician without reaching for a pencil. This does not mean that an extremely refined drawing skill is required, but you should be able to communicate ideas via the medium of drawing with ease. It is a skill that needs constant practice, just as even the finest concert pianist will always practise scales.

Drawing is a skill that can be learned and regular attendance at a drawing class with a good teacher can often produce startling results. Keep a sketchbook with you at all times, and get into the practice of drawing something every day, not an elaborate artistic creation worthy of being framed, but some simple object such as a teacup, a pencil sharpener or a friend's foot. You will be amazed at how quickly your drawing skill will improve, and your sketchbooks will often provide inspiration in a variety of unexpected ways.

Sketchbooks

Spiral-bound sketchbooks are probably the best. They will fold back flat when in use and you can tear out pages if necessary, without the book falling apart. Buy a large one and a small pocket one that you can easily carry with you. Do not buy books of very expensive paper, this can often be inhibiting and your sketchbooks are mainly for rough work, which

OPPOSITE: *The designer's work surface with a set model at an early stage of construction.*

will sometimes be mere scribbles to anyone other than yourself.

Pencils for Sketching

The standard pencil is the HB, but you will also need one or two softer ones for sketching, such as B or 2B or even softer. Try using some of the artist's

Pencils

Pencils are made from graphite, not lead as is often supposed. Graphite was first discovered in Borrowdale, near Keswick in Cumbria, around 1500, when some shepherds checking their flocks after a great storm, discovered that some trees had been blown down revealing a seam of a black substance which at first they thought was coal. It proved quite useless as a fuel, however, but was very convenient for marking the fleeces of their sheep. The first graphite pencils were not produced until 1662, when their manufacture became literally a cottage industry in Cumberland.

Finding the supply of English graphite severely curtailed as a result of the French Revolution, Nicholas-Jacques Conté in France in 1795 developed a method of mixing the powdery local graphite with clay, wax and water, then firing it in a kiln to produce the now familiar Conté crayons and pencils. For the first time, it became possible to control the degree of 'blackness' of marks made by pencils. They are graded by degrees of hardness: the harder grades are signified by the letter 'H' for 'hardness' and the softer grades by 'B' for 'blackness'.

pencils designed specially for sketching, such as a charcoal pencil. Good quality coloured pencils such as Caran d'Ache are also useful to give a rapid indication of colour.

Other Drawing Instruments

A wide variety of writing and drawing instruments is now available at most stationery stores. Experiment with them and discover those that work best for your own individual style. Felt-tip pens are excellent for rapid sketches, and the water-soluble variety can produce attractive, random effects when worked over with a little water. On the other hand, the large boxes of coloured felt-tip pens arranged according to hue and shade look attractive but are often an expensive trap. You will probably never use most of them, and the really useful colours rapidly get used up. It is better to buy a selection of individual colours, choosing ones that suit your style and the work you have on hand.

Erasers
Buy a good quality one; a cheap rubber eraser can leave black smudges behind that are impossible to remove. You should never have this problem with a vinyl eraser. You may also find a kneadable eraser useful for squeezing to a point between the fingers to add small highlights to a shaded pencil sketch, for example.

An eraser shield, simply a small sheet of very thin tin with a variety of small holes cut into it, is useful for erasing very small details while protecting the surrounding areas.

Pencil Sharpeners
A good sharpener is essential to maintain a good point. The type that has two holes of different sizes can be useful if you like to use the thicker type of artists' pencils, otherwise the kind of sharpener with a small container to catch shavings can be especially useful.

WORKING TO SCALE

The set designer must be at ease working to scale. This simply means that any object in a scale drawing or built in a scale model may be measured and then multiplied by a specific figure to obtain the actual size of the object. For example, if you are drawing a door that in reality is 2m high and 80cm wide, you may choose to draw it at a scale of 1:20, which means that the size of the door on your drawing is actually 10cm × 4cm (10cm × 20 = 2m and 4cm × 20 = 80cm). Note that the scale is correctly expressed as 'one to twenty' and written as '1:20'. Try to avoid 'one equals twenty' or '1 = 20', which are, of course, literal nonsense.

The Scale Ruler

Working at a scale of 1:20 means that the calculations are so simple that they may be done in the head. However, plans and working drawings at this scale can become inconveniently large, so the scale most frequently encountered is 1:25. When working on large stages 1:50 is often used. Now the calculations become more difficult. However, a wonderfully simple instrument is available that avoids the necessity for mathematical calculations:

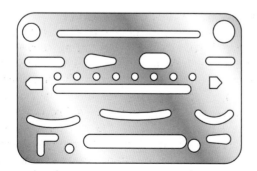

Eraser shield.

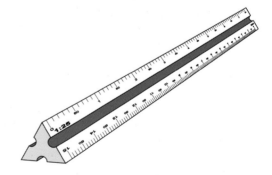

Scale ruler.

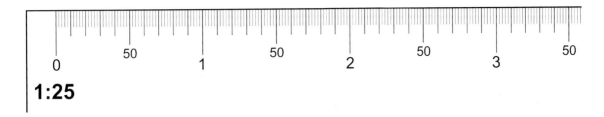

Reading a scale ruler.

the scale ruler. The instrument can look a little daunting at first glance, but it is really easy to use: the edge of the ruler is marked out, not in normal centimetres and millimetres, but in metres and centimetres at the specific scale in use. The main numbered divisions represent metres, usually sub-divided into 10cm divisions. The very smallest divisions usually represent 2cm since, at most scales, 1cm divisions would be too small and difficult to read. Each edge of the ruler is marked out at a different scale, so make sure you use the edge with the one you need. The scales will be marked near the zero end of each edge.

Scale rulers are available in various formats but the most useful type is the triangular or prism-shaped instrument capable of displaying several different scales along the three sides. Note that the sides are colour-coded to help prevent errors caused by accidentally using a scale on a wrong edge. Not all rulers contain the same range of scales, so make sure that you have the scales you use regularly (1:25 and 1:50) on your ruler. The edge of a scale ruler is easily damaged as it is designed for measuring rather than for drawing lines. Protect it by keeping it in the plastic box that usually comes with it, particularly if you intend to carry it about with you.

Imperial and Other Measuring Systems

Occasionally we still encounter the imperial measurement system, although the USA is now the only country in the world not officially using the metric system. On the whole, it is not a good idea to attempt to convert your dimensions. Instead, try to think in the new system and force yourself to forget the other. It is rather daunting at

first and you may find that you have to measure many common objects anew using metric. Now your 2m × 80cm door will be 6ft 6in high by 31½ in wide, and a metric scale such as 1:25 is extremely inconvenient. For this reason, the most common imperial scales are 1:24 (or half an inch to one foot) or 1:48 (or a quarter inch to one foot.) These scales are very close to the metric scales of 1:25 and 1:50 so take care not to confuse them. Imperial scale rulers containing these scales are still available, though you may have to hunt for them.

Remember that the scale does not specify any particular system of measurement. It is merely a ratio. So a drawing at 1:25 does not mean that you must measure in centimetres; it would still work even if you measured in inches (or finger-joints, lengths of string or whatever). You just have to multiply by 25 for the full-scale dimension. However, a scale of 1:25 or something similar usually means that the designer was working metrically, and scales of 1:24 or 1:48 usually indicate imperial dimensions.

Proportional Dividers

Occasionally there is no way to avoid having to completely redraw a technical drawing, converting it from one scale to another. You can do it by measuring each line, calculating the conversion and then redrawing the line at the new scale. However, a not very well-known instrument is available that will simplify the task considerably: proportional dividers. It looks disarmingly simple, consisting of two arms with points at each end and a moveable pivot point near the middle. There is usually a scale marked on one of the arms. To use

Proportional dividers.

Drawing board.

the dividers, first adjust the pivot point to the appropriate point on the scale and then measure the length of a line on the plan to be converted with the pointed ends at one side of the dividers, turn it over and the points on the other side will indicate the new dimension. In this way you can rapidly convert a whole drawing entirely without the use of mathematics.

TECHNICAL DRAWINGS

A technical drawing differs from a freehand drawing in that almost every line you draw will be produced with the aid of a guide instrument of some kind. This means that a wide range of drawing equipment is needed and, unfortunately, the more expensive brands are generally the best.

The Drawing Board

The term generally refers to a table of some kind. It is possible to use a simple board with a T-square, but the process is slow and you will need to take a

great deal of care to produce really accurate drawings. A drawing board on legs is a large piece of furniture, but most of the drawings you produce will be at least A1 size (59.4cm × 84.1cm) and your board should be big enough to accommodate size A0 (84.1cm × 118.9cm) if necessary. The angle of the drawing surface should be easily adjustable, for you will need to readjust it continually when drawing, depending upon which part of the board you are working on and whether you are working in pencil or ink.

The most useful piece of additional equipment is a drafting machine, consisting of two rules set at right angles to each other on an articulated arm that can be moved to any area of the surface, maintaining the same angle in relation to the drawing. This angle can be easily adjusted and locked, enabling not only accurate horizontal and vertical lines to be drawn but also lines set to any angle required. A drafting machine can be an expensive piece of equipment to buy, but it is one that will repay the investment in accuracy, ease of use and time saved. Several variations of this type of machine are also available, so try them out if possible and find which type works best for you.

Next best to a drafting machine is a parallel rule. This is a much simpler type of drafting machine, consisting of a straight edge spanning the whole board and running on adjustable cables at each side, allowing the user to draw accurate horizontal lines at any part of the drawing.

Vertical lines, and lines at the most frequently required angles, are drawn by holding a setsquare against the straight edge. Large setsquares are most useful here at the traditional angles of 45, 45 and 90 degrees, and 60, 30 and 90 degrees.

If you intend to use a T-square, buy one long enough to reach most of the way across your board. You will use it to draw the horizontal lines and setsquares (as above) for vertical or angled lines. Remember that to use a T-square you must hold the crossbar of the 'T' tightly against the side of the drawing board with one hand; this can sometimes cause problems if you are left-handed so check that your T-square is one designed to be used at either side of the board. Not all of them are.

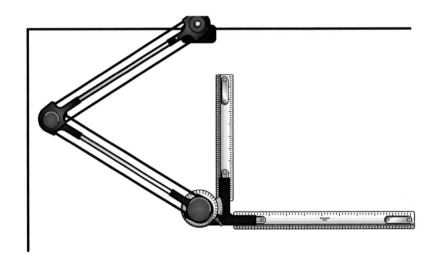

Drafting machine.

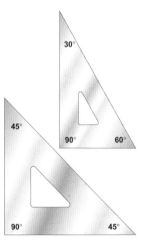

Setsquares.

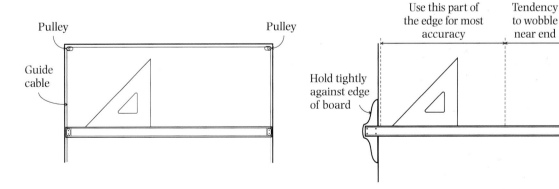

Parallel rule.

Using a T-square.

Drafting Stool

It is advisable to use a properly designed drafting stool when working at a drawing board. You will probably spend many hours doing this and back and neck problems are easy to acquire with bad posture. The trick is to keep adjusting the angle of your board, depending on the area you are working on and to take regular breaks, preferably with a few simple exercises, to relax tense muscles.

Point sharpener.

Clutch pencil.   *Drafting pen.*

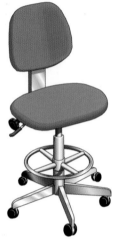

Drafting stool.

Pencils

You will need a hard pencil for technical drawing. Do not attempt to draw with anything softer than 2H. Clutch pencils are comfortable to use and allow a longer point.

You will need a special sharpener for clutch pencils. Small point sharpeners like miniature pencil sharpeners are available, but the container type is cleaner to use; these have a hole in which to insert the lead, which is then pointed by twirling it around, the messy graphite powder dropping into the plastic container. A drafting pencil is normally used with a long point (about 1cm or ½in), and the container type of sharpener has two little holes with which to adjust the length of lead for either a sharp or a slightly blunter point. Do not miss the handy little sharpener that is often hidden away in the button at the top of many common makes of clutch pencil.

Drafting Pens

For a really smart professional finish you should trace off your final drawings in black ink. The traditional drafting pens from manufacturers such as Rotring produce excellent results, but tend to be temperamental if neglected and allowed to dry up. Some are directly refillable with drafting ink and others have replaceable ink cartridges. Do not use Indian ink, it contains gum arabic and will clog up your pens. You will need a bottle of solvent for cleaning. The traditional drafting pen is quite expensive, but fortunately you can now obtain good felt-tip drafting pens in a wide range of sizes at little cost. Your completed plans will need to be photocopied so there is little point in buying any colour other than black.

A drafting pen is designed to give an even line of a specific thickness, so you will need two or three pens to produce other line widths: a medium width for the main lines of the drawing, a fine one for dimension lines and text and a thick one for borders and to render the permanent structure of the theatre building. You cannot produce a heavier line by just pressing down harder as you can with a pencil or a conventional pen. Note that an ink-filled drafting pen should always be held perpendicular to the drawing surface to work properly, so you should adjust the angle of your drawing board to not more than 30 degrees from the horizontal.

Compasses

This is an essential piece of equipment. It is worth buying a good quality instrument, with an extension arm (for drawing very large circles) and a device to attach a drafting pen to the compasses as an alternative to the graphite point.

Stencils and Other Instruments

A wide variety of stencils is available for drafting. Some of the most useful are shown here.

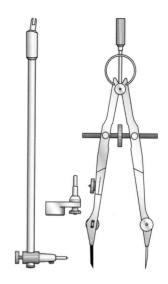

Compasses with extension arm and holder for drafting pen.

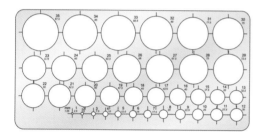

A circle stencil, containing a range of very small circles that are hard to draw accurately with compasses.

Lettering stencil.

Wavy-line stencil; very useful for drawing stage curtains on plans.

Flexible curve: a ruler you can bend to draw irregular curves.

French curves, used to draw smooth irregular curves; usually available in sets of three.

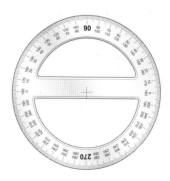

360-degree protractor.

MATERIALS

Paper for Drafting

You will need tracing paper for technical drawings so that you can work over drawings placed underneath it. You can buy tracing paper in large sheets, but it is far more economical to buy a roll and slice it off with a paper knife as needed. Tracing paper is usually sold by weight (in grams) so a roll of thin, lightweight paper will contain much more paper than a roll of thicker, heavyweight paper. A very lightweight paper is rather flimsy and will tear easily so buy one of medium weight, such as 90gsm (that is, a square metre weighs ninety grams. For more permanent drawings, such as master copies of stage plans that are intended to last for several years, use a plastic tracing medium which will not tear nor distort.

Drafting Tape

Never attempt to fix paper to your board with drawing pins. Most boards now have a vinyl surface that will not accept pins anyway, but the surface of a wooden board will soon be damaged by constantly being pierced in the same areas. Drafting tape is designed specifically for this job and will not hinder the use of drawing instruments. However, be aware that masking tape and drafting tape are different products, although similar. *Drafting tape*, with much less adhesive, is designed to be easily removed without damaging the surface of the paper; *masking tape* may tear your drawing when you remove it unless you are careful.

DRAFTING CONVENTIONS

The Stage Plan

The plan is probably the most important technical drawing you will produce, but it is limited in what it can show. Think of a map of your local town – it will show the streets and probably some of the main buildings such as hospitals or churches, but it cannot show what the streets or buildings actually look like. A map is not intended to show this. Similarly, a stage plan cannot show what your set really looks like but it can show its position on the stage, the footprint size of the various elements and their relationship to each other. Other drawings, such as elevations or sections, are always needed to supplement the plan.

A stage plan is not a top view of the set, neither, strictly speaking, is it a bottom view. If you draw the scenery literally at floor level then important elements that do not reach the floor (such as windows set in walls) would not show at all. Instead, think of the plan as representing a section through your set taken at somewhere between 1 and 1.5m (3 to 4ft) from the stage floor. Remember that a flat has thickness, usually about 2.5cm (1in) and this will affect the dimensions on your plans, thus your flats should be drawn with a double line to indicate this.

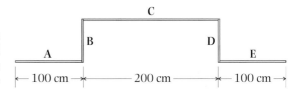

Plan of five flats forming an alcove. Note that flats A and E need to be built a little narrower than 100cm to allow for the ends of flats B and D forming part of these walls.

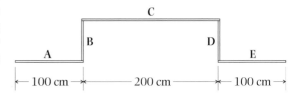

Alcove of the same dimensions as the one above. Now flats A and E need to be exactly 100cm wide, but flat C needs to be a little wider than 200cm as the ends are hidden behind the ends of flats B and D. Width of flats B and D needs to be similarly adjusted.

Note that the second arrangement is preferable to the first, for the ends of flats B and D are better concealed from the audience and any light behind is less likely to be seen leaking through the joins between the flats.

Joining flats at corners.

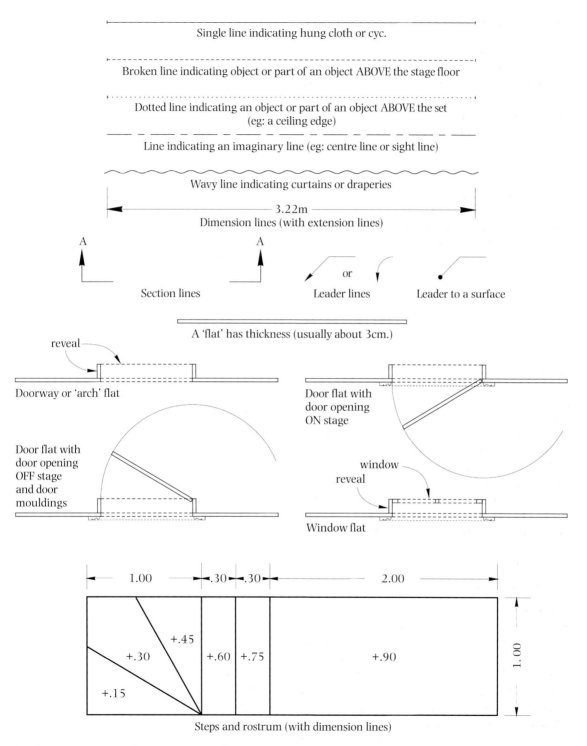

Single line indicating hung cloth or cyc.

Broken line indicating object or part of an object ABOVE the stage floor

Dotted line indicating an object or part of an object ABOVE the set
(eg: a ceiling edge)

Line indicating an imaginary line (eg: centre line or sight line)

Wavy line indicating curtains or draperies

3.22m
Dimension lines (with extension lines)

A   A

Section lines   or   Leader lines   Leader to a surface

A 'flat' has thickness (usually about 3cm.)

reveal

Doorway or 'arch' flat

Door flat with
door opening
ON stage

Door flat with
door opening
OFF stage
and door
mouldings

window
reveal

Window flat

1.00   .30   .30   2.00

+.45

+.30   +.60 +.75   +.90   1.00

+.15

Steps and rostrum (with dimension lines)

Drafting conventions for use on stage plans.

Very thin elements such as backcloths may be assumed to have no thickness and may be drawn with a single line. However, no line in a technical drawing should just 'stop', always draw a very small stopping line at each end to avoid the appearance of a merely casual break (see the diagram). Any elements that do not actually touch the stage floor should be drawn with a broken line. (Note that, for clarity, a broken line should always be drawn with the dashes longer than the gaps between them.) Thus a flat containing a doorway is rendered with solid lines on either side the doorway, but with broken lines indicating the doorway itself.

Doors are usually drawn partly open at an angle of 30 degrees with an arc indicating the area occupied by the opening door (note that this is not a direction line; it is not necessary to draw an arrowhead on a swing-line).

Reveals

There is often a need to conceal the fact that a piece of scenery is actually only 2 or 3cm thick, if, for example, the audience can see the top or side edges of a realistically treated brick wall. It is not necessary to build the entire piece to the desired thickness; instead, the builder will fix a strip of wood along the back of the edges that show to give the appearance of thickness to the unit. This thickness-piece is referred to as a 'reveal' and should be indicated on the stage plan. Thus a doorway flat (where the edges of the flat around the opening door will be seen) should have reveals of an appropriate width set around the doorway opening. The reveals at each side of the doorway will stand on the stage floor and so should be drawn with solid lines. The reveal above the doorway, however, will not touch the stage floor, so is rendered with a broken line, like the lines indicating the doorway itself. The accompanying diagram of drafting conventions should help to clarify this.

Reveals are not merely a technical requirement, they can be useful creative elements in your set. For instance, if suggesting a medieval castle really deep reveals at the windows and door openings will give a sense of ancient solidity. On the other hand, the use of very narrow reveals, or even their complete omission, can give the sense of a flimsy, artificial structure if that is needed.

Drawing Rostra and Steps

Put the heights of any changes in floor level on your stage plans. You may place the figure in a little circle or you may use a plus (or minus) sign before the figure and omit the circle (see the diagram of drafting conventions). All heights should be taken from stage level; thus any structure below the level of the stage, such as steps leading down from the stage to the auditorium, should be labelled with minus figures, still measuring from stage level. It is not usually necessary to indicate the precise construction of platforms, unless this is a specific design feature. Your builder will probably be more knowledgeable than you about this.

Elevations

An elevation may be drawn from any side, but the front elevation is probably the most useful view. It is not a perspective view, it is a 'paraline' rendering, drawn to scale and related to the plan. It is not difficult to construct if you have already drawn the plan.

Start the drawing by fixing your plan to the drawing board, with a clean sheet of paper immediately above or below it. Extend the centre line from the plan across the new page and construct a base line at right angles to the centre line near the bottom of the page. Next, extend lines vertically from the corners or intersections of objects on the plan, over the elevation sheet, and then draw the heights of objects by measuring up from the base line. Remove any lines that may be hidden by objects in front of them. If you are working on a proscenium stage it is a good idea to indicate the sides and the top of the proscenium with a heavy broken line.

Sections

The term suggests a cutting-through, and a sectional drawing, drawn to scale, illustrates the effect of taking an imaginary slice right through objects or a complete set and looking towards one of the cut edges. The type of sectional drawing

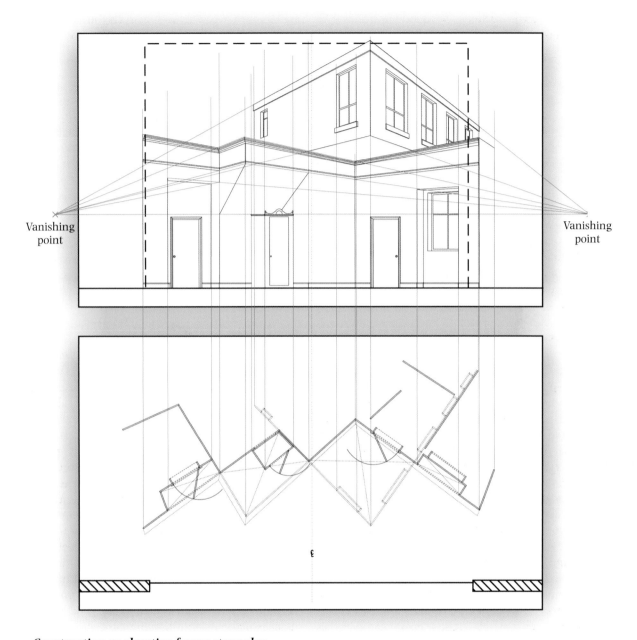

Vanishing point

Vanishing point

Constructing an elevation from a stage plan.

encountered most frequently is a centre line section, that is, the imaginary cut is taken along the centre line; but sectional cuts may be taken anywhere that is convenient and in any direction. Indicate on the plan where a section has been taken by using arrowed angle brackets labelled with a letter for reference. The arrows point in the direction of view (see diagram of drafting conventions). You can construct a sectional drawing in the same manner as the elevation, by

67

placing a new sheet of paper adjacent to the plan and the elevation, and extending lines across to the new page.

A sectional drawing of the entire set standing in position on the stage, including the front row(s) of seating, is particularly useful for checking vertical sightlines. The positions of any flown pieces should be marked, including borders and their heights from the stage floor. The lighting designer will certainly need a stage section when planning where to hang lanterns.

Working Drawings

These drawings are primarily for the set builder's use, they should show every piece of scenery he is expected to build for a show, with dimension lines and any relevant notes. It is not necessary to indicate precisely how the scenery is to be constructed, the builder will be much more knowledgeable than you in this respect. Draw each piece to scale as you wish it to appear from the front. The builder will probably make his own drawings of the back of each piece to show the construction details. Do not attempt to show painted detail, unless it is relevant to the construction, such as when it is necessary to cut around the outline of some organic or irregularly shaped painted object that may be difficult to appreciate before it is fully drawn. Complicated units, such as the *Hispaniola* truck described in Chapter 10, may need several drawings to describe them fully: side and front elevations, a plan and sometimes special sections. Any props to be built, such as the *Hispaniola*'s cannon, can usually be drawn by using a plan with linked side and front views.

Remember that technical drawings are intended to be read in conjunction with each other. No single type of drawing can give all the desirable information, but the drawings in combination should give any information that may be required.

Lettering

Good lettering for captions, dimensions and notes is important on any sheet of technical drawings. Use top and bottom guidelines ruled in pencil on your roughs to ensure consistency in height when you draw the text in ink on your final tracing. High quality freehand lettering requires a great deal of skill and practice and this is not the place to go into the finer details of developing a good hand. There are many specialist books available that offer good advice, but here are one or two basic pointers:

- Drawing letters far too big is a common fault. The maximum height of single-stroke letters should not be taller than 5mm (about ⅛in).
- Spacing should be consistent, but this does not mean that all letters should be equidistant from each other (see diagram).
- Each letter should fit into a well-proportioned, vertical rectangle. Do not make letters too wide nor too narrow.
- The two most important characteristics of good lettering are consistency and legibility. Do not attempt an over-decorative style.
- Lettering should be horizontal whenever possible to aid legibility. If vertically aligned lettering becomes a necessity, orientate all lines in the same direction, preferably with the bases of letters towards the right.

Lettering stencils designed for drafting may be used if you are unsure of your abilities (see the drawing above). Make sure that you buy stencils that are compatible in size with your drafting pens. Check the packaging. They are not suitable for use with a

NOT WAVING BUT DROWNING

Correct spacing – equal amounts of space between each letter, but varying amounts of space between the extremities of each letter.

NOT WAVING BUT DROWNING

Incorrect spacing – equal amounts of space between the extremities of each letter results in apparent unequal spacing. (Compare A–V with I–N)

Spacing lettering.

pencil. The stencils are designed to be used by sliding against a straight edge, thus obviating the need for guidelines, and allowing the user to concentrate solely upon good spacing.

Dimension Lines

Although dimension lines are important, especially on sheets of working drawings, great care should be taken to avoid confusion. A multitude of dimension lines can easily obscure the drawing so use a distinctly lighter weight than for the outlines of objects to make sure that they are clearly differentiated. Leader lines and extension lines should be similarly very light in weight. Place the actual dimension in the centre or immediately above the dimension lines, using a consistent unit of measurement whenever possible.

Stage plans in particular may easily be obscured by dimension lines, so on these they are generally

Extensions and Leaders

Extension lines are the lightweight lines on technical drawings that extend from the ends of an object to enclose and define precisely the extent of a dimension line. They should extend to just beyond the dimension line's arrowheads, and there should always be a tiny gap of about 1mm (or ⅟₁₆in) between the extension line and the object itself. Leaders are the lines that point from a piece of textual annotation or a related detail drawing to the object referred to. The line should be lightweight and either angled or curved to differentiate it clearly from an outline. Leaders usually terminate in an arrowhead, but when specifically referring to the surface area of an object, as opposed to the object itself, it is usual to end it with a clearly drawn, solid dot on the actual surface indicated. Some designers prefer to use freehand wavy or 'serpentine' leaders which are perfectly acceptable, but care should be taken to avoid an over-elaborate flourish that can obscure the drawing beneath. The primary rule is always clarity.

kept to a minimum or even omitted altogether. The preferred solution is to offer stage plans in alternative formats: fully or partially dimensioned, or completely un-dimensioned.

Borders and Title Boxes

The drawing should be completed with a border drawn as a heavyweight line about 2cm (¾in) from the edge of the paper. Draw a title box in the bottom right-hand corner to contain any relevant information such as the name of the show, the production company, the venue, the director and the designer. Always clearly specify the scale and date each sheet.

TIMMS CENTRE FOR THE ARTS		
"WE WON'T PAY! WE WON'T PAY!" by Dario Fo		
STAGE SECTION		
Director: Kim McCaw	Scale: 1 : 48	
Designer: Colin Winslow	Sheet: 2 / 3	
Lighting: Lee Livingstone	Date: 08/10/03	

Typical title box.

Perspective Renderings

A perspective rendering can be constructed technically by using a stage plan and will often be found useful to give a general impression of a set on stage. Follow these steps:

1. Draw the proscenium opening to scale and mark the vertical centre line.
2. Mark off intervals of 50cm (or 1ft, if working in imperial measurements) at the same scale along the base line and up one side of the proscenium opening.
3. Assume the viewer to be standing at the centre of the auditorium and, estimating the viewer's eye level, mark the horizon line at eye level right across the page. If the viewer is standing centrally, the vanishing point will fall at the intersection of the horizon line with the vertical

centre line. Draw perspective lines through the marks along the base line of the proscenium to the vanishing point.

4. Mark a point on the horizon line equivalent to the distance from the viewer to the proscenium,

measuring outwards from the vanishing point to left or right along the horizon line (DP).

5. Extend a line from DP to the bottom corner of the proscenium on the opposite side.

6. Draw horizontal lines through the points where

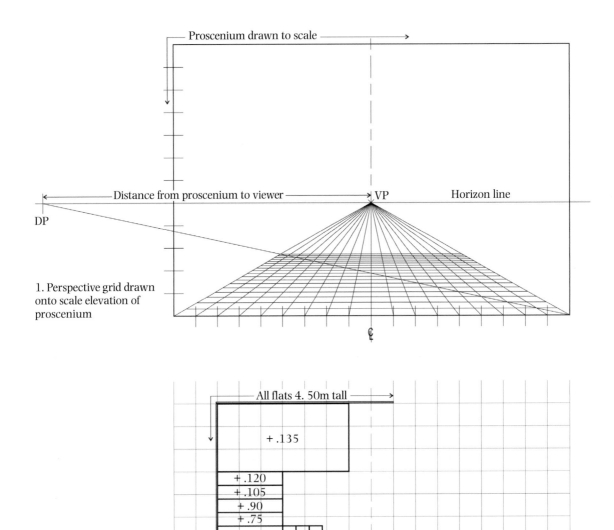

Proscenium drawn to scale

Distance from proscenium to viewer → VP   Horizon line

DP

1. Perspective grid drawn onto scale elevation of proscenium

All flats 4. 50m tall

+.135

+.120
+.105
+.90
+.75

+.60   +.45 +.30 +.15

2. Plan of structure with superimposed grid of 50cm squares drawn to scale

Perspective rendering.

70

the diagonal intersects the perspective lines to construct a grid of 50cm (or 1ft) squares in perspective.

7. The set may now be plotted on this perspective grid from a similar (non-perspective) grid drawn on the stage plan.

8. Take all vertical measurements from the proscenium and extend the lines back towards the vanishing point to estimate the heights of objects in perspective.

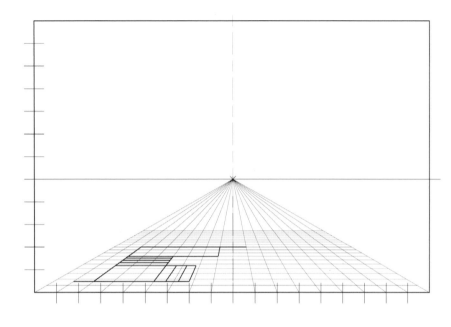

3. Plan transferred to perspective grid

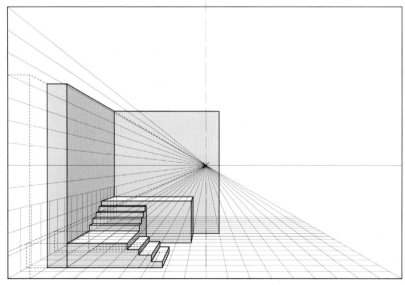

4. Structure rendered in perspective before removal of construction lines

Presentation of Technical Drawings

Obviously, technical drawings should be as precise and accurate as possible. You may find it useful to draw up all the several elements of the set on small sheets of paper and then assemble them on your drawing board to fit neatly on to a standard size sheet (usually A1 size). Lay them out carefully, lining them up with the straight edge of your drafting arm or T-square, and leaving a consistent space between each object to allow sufficient room for dimension lines and labels. Fix them to the board with masking tape. When everything is arranged in order, lay a fresh sheet of tracing paper over the whole assembly and make your final tracing, preferably in ink.

The final tracing is merely mechanical, so it is helpful to trace lines in the following order:

1. All horizontal lines from the top of the board to the bottom.
2. All vertical lines from one side of the board to the other (depending on whether you are right- or left-handed.)
3. All angled lines.
4. Any curved or irregular lines.
5. Dimensions and lettering.

This is the quickest way to trace off a final drawing, but note that, when working in ink, lines must have time to dry before you work over them again when there will be little chance of smudging.

A human figure drawn to the same scale is not merely an attractive addition to set elevations, sections and perspective renderings but it is also great help in visualizing scale. Use a simply drawn male or female figure of average height, perhaps suggesting a character from the show you are designing. Remember to keep a copy of it to trace off on to subsequent drawings.

Duplicating Technical Drawings

The cheapest method of duplicating drawings is by dyeline copier; however, the drawings must be on a translucent medium such as tracing paper or drafting film in order to use this method. The drawing is laid on a special light-sensitive paper and exposed to a bright light that produces a positive imprint on the paper. A disadvantage of this method is that the copies tend to be somewhat impermanent and discolour and fade with time. (They also smell quite disgusting when newly printed.) Very large photocopies may be made on industrial copiers. They are rather more expensive than dyeline copies but the image tends to be crisper and more permanent.

Drawings may be rolled or folded for storage. The lighting designer and the workshops will probably prefer rolled copies, but folded copies are easier to slip into a folder to carry about with you.

The standard method of folding is as follows:

1. Fold both short sides to each other, with the drawing inside.
2. Fold both short sides back again towards to the centre-line fold.
3. Fold horizontally to display the title box on the front of the folded drawing.

CAD

Hand-drafting, such as that described above, is now rapidly being replaced by computer-aided techniques and, correctly handled, these can

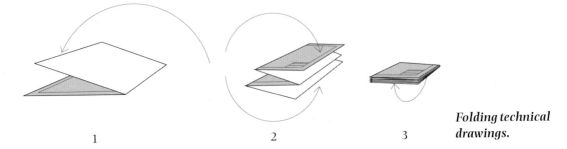

1   2   3

Folding technical drawings.

produce excellent results. AutoCAD has become the industry standard in recent years, but, unfortunately, is a very expensive piece of software. Other programs can produce equally successful results: TurboCAD is a very good drafting program, which, although it does not have all the remarkable facilities offered by AutoCAD, is much cheaper to buy and simpler to learn. The CorelDRAW graphics suite offers basic but thoroughly practical drafting tools, together with a wonderful assortment of other pictorial techniques that are useful to the set designer; most of the drawings in this book were created in CorelDRAW.

CAD drafting standards have now been established under the auspices of the Association of British Theatre Technicians (ABTT) and may be freely downloaded at: www.cad4theatre.org.uk

See Chapter 7 for a more detailed discussion of the use of computer techniques in set design.

BUILDING THE MODEL

Equipment

It is impossible to give a comprehensive list of all the tools needed for model-making. Such a wide range of techniques is involved that almost any tool or utensil you own will be useful at some time. The list below contains the basics, but the first three items (knife, cutting edge and mat) should be considered essential.

Cutting knife

This will probably be the tool you use most frequently. Scissors are not suitable for making really accurate cuts, so pieces of card, paper or thin wood should always be cut with a knife and straight edge. A wide variety of craft knives are available and you should experiment to find the one that suits you best. Surgical scalpels (available from art and crafts suppliers) are cheap to buy and have easily replaceable blades. Handles come in several different styles, so try them out to find the type that fits your hand most comfortably. The blade illustrated is a 10a. But whichever type of knife you use, choose a blade with a long, thin point like the one shown in the illustration for getting into corners.

Scalpel with 10A blade.

A cutting knife that is not extremely sharp is useless for accurate cutting. The blade should be changed frequently. If you have two knives you can keep one with a new blade for really accurate cutting and another with an older blade to be used for tasks such as rough cutting, gouging, whittling wood or sharpening pencils, thereby ensuring that you always have the sharpest possible blade in your better knife.

Cutting Edge

Use a metal straight-edge for cutting straight lines. Never use a wooden or a plastic ruler as a cutting guide for the edge will be rapidly ruined. Some metal rulers intended for use as cutting guides are designed to resist slipping, either by the shape of the ruler (as shown here) or by the addition of a backing of thin cork. Others consist merely of a thin strip of flat steel. You may find that this type offers greater accuracy, even though it does have an unfortunate tendency to slip when in use. Find the type that suits you best.

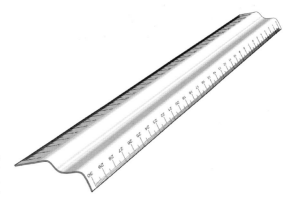

Metal-cutting rule.

Cutting Mat

A cutting mat of some kind is an essential piece of equipment. Never cut on the surface of your drawing board or a table top direct. Vinyl cutting mats are available which offer an excellent non-slip, self-healing surface for cutting on. It is not really necessary to buy a very large size since most of the pieces you will be cutting will be very small. Look for a double-sided mat so that you can turn it over when one side becomes worn and thus double its life. There are several materials you can use to make an improvised cutting mat, but wood is never really satisfactory because your knife will tend to follow the grain and veer away from the cutting edge. The thick strawboard back of an old sketchbook makes a good cutting mat, but will not last as long as vinyl.

Saw and Mitre Box

A miniature saw blade that fits into the handle of a craft knife is extremely useful for cutting wood strips. These are available with a small matching mitre box that can be used for cutting accurate 90- or 45-degree angles to create a really snug fit at butting corners.

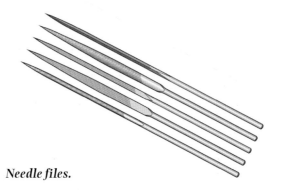

Needle files.

Needle Files

A selection of slim, model-makers' files may be useful. They are available in a variety of shapes – rounded, flat, square, triangular. Look for a set of about ten assorted files, preferably in a plastic storage case. The files are brittle and the points can easily snap off.

Soldering Iron

An electric soldering iron is indispensable when working with wire or metal, together, naturally, with a supply of solder and a pair of wire-cutters. Remember that a soldering iron can be a fire hazard, especially in a workspace littered with paper and inflammable adhesives. Most irons are designed so that the hot tip does not touch the work surface when you set it down, but a small metal stand to hold your hot iron is a good safety precaution. Always solder in a well-ventilated area.

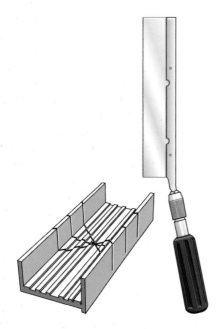

Model maker's saw and mitre box.

Soldering iron.

How to Solder in Twelve Easy Steps

1. Use a piece of hardboard or plywood to protect your work surface.
2. Use a scale drawing of the object you are making as a template. Make several copies because the drawing can become charred and difficult to read as you work.
3. Cut the pieces of metal rod or tubing to size with a metal saw or side-cutters.
4. Lightly sand or rub with steel wool the areas to be soldered to etch the surface slightly and remove any oxidation or grease that would contribute to a poor joint.
5. Fix the pieces to be joined to the template drawing with drafting tape, keeping the tape away from the areas to be soldered.
6. Apply soldering flux to all joints. The flux etches the surface and allows the solder to flow more freely through the joint. Soldering flux is corrosive and poisonous, if you get any on your skin, wash immediately with plenty of soap and water. Do not breathe the fumes of zinc chloride given off by the heated flux.
7. Use a 'tinned' soldering iron. To tin an iron first wipe the hot tip with a wet cloth, then melt just enough solder on the top to cover the surface. Quickly wipe again with the cloth. If the iron starts to look uneven or has black spots on it, it may need to be retinned.
8. Using the tinned soldering iron, heat the metal surface just beside the joint to be soldered. The heat will be transmitted to the joint.
9. Touch the solder to the joint and remove the iron when the joint appears to be complete.
10. Wipe with a damp cloth to cool the area.
11. A good joint looks shiny, while a weak joint will look dull.
12. When the joint is complete and thoroughly cool, wash with warm soapy water to remove the flux and allow to dry.

Materials

Adhesives

Choose a glue that is best suited for the job in hand; some offer a quick initial bond or 'fast grab' before hardening to full strength, but this can sometimes be a disadvantage when a part needs to be carefully and accurately positioned. Other glues need some time to take hold and then much time is wasted holding the pieces together until the glue begins to grab. It is important to use an adhesive that is not water-soluble when dry or you run the risk of its being dissolved by the paint you will apply later and that the model will literally fall apart.

Emulsion-based 'white' glue is the most popular adhesive for model making. It is clean to use, non-toxic, water-soluble (until set) and is almost invisible when dry. It is readily available from a wide range of manufacturers. Synthetic resin adhesives such as UHU have a fast initial grab, form a strong bond and will stick almost anything (UHU was developed in 1932 as the first all-purpose adhesive capable of sticking the new plastic material Bakelite). Bear in mind that the fumes are slightly toxic and work in a well-ventilated area. Plastic cement is something of a misnomer. It is a clear, watery liquid that rapidly dissolves a very thin layer of the surface of the plastic it is applied to and re-fuses it as it dries. Use it by holding the pieces together in position and painting the liquid along the join with a tiny brush. The adhesive will be drawn into the join and weld the parts together. Take care, for repeated applications will eventually damage the plastic. As with the synthetic resin adhesives, the fumes are slightly toxic. Spray adhesives such as Spraymount are extremely useful for gluing large areas of paper to a surface. This is the only kind of adhesive that will not stretch the paper and cause irremovable wrinkles. Unfortunately, it is expensive to buy and messy to use. Follow the instructions on the can and always spray over a protected surface in a well-ventilated space. When you have finished spraying, turn the can upside-down and press the spray button until the spray stops, this will clear the adhesive from the nozzle and prevent a wasteful blockage. Pastes such as Gloy or wallpaper paste are unsuitable to glue parts of the model together, but, being water-based, are useful for small papier mâché effects (see below).

Card

Your basic model-making material will almost certainly be cardboard. It is worth buying a good quality card that will not separate when cut into small pieces and has a good surface for watercolour paints. You will need several different types:

Mounting card A good stout card, usually available with one side white and the other coloured. White/black is a good combination since you will inevitably need a supply of black card for masking pieces. The most useful thickness is one that is as close as possible to the thickness of a flat at the scale you are using.

Art boards You will also need some thinner card to use for smaller architectural details and for building up panelling and mouldings in layers. Many different types are available. A range of thicknesses of the same type of card is preferable to an assortment of different makes, which may each react to the paint in a slightly different manner, tending to cause variations in tone.

Foam-core board A thick, but lightweight board consisting of a sheet of polystyrene foam with a thin card backing on each side. It is usually available in black or white and in thicknesses from about 5mm to 1.5cm (about ¼ to ½in). Black foam-core board is particularly useful for building model boxes, representing the architectural stage-house containing a set model.

Plasticard A special plastic-impregnated card designed for use in architectural models. Available in a wide range of thicknesses, it does not separate into layers when cut into very small pieces as some cardboards do.

Wood

Balsa wood is frequently used by model makers but is often too soft and fragile for many purposes. Hardness is usually indicated by the colour-coded ends on each piece: red is harder than green. Hard woods are available from model-making suppliers, ready prepared and finished for use. They include fine decorative woods such as mahogany, walnut and ash; for general purposes, look for obeché wood, which looks similar to balsa but is much harder, with a fine, straight grain. Most model-makers' woods are available cut into strips from about 1.5mm square section to 1cm square section (⅟₁₆ to ⅜in square) or in planks of 10 to 15cm wide (4 to 6in). Many of the exotic trees from which these woods are cut have very thin trunks, consequently only very few wide planks can be cut from a single trunk and for this reason planks tend to be much more expensive than the equivalent number of thin strips, making it uneconomical to buy planks of wood merely to cut up into strips.

Architectural Model-makers' and Dolls' House Supplies

Specialist shops for architectural model makers offer a wide array of materials and useful parts, including scale furniture and people, steps, ladders and handrails made from plastic. However, useful though they are, they are usually expensive and tend to be available only in contemporary styles.

Dolls' house shops sell beautiful miniature reproduction furniture, but inevitably at the wrong scale (the most popular scale for dolls' houses is 1:12). However, there are many small parts that can be extremely useful, such as the tiny brass knobs intended for model furniture: The doorknobs tend to be too big, but the smaller drawer knobs are much closer to doorknob size at 1:25 or 1:24.

Miniature hardwood mouldings, skirting boards, banister rails and suchlike are also available. Again, they are usually produced at a larger scale than that required for theatrical models, but can be carefully cut down to the size needed.

Useful Odds and Ends

Make a collection of objects that may come in handy: broken pieces of jewellery, brooch mounts, earring 'butterflies', broken toys and the contents of Kinder Surprise chocolate eggs (which have useful little knobs, wheels and so on) may all be useful to the model maker. Include a selection of beads, pins, dress hooks and snaps. Sometimes advertisements in magazines offer reproduction paintings for sale and print postage-stamp size illustrations of the paintings on offer: These may be used to make tiny pictures to hang on the walls of your model set. Similarly, magazine photographs of carpets offered for sale may be pasted on to a J-Cloth with an adhesive such as Gloy for added thickness and texture and then trimmed to make an impressive-looking carpet in a set model. You will, of course, always save any furniture you make for recycling in future models, and so gradually build up a useful collection.

TECHNIQUES

The Baseboard

Always use a sturdy baseboard that will hold your model firmly together. Foamboard or mounting card will inevitably bend and warp; never underestimate the power of paint and water to warp cardboard. If the baseboard warps or bends,

your model will be ruined, so it is worth getting a piece of thick plywood or blockboard cut to a size suitable to contain the complete model, including any elements of the theatre building you wish to include. Make sure that there is no risk of splinters, then glue a sheet of mounting card over the wood and trim neatly. Make sure the bottom is really clean and smooth: You may have to show your model on a beautifully polished desk or table and scratches will not be appreciated. It is sometimes a good idea to glue a piece of felt or baize to the bottom of the baseboard.

Transferring Designs to Card

It is a good idea to build the model at the same scale as your technical drawings. If you have already completed the working drawings, transfer any flat elements to card with graphite paper; this is rather like carbon paper, but, whereas carbon paper is indelible and difficult to cover with paint, graphite paper provides a transfer very similar to the effect of rubbing the back of paper with a soft pencil to trace off a design on to another sheet. It produces a grey, pencil-like, erasable copy. Transfer the stage

Detail of set model for Rookery Nook, *showing brown carpet made from flocked paper, a rug cut from a catalogue and thickened with J-Cloth and stair carpet made from painted blotting paper. The pictures are cut from advertisements in magazines and the doorknobs made from the cut-off heads of black, round-headed dressmaker's pins.*

plan to the baseboard by first marking the centre line and the edge of the stage, then you may be sure that the model will sit squarely on its base. It is often convenient to paint the base before starting to fix the set units in place, so mark the corners of the set by pricking the card with a pin so that you can paint over the lines and still see where the elements are to be positioned from the pinpricks, which will show through the paint.

It is sometimes possible to glue a sheet of working drawings to a sheet of card with Spraymount, but, if you do this, make sure that the paper is stuck very firmly to the card; it has an annoying tendency to separate when being painted.

Cutting

Accurate cutting is essential and there are one or two rules you should follow:

- Always be sure to hold the blade at right angles to the card. This is most important, so get into the habit of locking your hand holding the knife into position so you can make several cuts along the same line without any variation in the angle of the cut.
- You should always press down more firmly with the fingers of the hand holding the metal straight-edge than you do with the knife in the other hand. If your ruler slips, it is tricky to

Using a scalpel and metal ruler for cutting card.

replace it in exactly the same position and the result will be an inaccurate cut.

- Do not try to cut right through a piece of card with a single cut by applying heavy pressure on the knife. If your straight-edge is held firmly in position you can make several cuts in exactly the same place and produce a neatly cut edge with no tearing.
- You can cut through thin pieces wood with a craft knife or scalpel in the same way, but be aware that the knife will have a tendency to follow the grain of the wood and possibly veer away from the straight-edge. Take care to counteract this tendency as you cut.
- Cutting curves, circles or irregular shapes must be done freehand. Start by following the line carefully using the extreme point of the blade and making only a very shallow cut. Cut from the inside of the circle or curve and revolve the card as you do so. This first shallow cut becomes a guide for the second one and successive cuts can be made slightly heavier and deeper until you are completely through the card. Circle cutters, which work rather like a pair of compasses with a cutting blade instead of a drawing-point, are purchasable. They work quite well with paper or thin card but are not very successful when cutting the thicker mounting card.

It is hardly necessary to point out that the use of a very sharp knife in close proximity to your fingers offers a strong possibility of accidental cuts. Make sure that the fingers of the hand holding the metal cutting guide are always kept well away from the edge. Apart from the fact that your fingers are one of your most valuable assets as a designer, you will find that to get blood on to the surface of a model can be disastrous since it has a tendency to bleed literally through any of the usual types of paint.

Gluing

The most common mistake is simply using too much glue; no glue should encroach upon the surface of the model, and this means maintaining glue-free fingers as you work. Do not attempt to squeeze glue from the container nozzle directly on to the model. Squeeze a very small amount on to a scrap of card or a plastic lid and transfer it to exactly the right spot with the point of a cocktail stick, a sharpened matchstick or a pointed scrap of card. White glue may be removed with a damp cloth before it sets, and the synthetic resin glues may be left until they are partially dry then rubbed or peeled off. Try to avoid this, however, as the surface will always be damaged to some extent.

When gluing the end-grain of wooden pieces, you may find that the glue soaks right into the grain leaving little on the surface so a weak join is the result. This is particularly noticeable when gluing objects such as wooden banisters or the legs of furniture into place. Prevent this by applying a little glue to the end-grain, letting it dry to create a seal then reapplying glue before setting the piece into position.

Some model makers like to use a syringe for really accurate gluing. Syringes designed specifically for model makers are available from specialist suppliers but they tend to be expensive. A cheap alternative is to buy disposable hypodermic syringes from a chemist. The needles are bought separately and are colour-coded for thickness. Use a fairly thick needle. You will need to cut off the sharp point before use, disposing of the tiny cut-off point carefully. Cutting it off with wire cutters will squeeze the very thin tube together, but it is easily opened again by tapping a pin into it. Remove the plunger, half fill with glue and then replace the plunger. Turn the syringe point upward, expel the air bubble and it is ready for use. You can now place a tiny dab or trail of glue in exactly the right position without its dripping or getting on to your fingers. Insert a pin into the needle when you have finished working with it to prevent the glue from hardening. Some of the refill kits available for printer ink cartridges contain a blunt syringe that is ideal for model making.

Resist the temptation to glue all the pieces of the model together before painting or you may find that there are areas that you are unable to get into with your paintbrush. Decide which parts it will be safe to assemble without making them difficult to paint and leave the final assembly until all the individual sections are completely finished.

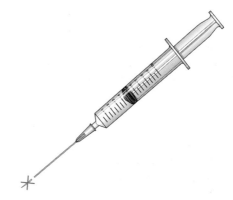

Disposable syringe with point cut off for applying glue.

A Dreadful Warning!

Cardboard is manufactured by gluing layers of thin paper together under pressure, and paper, when wet, will always expand. So, when the surface of a sheet of card is painted with a water-based paint, the water will soak into the top layers causing them to expand. The dry layers beneath will try to prevent this, causing the card to curl. This warping effect is surprisingly strong and difficult to prevent, and, once it has happened, it can be almost impossible to straighten it out again effectively. Always take stringent measures to prevent warping by supporting any large areas of card with a grid-work of thin strips of mounting card glued on edge to the back. Mounting card on edge is actually stronger than equivalent strips of wood. This is a great bore to do, but is usually essential to maintain the shape. There are few things more disheartening than a beautifully built, white card model which has been completely pulled out of shape by the application of a first coat of watercolour, ruining hours of work. It *will* happen to you – at least once.

Curved elements

It is often necessary to bend pieces of card to make elements such as curved walls or the sides of curved steps and rostra. Card will not bend easily (unless, of course, you actually want it to remain perfectly flat; see 'A Dreadful Warning!' above). If you try to bend it, the layers of paper comprising

Strips of card glued on edge to the back of a set model to prevent warping and for reveals to suggest the thickness of walls around doorways and other exposed edges.

the thickness of the card will be stretched on the convex side and forced to contract and pucker up on the concave side, causing unsightly wrinkles and an uneven curve. Therefore before bending, the card needs to be carefully scored, or cut only part way through on the convex side at right angles to the direction of the curve. Make the score lines with a cutting knife and metal straight-edge, cutting all lines to approximately the same depth. Space the cuts fairly close together, about 3 to 5mm (⅛ to ¼in) apart, depending on the severity of the curve, making sure that they are all parallel. It helps to mark them out in pencil before cutting. Treated in this way, the card should bend easily in the direction required.

To maintain a specific curve on a large piece cut curved formers from mounting card. Make them as long as possible and glue them horizontally at regular intervals from top to bottom, on the back of the piece, avoiding any openings such as doorways or windows. Space the formers with straight, vertical strips of card glued on edge between them to help to maintain the shape and prevent warping. If you intend to display the convex (or

scored) side of the curve, glue a piece of paper over the piece to hide the score lines and provide a good surface for painting. Trim off surplus paper along the edges when the glue is dry.

Panelling, Mouldings and Doors

Models for period sets will inevitably require some panelling, even if only on the doors. This can be made from layers of thin card: cut the panels out of a sheet of card then place it over a second sheet, draw around the inside of the cut-out panels and cut the second set of panels slightly smaller than the first. Repeat this for deeper, more elaborate panels. When all the panels have been cut out, glue all the layers together on to a plain sheet of card, aligning all the panels carefully so that the edges of each successive layer suggest a thin strip of moulding around the inside of each panel. Finally, trim the whole sheet to the dimensions required, cutting right through all the layers to produce a neat edge. You will need to use particularly thin card for this technique to avoid excessive thickness when all the layers are assembled.

Doors can be hinged to open correctly with a paper flap glued to one side and hidden under the top layer of panelling, if possible. Glue the other side of the flap to the side of the doorway opening, to be hidden under a strip of architrave moulding.

A similar technique may be used to make strips of cardboard mouldings for architectural details such as chair rails, plaster moulding, skirting boards or to fit around doorways. Glue thin strips of card together in layers, leaving a thin strip of the lower layer showing below each subsequent layer. Finally, trim the flat side, cutting through all the layers together.

Glue strips of card to the back of doorways to represent reveals. The reveals at the sides of the model doorway may be extended up the entire height of the flat to perform the double function of door reveal and strengthener.

Prevent the doors from being pushed right through the door opening by gluing a very thin strip of card along the inside of the reveal at the top and the opening side to act as a doorstop. Finally, add a doorknob. If you do not have a dolls' house knob available you can cut the head from a round-

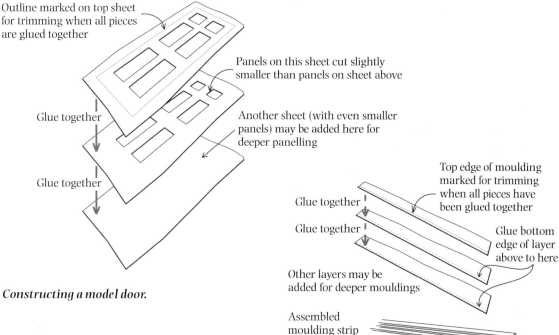

Outline marked on top sheet for trimming when all pieces are glued together

Panels on this sheet cut slightly smaller than panels on sheet above

Glue together

Another sheet (with even smaller panels) may be added here for deeper panelling

Glue together

Glue together

Top edge of moulding marked for trimming when all pieces have been glued together

Glue together

Glue bottom edge of layer above to here

Other layers may be added for deeper mouldings

Assembled moulding strip

Constructing a model door.

ABOVE: Making model mouldings from cardboard.

headed pin, leaving a short length of it to glue into a hole pierced in the door. Make sure that you glue on doorknobs firmly; they seem to hold an irresistible attraction, and it is almost inevitable that someone will try to open a door on your model by tugging on the doorknob with their fingernails.

Windows

Window frames must be made by carefully cutting out each pane from a piece of thin card. This is a lengthy and tedious process which needs to be done very carefully. Mark out the window frame care-fully, then first cut all parallel lines in one direction, turn the card through 90 degrees and cut all the parallel lines in the other direction. Work with a very sharp blade and make sure that you get the point of your knife right into the corner of each pane to avoid messy tears.

Windows on stage are frequently left unglazed to avoid the problem of light reflected from the

RIGHT: Cutting out model windows requires a great deal of care. This one is 18cm (7in) tall and is made entirely from painted cardboard with wooden beads for finials.

glass, but if glass is required it may be represented on the model by gluing clear acetate to the back of the window frame, thereby also strengthening the whole window. If you do this, remember to paint the window frame before gluing on the acetate.

Windows with leaded glazing or stained glass can be made by drawing the leading on to acetate direct with a drafting pen, then filling in areas with coloured varnishes or inks to suggest stained glass. If you have several windows to make you can speed up the process by drawing the leading on a sheet of paper and simply photocopying it on to the acetate.

Making Organic Objects and Other Architectural Features

Organic shapes such as rocks or tree trunks may be carved from wood or polystyrene and covered with paste and thin paper to form a suitable surface for decoration. The cheap, absorbent tissue paper used by wine merchants to wrap around bottles is excellent for this. Glue thin string or thread vertically up and down tree trunks before pasting with paper for a gnarled appearance. A coat of artists' gesso will provide an excellent painting surface.

Pillars can be made from dowel of an appropriate diameter and finished, if necessary, with rectangular bases built from card and circular mouldings made from thin, smooth string or plastic-coated electrical wire wrapped around the dowel where appropriate. The accompanying illustrations show simple methods of making miniature capitals.

Miniature, turned balusters and newel posts can be bought from dolls' house suppliers or shops selling materials for building model galleons. It is possible to buy a model-makers' lathe and turn these elements yourself, but they tend to be expensive and require a good deal of skill in use. If you only need only one or two turned items, perhaps for a newel post or a period lamp post, you can make them by wrapping thread around a length of stiff wire to build up the silhouette required, brushing the thread generously with

The Classical Orders

There are three main 'orders' of ancient Greek architecture, which are easily identified by the 'capitals' or the decorative tops of pillars. In chronological sequence of their development they are:

Doric The simplest of the three orders, consisting solely of rings of moulding running around the column, and a square block at the very top; typically, the pillars have no base nor plinth.

Doric

Ionic The one which looks like the top of a capital 'I'; note that the pillar looks quite different when viewed from a side rather than the front.

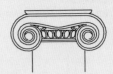

Ionic

Corinthian The most decorative and elaborate of the three orders and the one that has been most frequently adapted (and bastardized) by later generations.

Corinthian

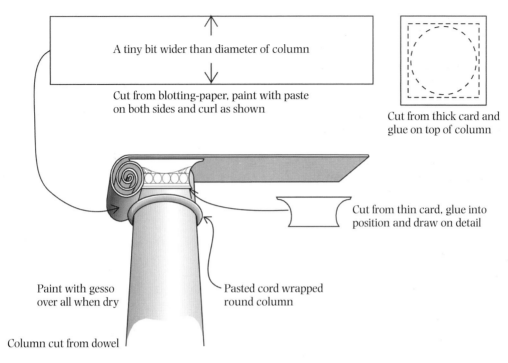

A tiny bit wider than diameter of column

Cut from blotting-paper, paint with paste on both sides and curl as shown

Cut from thick card and glue on top of column

Cut from thin card, glue into position and draw on detail

Paint with gesso over all when dry

Pasted cord wrapped round column

Column cut from dowel

Ionic capitals for model columns.

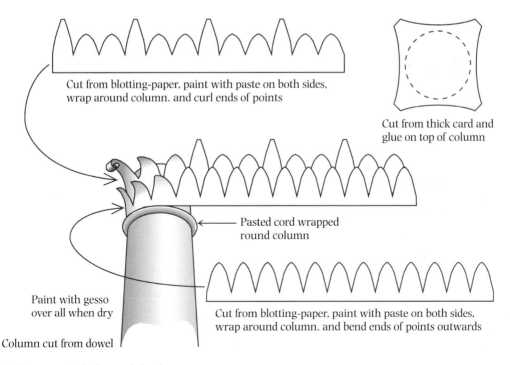

Cut from blotting-paper, paint with paste on both sides, wrap around column. and curl ends of points

Cut from thick card and glue on top of column

Pasted cord wrapped round column

Paint with gesso over all when dry

Column cut from dowel

Cut from blotting-paper, paint with paste on both sides, wrap around column. and bend ends of points outwards

Corinthian capitals for model columns.

ABOVE: *Model with architectural details (eagle balcony support and flower urns), cast in plaster from latex moulds.*

LEFT: *Model banisters made from beads and wire wrapped with thread.*

paste as you work and finishing with a layer of artists' gesso when the paste has dried to present a smooth surface for painting.

Casting Architectural Features

Elements such as corbels, balusters, decorative capitals and urns may be cast in fine plaster. Draw the outline of the object to scale on a piece of wood or card to use as a guide and model on to it directly, using a modelling material such as Plasticine. Take care to avoid undercuts which will make the cast difficult to remove from the mould. Place the Plasticine model on a flat base and paint it with Vaseline as a barrier before painting with several coats of liquid latex (a synthetic rubber solution available from craft shops). Allow the latex to dry between each coat. When the rubber mould is thoroughly dry, discard the Plasticine model, clean the mould and you are ready to take

a cast. Craft shops sell a fine plaster ideal for this type of work. Wet the inside of the mould and mix a small quantity of the plaster with a little water (always add the plaster to the water, not vice versa). The mixed plaster needs to be about the consistency of cream, to make sure that it runs into all the little crevices in the mould. Flex the rubber mould to remove air bubbles as you add the plaster, then leave to set. The plaster usually takes about an hour to set thoroughly, after which you can carefully remove the hardened cast, clean the mould and make more casts as required. The whole process is somewhat lengthy, but is a good way to make a series of identical objects. The latex moulds will last indefinitely, so you can gradually build up a library of moulds for frequently used objects.

Tiny rococo swirls can be made by piping them directly on to the model with thin plaster

84

from a disposable syringe. This will, of course, ruin the syringe so do all the work in one session, if possible.

Curtains and Other Fabrics

Do not attempt to use actual fabrics on models to represent stage drapes or features such as window curtains or tablecloths. This is never really effective, for even if you use the finest possible fabrics the small scale will always prevent them from behaving like real drapes. Use black card for black borders or flat black drops. Drapery such as the black legs used for side masking may be represented in the same way or by using corrugated cardboard painted black to suggest the vertical folds of hanging drapery.

The amount of fullness in window curtains is so very small when working to scale that they can often best be suggested by merely drawing or painting the folds on to a scrap of coloured paper cut to the appropriate shape and then glued into position. Swags may be made by modelling and casting as described above or carved from balsa wood. Blotting paper, painted with a paste such as Gloy to make it floppy, makes good table cloths and bedspreads and hardens to shape as it dries. 'Blackwrap', the thin, black, metal foil used by stage electricians to confine the spread of light beams, makes good miniature tablecloths. It can easily be cut to the appropriate size and shape with scissors, then pressed over the model table to suggest realistic folds. The matt black surface accepts paint quite well. Upholstered furniture such as armchairs or sofas may be carved from balsa wood and upholstered in pasted blotting paper. Cushions and pillows may be made from little pads of pasted blotting paper, rolled or folded to the desired shape and size, and allowed to harden before being painted.

'Flocked' paper, with a velvet-like pile, is useful for making fitted carpets. The range of colours available is somewhat limited and tends to be too intense for most model work, but you can buy

white or grey and spray it to the colour required with a diffuser. Patterns can be drawn on it with coloured felt-tip pens if required.

Gauzes

Gauzes can be difficult to represent in models since these become effective only when appropriately lit. A piece of silk organza of the desired colour can be used to suggest a plain, sharkstooth gauze. Iron the organza to remove any creases and mount it into a frame cut from a sheet of stout card so that it will hang properly and flat in the model box. You can omit the cardboard frame at the bottom edge if it is visible and either leave it hanging loose or support it by neatly gluing the fabric around a length of very thin metal rod.

A painted gauze can be suggested by first preparing a colour rendering on paper or card, then scanning it into your computer and printing it out on to a sheet of the specially coated acetate available for whatever type of printer you use. This

Detail of set model showing rococo details made by applying fine plaster from a syringe.

will provide a semi-transparent image that you can use in the model box; but it will not behave exactly like the full-scale, sharkstooth gauze on stage. However, an advantage of this method is that it leaves you with the original colour rendering for the scene painters to work from.

People

One or two miniature people at the same scale as the model are a great asset. They are especially useful when showing a model as they give an instant impression of scale. You can buy figures from architectural model suppliers, but they are expensive and are available only in modern clothes. You can easily sketch generic male and female figures to scale on a small piece of card and cut them out. Make them stand up by gluing a small triangular support at the back or by gluing a needle to the back with the point protruding just a tiny distance below the bottom edge so that they can be stuck into the model wherever they are required.

Probably the most effective method of making scale figures for a specific show is to take the costume designs, scan them into a computer and then reduce them to the correct scale with your favourite graphic software and print out a miniature version of the figure in costume in full colour. These can then be mounted on to thin card, cut out and supported as described above.

The Model Box

A well-presented model should show any relevant parts of the architectural structure of the stage house. Usually, on a proscenium stage, this will consist of the stage walls and the proscenium. Black foam-core board is useful here, but make sure that your model does not become too difficult to handle or view properly when these elements are added. It may be useful to make the model proscenium removable. Scenery that is not intended to move should be glued into position. But do not glue down furniture – the director may want to try out alternative arrangements on the model and you will probably want to save it for recycling. Flown items such as backcloths can be hung in position from lengths of wood or metal rods made to span the model box and drop into numbered slots at the top of the side walls. This makes them easy to remove or drop into their correct positions when demonstrating your design from the model.

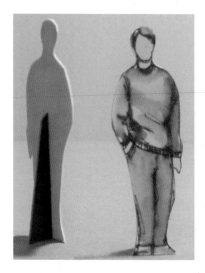

A simple cut-out figure can give scale to set models.

Costume designs scanned, reduced to scale, glued to thin card and cut out to populate a set model and give a sense of scale.

The giant's hands – often observed when the designer is presenting his model. Photo: Fat Chance Productions

Do make sure that the completed model is firmly glued together and that any movable parts are sturdily supported so that they cannot topple over. Presenting your work to the actors and technicians can be a rather nerve-racking experience and pieces that fall over or drop apart in your hands will only make you more nervous and not show your work in its best light.

PAINTING THE MODEL

Equipment

Palette
Many designers use plates, old tin lids or whatever comes to hand for mixing colours, but it is worth buying one or two porcelain palettes conveniently designed to hold little pools of paint in the indentations. Whatever you use, having some-

thing white will make it easier to assess the colours you are mixing.

Brushes
The very best brushes for use with watercolour have red sable bristles, made from the tips of the tail hairs of the Siberian mink. Second to these in quality are camel hair brushes (really squirrel hair). However, really good brushes are extremely expensive, and to use them to paint set models that are often rough textured and painted by using deliberately unconventional brush techniques, will quickly ruin them. Fortunately, good synthetic brushes are available which are much cheaper and excellent for model work. You will need brushes that will form a good point when wet and not all brushes will do this. (Many artists buying brushes wait until nobody is looking and wet the bristles between their lips to check the point, but sensitive suppliers place a little water in a handy position to discourage this unhealthy habit.) Gently press the side of the bristles on to a surface to check that they will spring back into position again. Some cheap brushes will have no spring in them at all and will stick out annoyingly at an angle after each stroke. You will need a range of three or four brushes, in sizes ranging from thick to thin. A good selection might be sizes 9, 4, 2, 1 and possibly 00 (very thin). Keep your old, worn brushes for painting very roughly textured models, and buy one or two cheap children's paintbrushes that you can treat as disposable for use with substances such as spirit varnishes that you know will ruin them.

Ruling Pen
This type of pen is often packaged with a compass set since it may be used with a pair of compasses

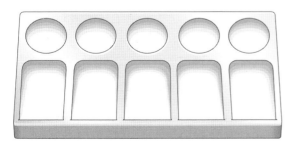

ABOVE: *Ruling pen.*

LEFT: *Palette for mixing watercolour paints.*

87

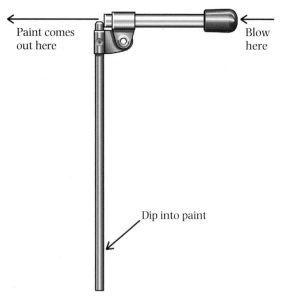

Paint comes out here ← ← Blow here

Dip into paint

ABOVE: *Diffuser for use by mouth.*

RIGHT: *Using a toothbrush for a spatter effect.*

for drawing circles in ink. It is used only rarely now, and many people do not realize exactly what it is for; however, it can be a handy tool for drawing lines of any reasonable thickness and with almost any liquid medium you wish. In model making it is useful for painting thin gold lines along period mouldings, highlighting panelling or painting miniature, striped wallpapers. Mix a little paint to a suitable flowing consistency but do not dip the pen itself into the paint or ink, instead, fill the pen with a sable brush by drawing the bristles along the side of the claw nib so that a small amount of colour is held between the prongs. Adjust the thickness of the line with the screw at the side. The pen may be used with a ruler or, of course, fitted into a pair of compasses for drawing circles.

Diffuser

This simple and inexpensive instrument designed for spraying fixative is very useful for producing sprayed textures with any liquid medium. Just hold the long end in the ink or paint, adjust the angle and blow into the end with the little plastic mouthpiece. The spray will come out of the end opposite the mouthpiece. The spray is not narrowly controllable so protect your work surface when using the diffuser.

Sponge

A small piece of natural sponge is useful for applying a painted texture to surfaces. Buy a very small one, you will not be able to get into tiny corners with a large sponge. Roll the sponge around in your fingers when texturing to avoid a repetitive pattern. Avoid messy fingers by wearing a rubber glove. Wet the sponge to soften it before use and clean it as thoroughly as possible as soon as you have finished.

Toothbrush

Not a tool intended for painting set models, but useful for producing a fine spatter effect. Dip the ends of the bristles in the paint medium and draw your thumb along them, with a little practice a surprising variety of spatters may be produced. Again, wear a rubber glove to avoid messy fingers, and, it should hardly be necessary to say, do not use the brush for teeth cleaning afterwards ...

Airbrush

This is an exciting instrument that is capable of producing some wonderful effects. It is particularly useful for painting set models as we frequently need to gradate the paintwork on scenery to black at the top and sides. The scene painter will probably use a paint spray to do this and the airbrush can produce the same effect in miniature. Spraying obliquely across a textured surface with a highlight or shadow colour can emphasize a rough texture dramatically. However, the airbrush has many disadvantages: it is expensive to buy, temperamental in use and requires a degree of skill to produce the best results. A really thorough cleaning each time it is used is absolutely essential; use a special solvent sold for the purpose and spray through the brush until you are quite sure no pigment at all remains. You will probably find that you spend more time cleaning the airbrush than you do painting with it, but, if you neglect it, you will need to buy an entire new matched needle–nozzle assembly.

Air for use with airbrushes is available in pressurized cans. However, these are expensive and you will use up most of it in cleaning the brush. A small compressor is a good investment if you are planning to do a lot of airbrush work, but make sure that you buy one that is compatible with your make of brush.

You can use almost any type of paint (diluted to about the consistency of milk) in an airbrush, but the ready-mixed colours made especially for this kind of work are best. They are less likely to clog the brush and usually come in a bottle with a convenient dropper in the cap. Take great care if you decide to use acrylic paint, it is not water-soluble when dry and can easily ruin an airbrush if it is not cleaned out really thoroughly and often.

Materials

Paints

The type of paint you use depends to a large extent upon personal preference. It is advisable to use water-based paints for compatibility and ease of use, and gouache, acrylic or watercolour paints are all popular.

Gouache or designers' colour has good opacity and brilliance and may be bought in small tubes from art stores. This is probably the most popular type of paint for set design work generally. An extremely wide range of colours is available, but note that some colours, such as those made from rare natural pigments, are much more expensive than others. Acrylic paints are also available in tubes. They do not have quite the same degree of opacity as gouache, have a slight eggshell finish when undiluted but are less easily damaged by handling and are excellent for large areas of flat colour.

Watercolours are available in tubes or in tablet form. They contain no body colour, as lighter tones are obtained by thinning the paint with water to allow the white paper to show through. They are always transparent to some degree, and will never completely paint out a colour beneath. They are excellent when used to produce layered effects with consecutive transparent washes of colour.

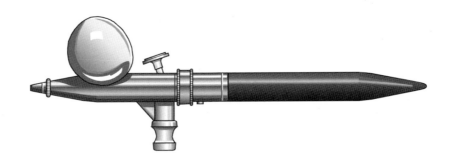

Airbrush.

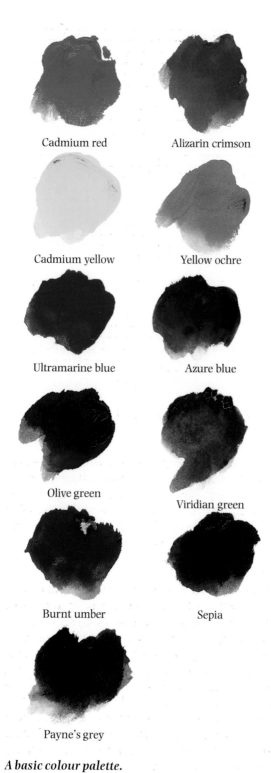

Cadmium red   Alizarin crimson

Cadmium yellow   Yellow ochre

Ultramarine blue   Azure blue

Olive green

Viridian green

Burnt umber   Sepia

Payne's grey

A basic colour palette.

It is a good idea to keep a wide selection of colouring materials, including artists' inks, coloured pens, pencils, wax crayons, felt-tipped markers and a range of metallic colours. The fine artist may want to avoid mixing different media, but the stage designer is primarily interested in indicating his intentions by whatever means necessary and is usually unconcerned about maintaining the purity of the medium.

A basic palette might consist of the following pigments:

- two reds: cadmium red and alizarin crimson
- two yellows: cadmium yellow and yellow ochre
- two blues: ultramarine blue and azure blue
- two greens: olive green and viridian green
- two browns: burnt umber and sepia
- a grey for mixing with colours to reduce intensity: Payne's grey.

You will need large amounts of white and black so buy them in large tubes. Somewhat confusingly, several different kinds of black and white are available. Most useful are permanent white for greatest opacity, zinc white (which is slightly transparent but produces clearer tints when mixed with other colours) and ivory black (a rich black that mixes well with other colours to produce darker tones); lamp black is more opaque but tends to turn colours slightly muddy when mixed.

Gesso
This is available ready-mixed as a fine white paste, intended for use by artists to prepare a surface for painting. It is excellent for unifying several different types of surface, such as card and wood, and to hide the exposed cut edges of card when it is joined at corners. A spray-on version is available, but usually the gesso is applied with a brush. It dries quickly and gives a very good, slightly toothed surface suitable for most types of paint. However, do not just automatically cover the entire model with gesso; any surfaces intended to suggest very smooth, reflective textures such as polished wood or marble are best left untreated. Gesso has a tendency to create a slight chalky effect that may not be desirable in all cases.

Polyfilla

A useful material for texturing models and creating effects such as distressed plaster, brick walls, stucco and a variety of abstract textural effects. Do not be tempted to buy the ready-mixed kind, the powder form is much more useful since it may be mixed to any consistency desired, or even deliberately badly mixed for a particularly uneven texture. A yogurt pot is a good container for mixing. Do not mix too much at a time since it dries remarkably quickly, and always remember to add the plaster to the water, not the water to the plaster. Polyfilla contains an adhesive to prevent flaking and chipping. If you use plaster of Paris or a similar material you will need to add a little white glue to the mixture or it will crumble away when dry. A coat of Polyfilla can be easily inscribed with a cocktail stick or a sharpened matchstick as it dries to produce pointing lines. Choose an appropriate bond.

Pay particular heed to the Dreadful Warning above: a surface with any kind of plaster applied to it will have a much stronger tendency to warp than with paint alone. Apply plenty of extra support wherever possible to avoid a ruined model.

Varnishes

Very smooth or polished surfaces can be greatly enhanced with one or two coats of suitable varnish. Several types are available from art suppliers; Winsor & Newton make a poster colour varnish that is particularly useful. Varnish will soak unevenly into most cardboard or paper surfaces so treat the first coat as a sealant and apply a second one for a good gloss finish. Matt varnish may seem a slight contradiction in terms, but, although producing only a very slight sheen, a matt varnish will enrich colours and textures, restoring some of the intensity of the wet paint that is often lost as it dries. Most varnishes are spirit-based, so you will need the appropriate solvent, usually methylated or white spirit, to clean your brush after use. This is a task for one of your cheap, disposable brushes, but, since these often shed their bristles easily, make sure that you do not get unsightly loose hairs trapped in the varnish.

Emulsion glazes are available which have the

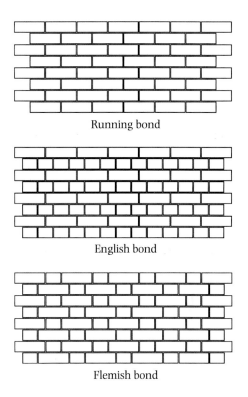

Running bond

English bond

Flemish bond

Some common masonry bonds.

advantage of being water-based and therefore capable of being diluted. However, they will never produce the same high gloss as a spirit-based varnish and are somewhat unpredictable, often picking up the paint beneath and creating nasty smears. Always test carefully before use.

Techniques

A primary rule is always to test colours in combination before applying any paint to a model. Paint will often dry a few degrees lighter or darker than it appears when wet. A small quantity of colour seen against a white surface looks quite different from the same colour when seen among other colours, and you will inevitably need to make some adjustments to take this into account. You can, of course, apply successive coats of paint to a model to adjust the colours, but not indefinitely. You will find that the surface quality rapidly deteriorates. Lay in your largest areas of colour first so that you may judge smaller areas of colour in relation to them.

Good quality paints will permit a great degree of mixing before losing integrity. Cheaper paints such as children's poster colours rapidly turn to mud when mixed. Artists' colours are extremely intense so you will only rarely need to use a pigment directly from the tube. Mixing the colours and adding white, black or grey in varying amounts will produce a literally infinite range of hues, tints and tones.

Carefully analyse the colours around you in everyday life, check the greys in a streetscape for example; they are rarely simply a mixture of black and white: a type of grey generally confined to the sides of battleships. The greys we see about us inevitably contain an amount of other colours in the mix. Do not make assumptions about colours, for instance, you probably think that tree trunks are brown, but if you examine them you will find that they are grey, green, silver and cream. In fact, they are almost any colour except brown. The wood that we see about us in our living rooms often appears to be brown, but this is usually the result of staining and polishing, and, even then, the finished surface can vary between a deep, rich red and a very pale beige.

Observe a plain wall painted in a single colour, features such as mouldings, recesses or corners may all be painted in exactly the same colour, but are still readily discernible to the eye, even though there is no kind of line around them to give definition. This, of course, is because the light hitting them is directional, often from a window or an artificial source such as a lamp, supplemented by an amount of reflected light, usually from the ceiling. In the theatre, the stage is lit from a great number of artificial sources, often coming from all directions and so natural shadows tend to be eliminated. A good lighting designer will try to counteract this effect, of course, and balance the light levels to obtain the best definition, but the set designer and the scene painter can also help by suggesting a little of the effect of directional lighting by darkening inside corners, running subtle lines of painted shadow under features such as mouldings and sometimes enhancing the effect with painted highlights. Dragging a brush containing a little highlight colour, considerably lighter in tone than the base colour, over a textured surface will dramatically emphasize the roughness of the texture. Similarly, steps and staircases can be enhanced by painting the risers slightly darker than the treads for added definition.

Not only is stage lighting multidirectional, it is also often heavily coloured. Discuss with the lighting designer how best to enhance your colour scheme, not necessarily to make it more appealing but how to achieve the particular tone, mood or atmosphere you are aiming for. Sometimes you may decide, say, to use slightly cooler colours than you had originally planned so that they will accept warm, tinted lighting without becoming overly hot. At other times you may choose to intensify

Some Colour Definitions

hue another name for colour

tint any colour with white added to make it paler

shade any colour with black added to make it darker

tone the lightness or darkness of a colour as opposed to its hue

intensity the strength (brightness or dullness) of a colour

primary colours red, yellow, blue; three colours that cannot be mixed from other colours

secondary colours colours such as green, orange and purple that can be made by mixing two primary colours together

intermediate or tertiary colours colours such as orangey-reds or yellowy-greens, made by mixing a primary and a secondary colour together

complementary colours two colours that, combined together, contain all three primary colours, such as red + green, orange + blue or blue/green + red/orange; complementary colours are situated directly opposite to each other on a conventional colour wheel

key colour the dominant colour in a colour scheme or mixture of colours.

your colour scheme, emphasizing contrasts, so that it may be deliberately toned down by the lighting designer, without reducing it to visual atonality.

Remember that, although you may be creating designs on a white surface at home in your workplace, the background colour in a theatre is black. This may affect your choice of hue and intensity. Sometimes it is helpful to spray some black on to the periphery of your set at the top or the sides or both, softening the harsh division between the edges of the set and any black masking adjacent to it. It can reproduce, to some extent, the effect of a concentration of light at the centre, focusing the audience's attention on the acting area.

The amount of painted light and shade you use will depend upon the style of the design. A degree of deliberate artificiality is sometimes appropriate, but at other times this may be toned down to be hardly noticeable or ignored altogether. There are no rules here. You must use your best judgment as a designer.

The textural qualities of the surfaces in the model are as important as the colour quality, arguably more so, and you should pay careful attention to reproducing these as effectively as possible. Is a wooden surface rough or smooth? Has the wood been polished? Exposed to the weather? Worn with age? Are stone surfaces rough or smooth? Is the surface natural or artificial? Highly polished surfaces such as marble and some woods benefit greatly from a high gloss finish. Experiment with the different types of artists' varnish available at your art store, and with different methods of application to achieve the effect you need.

For distressed surfaces try painting on layers of thin, tinted washes of dirty water: Try adding a little blue and some brown to a lot of water to produce a useful *mouse* colour, somewhere between brown and grey. Work the wash into corners where grime would tend to gather. Do not be overhasty, effective distressing is a gradual process.

Remember that it is much easier to paint the floor of your model *before* gluing the set to it.

PHOTOGRAPHING THE MODEL

When the model is complete you will probably want to photograph it. Photographing a scale model works a little special magic on it, for the sense of the 'miniature' is removed in a photograph and it becomes easier to visualize your model as a full-sized set.

Set up the model at a convenient working height and light it with one or two small, adjustable lamps, eliminating unsightly shadows as much as possible. Small halogen desk lamps are ideal for this. If you wish, experiment with a few coloured frosted lighting gels. These can be particularly useful for lighting a model cyclorama or sky cloth.

Polaroid or digital cameras, offering the advantage of instant results, are excellent. Digital images, either direct from a digital camera or scanned from a print, can be usefully manipulated by using computer techniques, not only as a way to eliminate inaccuracies but also to add digital furniture and set dressings from other sources, or to populate the set with digital actors to give a sense of scale.

Keep photographs for your own records, of course, but also circulate copies to all the departments working on the show. The model will not always be available when needed and a photograph can be a useful reference. Make sure that a photograph of the model is pinned to a wall in the rehearsal room. Actors will appreciate the opportunity to familiarize themselves with the set they are to work on.

krill
often

6 STYLE AND CREATIVITY

WHAT IS MEANT BY STYLE?

Theatre is probably the only art form that is firmly based on *fakery*. Actors may devote much time and effort to create a character built upon truth and rooted in reality, but, in order to present that truth and reality convincingly to an audience, they must employ a wide range of techniques that are actually calculated to deceive. Juliet is not really in love with Romeo and the actor playing Macbeth is not really a murderer. It is all fake.

The same might be said of the set designer's work. Even if we decided to present Macbeth's castle at Dunsinane as realistically as is humanly possible, built from real stone and timbers, it would still be an obvious fake for we would need to remove at least part of the castle wall so that the audience could see what goes on inside. We would also need to remove a large part of the roof to light it efficiently, and through the windows we would see the back wall of the theatre, unless we placed a fake sky behind them. In any case, the actors would not be speaking nor behaving like real people and so would not belong to the realistic world we have attempted to create.

Theatrical truth goes far beyond the mere reproduction of reality. The theatre works special magic, and scenery, costumes and lighting all combine to convince us that what the actors present for us has a particular kind of reality. We are persuaded to participate in the obvious

OPPOSITE: Collages are very quick to create and can sometimes be a help in establishing colours or tonal and textural qualities appropriate to a production. This one was for J.M. Synge's play Riders To The Sea.

deception happening in front of us. In musical theatre the deception is even more obvious, for here the performers will break into song or dance in a manner that is ostensibly quite ridiculous but actually has the power to move us through a gamut of emotions from laughter to tears.

The set designer is one of the most significant conspirators in this deception since it is he or she who creates the world in which it can take place. The designer, in collaboration with the director, must carefully consider the nature of this artificial world of the play (or opera or ballet) and create a special space that not only provides the physical requirements of the action but actually goes much further than this, becoming an integral element of the whole artistic creation.

It is not sufficient merely to present the physical location of a scene in a realistic manner. In his book *The Dramatic Imagination*, the American stage designer Robert Edmond Jones wrote:

> Scene designing is not what most people imagine it is – a branch of interior decorating. There is no more reason for a room on a stage to be a reproduction of an actual room than for an actor who plays the part of Napoleon to be Napoleon or for an actor who plays Death in the old morality play to be dead. Everything that is actual must undergo a strange metamorphosis, a kind of sea-change, before it can become truth in the theatre.

Compared with the interior designer, the set designer is in a quite extraordinary position for he knows in advance every single event that will take place in the space he designs. Thus a room on stage will have different requirements and a totally different style if designed for, say, a comedy by Noël Coward, a drama by Strindberg, a tragedy by

TOP LEFT: *A realistic room set for Sherlock Holmes's study at 221b Baker Street in* Sherlock's Last Case *at the Pitlochry Festival Theatre. Directed by Brian Shelton. Lighting by Paul Covell.*

MIDDLE LEFT: *Decaying columns and dust sheets defining the floor create this only partially realistic room in a literally crumbling hotel for the second Act of* The Ends of the Earth *at the Timms Centre for the Arts in Edmonton, Canada. Live video of the actor upstage behind the window was projected at the back of the set and to on-stage TV sets. Directed by Beau Coleman. Lighting by Lee Livingstone. Photo: Ellis Bros*

BOTTOM LEFT: *This room in the pantomime* Little Red Riding Hood *at The Theatre, Chipping Norton, consists of nothing more than a single painted frontcloth.*

Shakespeare or a Christmas pantomime. Indeed, the room may not physically resemble a real room at all.

The designer must decide upon the dramatic purpose of the room in each case. The Coward play may need to present an air of period elegance and sophistication, with a carefully considered arrangement of doors and furniture in which the action can take place. It may not be totally realistic, but will probably have at least some elements that suggest room-like qualities. The Strindberg room might contain little to suggest location. The dramatist here is not merely relating a story, he is giving us psychological insights into his characters and expects us to consider their actions and reactions in the situations in which he places them. The set needs to reflect this, and the designer and the director will need to discuss what degree of emphasis is to be placed upon the re-creation of a realistic period room. A room in a play by Shakespeare may simply not exist physically at all and furniture and dressings may be minimal. It is Shakespeare's poetic words and ideas, as interpreted and presented by the actors, that work the magic here. His plays may be performed in literally any period and a great range of possibilities exists for the set, from hardly anything at all to a highly conceptualized design like nothing ever seen before. A room in a pantomime may consist of nothing more than a painted backcloth or it may be an elaborate built set full of tricks and surprising special effects. The dramatic action that this 'room' might be required to accommodate could involve characters such as a Demon King, two actors pretending to be a cow and a dozen dancing fairies. It will almost certainly be very colourful and any suggestion of period will not be hampered by an undue regard for historical accuracy.

REALISM AND NATURALISM

A distinction should be made between *realism* and *naturalism*. Realism was an artistic movement in late nineteenth-century drama, reacting against the highly romanticized productions typical of the period and replacing them with plays about ordinary people in real situations. Previous theatrical conventions were cast aside in favour of a style of performance that gave a greater illusion of reality. It was, however, still an illusion.

Realism, as presented on stage, can never be entirely complete. The boundaries of a set and the surrounding architecture of the theatre are always apparent. Therefore we need to consider exactly how and where the realism ends. Today, many settings in the commercial theatre show a degree of simplified realism in which many of the non-essential elements are eliminated, but features such as doorways or window frames are retained.

Selective realism for Dr Stockman's house in a production of Ibsen's An Enemy of the People, *set in the Canadian prairies at the Manitoba Theatre Centre in Winnipeg. Directed by John Hirsch. Lighting by Joe Stell.*

These fragmentary features are sometimes combined with abstract elements. The term 'selective realism' is often used to describe settings of this type.

Realism can also include composite settings, showing several locations on stage at the same time. These may be closely related to each other, as, for example, in a setting showing a cross-section of part of a house or it may consist of an arrangement of geographically disconnected spaces. Each individual space may be suggested in a realistic manner and the audience is expected to ignore the fact that walls are removed or spaces geographically compressed to a remarkable extent.

Naturalism was also an artistic movement in late nineteenth-century drama, but one that aimed to present ordinary life as accurately as humanly possible, with little or, ideally, no illusion. However, the rather depressing plays associated with the movement shocked and alienated audiences with their subject matter and the movement was comparatively short-lived.

Nowadays, the term realism is used in the context of set design to describe a style of setting or production that presents some illusion of reality, using any appropriate theatrical devices, whereas naturalism suggests a production presented with as little artifice as possible.

By the early years of the twentieth century naturalism was considered out of date and symbolism, originating in France, became the fashionable artistic movement. Symbolism attempted to present an inner reality, freed from the trappings of realism or naturalism. Plays were presented in a completely non-realistic style, often in heightened or poetic language. Symbolism is still a viable style today but one that holds traps for the set designer: a concept that may intellectually appear to be ideally appropriate to a production can easily prove inadequate or even completely ridiculous when brought to a logical conclusion on stage. A setting for Chekhov's *The Seagull* consisting solely of a giant seagull might be an extreme example of this.

Abstract settings became popular during the early twentieth century. The style gives no indication of location or period but consists mainly of non-specific elements such as rostra, steps and panels, creating a sense of universality. It is a style that is particularly applicable to classic drama, where locations are not specific and a sense of period is not considered to be significant in the set, such as in the plays of the ancient Greek dramatists.

In the end, attempts to define style precisely are probably futile. Many of the commonly recognized

Setting for Act 2 of Chekhov's **The Cherry Orchard** *at The Royal Lyceum Theatre, Edinburgh. Directed by Stephen McDonald. Lighting by André Tammes.*

A completely abstract setting for a production of The Tempest *at the Thorndike Theatre, Leatherhead. Directed by Robert David MacDonald. Lighting by David St John.*

terms suggest a period rather than a style (such as baroque or art nouveau), or tend to be vague and imprecise (such as deconstructivism or post-modernism), or merely refer to the work of other artists (such as surrealist or Brechtian). It is probably better to work instinctively rather than to make a conscious decision to adopt any specific style. However, it is useful to be familiar with the terms since they are frequently bandied about in discussions with the director.

COLOUR, TEXTURE AND FORM

Anyone visually orientated will probably be unable to resist associating colours with design ideas at a very early stage. However, do not be overhasty to establish a precise colour scheme. Try considering the appropriate *types* of colour before selecting particular hues. Should they be dark or light? Warm or cool? Pale or intense? Allow colour schemes to develop as you work on a design, instead of pre-selecting the colours as you would, perhaps, if you were decorating your living room.

Often the choice of colours will be suggested by the materials you select for your design. Try associating textures with the play. Do you see wood? Stone? Metal? Is the wood finished and polished? Is it in a natural state? Is the stone sharp and jagged or worn and smooth? Is the metal shiny or corroded? Perhaps you visualize the texture of more sophisticated materials such as plastic, chrome, glass or mirror. Can these be translated into a stage setting that is practical, appropriate and artistically satisfying?

The types of shape contained within your set (geometrical, rounded, organic); the proportions

99

(tall, narrow, wide, low); and the quality of the lines you choose (straight, curved, angular, undulating) will subliminally affect the way the audience reacts to your design. Speaking very generally, horizontal lines and proportions can give a sense of ease and relaxation (think of waves at the seaside), whereas strong, vertical lines and tall shapes tend to suggest awe and grandeur (think of the pillars in a Gothic cathedral or giant redwood trees in California). Lines and shapes that appear angular and disorganized create a sense of unease (think of fallen timbers in a bombed building). The designer will often discover ways in which these subconscious reactions can be subtly exploited.

In selecting colours for stage settings we need to be aware of their emotional content in various strengths and combinations. The subliminal effects suggested by the abstract qualities of lines and shapes as suggested above can be reinforced by a complementary use of colour. The sense of ease and relaxation suggested by undulating, horizontal lines can be emphasized by the addition of, say, a cool, bluish colour scheme, a sharp contrast to the effect of vertical shapes when coloured in hot colours such as reds, yellows and orange. Note the effect of randomly selected colours applied to angular compositions when contrasted with the same composition coloured in hues containing only red and blue. The yellow shape near the centre leaps to claim attention, although in the multicoloured composition the same yellow shape is lost in the general confusion. These ideas can be subtly exploited in the colours, tones and textures selected for a stage set. Try excluding one of the primary colours from the design; excluding red, for example, will still permit dark blue, light blue, pale yellow, gold, olive green, sea green and a large number of other hues produced by mixing blue, yellow, black and white in various combinations. The colour schemes resulting from this simple trick will be more harmonious, and the colour omitted may then be used in specific areas for particular emphasis as required.

This restricted palette technique has obvious advantages when designing shows containing a series of colourful painted scenes, but it may also be useful when selecting more subtle colours and textures for settings in serious drama. However, it is not suggested for use as a rule. It is merely a device that can sometimes help to bring an unruly colour scheme under control.

USING THE CREATIVE IMAGINATION

The set designer should not underrate the value of the audience's imaginative ability. Albert Einstein wrote, 'Imagination is more powerful than knowledge', and audiences are generally remarkably willing to become eager accomplices in their own deception. We are familiar with the ease with which an actor can move an audience to tears or laughter by an emotional appeal to the imagination. In a similar way, the set designer can often create physical architectural or geographical features better by suggestion than by showing them in complete, realistic detail.

You may have experienced children playing with found objects such as an old car body, a heap of cardboard boxes or a fallen tree trunk and seen it turned into a cowboy fort or crusader castle merely by a creative leap of a child's imagination. The same magical effect can occur in the theatre, if we provide some appropriate clues, such as those offered by the old car body or fallen tree trunk. A scene taking place in a forest, for example, does not necessarily need to contain a physical representation of trees. You may prefer to suggest the quality of 'forest' by your design; conspire with the lighting designer to produce the appropriate mood and leave the trees to the audience's imagination.

Rather than attempting to design a realistic Dunsinane for *Macbeth*, it might be more appropriate to find a way to create the non-physical world suggested by the play: a world of political intrigue and assassination, the inevitability of a preordained fate, the machinations of mysterious dark forces and the omnipresent imagery of blood. Let the audience's imagination supply the stones and the timbers of the medieval castle.

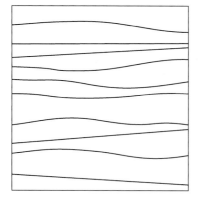

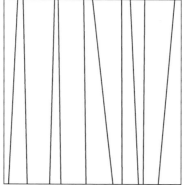

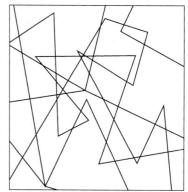

Gently undulating, horizontal lines can produce a sense of ease and relaxation.

Vertical lines can produce a sense of awe and grandeur.

Angular, disorganized lines can produce a sense of unease.

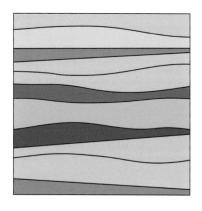

Horizontal lines plus a cool colour scheme.

Vertical lines plus a hot colour scheme.

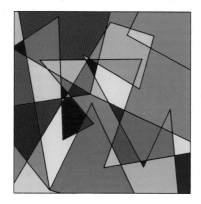

Angular lines plus a random colour scheme.

Angular lines with restricted colour scheme.

101

PRACTICALITIES

Stability and Safety

It should hardly be necessary to point out that your scenery must be stable. All scenery is, by its nature, a temporary structure and this means that there is an ever-present risk of parts shaking, wobbling or even collapsing altogether. Your builder can give good advice about this, but you can help by taking stability into account when designing the structures. Make a note of any parts of the set that may require special reinforcement, such as a door that will be slammed heavily or a wall that an actor is to fall against. You should not expect the builder to solve all your structural problems for you, and, if any necessary supporting features are considered at the design stage, they can be integrated into the design scheme as a whole. Often you will find that the necessity of incorporating these supporting elements into your structures can actually be a spur to the creative imagination rather than a limitation, guiding you into directions you would not have considered otherwise. It can be useful to take careful note of any unstable features in the model. Elements that tend to fall over or easily collapse in a well-made scale model will probably have a tendency to do the same thing when the set is built at full size.

Handrails should be provided on any high levels or along high runs of steps. An actor who feels unsafe will not be able to perform to the best of his ability, and a handrail in sympathy with the style of the set can often become a valuable design feature. However, occasionally you may feel that a handrail is not desirable for artistic reasons and you should then anticipate a possible problem and discuss the matter with the director, the cast and the production manager. Much will depend on the type of action planned and whether the actors feel confident. Often just a thin strip of wood fixed along the edges of rostra so that performers can easily feel the edge with a foot will help. Bear in mind that theatre differs from real life in that every action taking place during a performance is rehearsed in detail, so some of the safety precautions required in everyday life are not always necessary on stage. However, if performers express doubt or insecurity, play safe and provide handrails.

Note that off-stage access steps should always be provided with sturdy handrails with a white or luminous edge to each step. An actor leaving a brightly lit stage for the comparative darkness of the wings may be momentarily blinded by the abrupt change of light level.

Furniture

Stage furniture is not governed by the same considerations as furniture in real life: To begin with, on stage the term 'furniture' includes boxes, rocks, wooden blocks, tree stumps or, indeed, anything that may be sat on, stood on, leaned against or generally treated in the way a piece of furniture may be treated in reality. All stage furniture and props need to be arranged in a manner not only to be appropriate to the location and the period in which they appear, but also to supply the needs of the action required to take place on and around them. Sometimes even the number of paces an actor needs to take between a chair and a table may be crucial. Many of Alan Ayckbourn's plays are notable in this respect. Remember that in a period play actors may be wearing restrictive costumes or required to behave in a much more formal manner than we do today. Small chairs can easily be knocked over and low-seated sofas can make it impossible for an actor to sit down or stand up with any degree of grace.

Edward Gordon Craig, in his book *Scene*, wrote that Molière could arrange three or four chairs on his stage so that they seemed to act '... and plead for the actor to use them', and indeed, the design of a whole set can sometimes be developed around a particular arrangement of furniture and props. Two characters discovering mutual feelings of love during a scene, for example, may begin by sitting apart on separate seats, but gradually move physically closer as the scene progresses. In this case the furniture needs to be carefully arranged to permit this, and allow the actors to communicate their emotions to the audience at the same time. The furniture arrangement can provide the ostensible motivation for each step in the move towards each other. Perhaps drinks are

The Death of Mrs Condomine

Act 1, Scene 1

Summer, 7.00pm. The elegantly furnished drawing room of a large country house in Sussex. French windows at the back open onto a well-kept garden. There is a door leading to the entrance hall in the stage left wall. As the curtain rises, the dead body of Mrs Condomine is discovered lying on the Persian carpet at centre stage.

The door L. opens and Mr Condomine enters. He stands, horror-struck, his hand on the doorknob:

MR CONDOMINE: My God! Mabel! ...

The door at stage left could be hung to open in one of several ways. Which do you think would be most effective?

Example 1

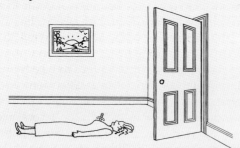

We can see the door opening, but Mr Condomine is completely hidden. We cannot see who actually says the line.

Example 2

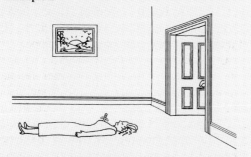

Again, we can see the door opening, and possibly see part of Mr Condomine as he discovers the body,

but the action of opening the door forces him to step backwards from the direction in which he is moving.

Example 3

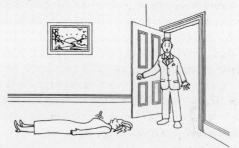

This time, the action of opening the door propels Mr Condomine onto the stage. We can clearly see him and his reaction to the horrifying discovery of his wife's body.

You may think that Example 3 is the obvious choice. However, Example 2 does have the possible merit of suspense: the door opens, but there is a short delay before we see who is entering and we wonder who it can be. Is this the effect required at this particular moment? In a thriller it could be important that the audience does not know who discovers the body. In this case, Example 1 may be the preferred choice. Discuss your choice with the director so that you both agree upon the effect intended.

poured? The position of the drinks table in relation to other pieces of furniture then becomes important, providing intermediate steps in the sequence of moves. Where are the actors to put down their glasses? A small table placed in just the right position could draw them towards each other by the mere act of setting down a glass.

The specific style of each piece of furniture can also play an important role. For example, a scene in which two characters have an argument may benefit by having one sitting on a chair which is a little higher or obviously more comfortable than the other, placing him physically in a slightly superior position. A scene between a man and a woman in a small flat may acquire particular overtones merely by the presence of a bed in the room, especially if it is a double bed.

Even a scene containing little or no furniture will inevitably contain elements that dictate the actors' movements to some extent. The balcony in *Romeo and Juliet*, for example, must be placed so that Juliet on the balcony and Romeo below can both be clearly seen as they interact with each other, and as Juliet reacts to the off-stage voice of the Nurse, but also allows them to react indirectly with the audience. The characters occupy separate yet united worlds. Creative lighting, with perhaps a stream of warm light from the window striking Juliet and cool moonlight on Romeo below, would be invaluable here, making a distinctive colour separation between the two characters, which is eliminated when Romeo draws physically closer to Juliet on the balcony and shares her warm light. Careful positioning of the various scenic elements to permit this and their integration into the overall production style is of vital importance. It cannot merely be left to chance.

Play a mental game of 'what if?' with your ideas. What if that platform were twice as high? What if it were curved? Made of glass? What would happen if the set were painted entirely in red? – or white? – or black? Stretch your imagination. Sometimes the exercise can be remarkably productive.

Let There Be Light!

Generally speaking, stages are windowless and dark. Everything we see during a performance is revealed to us by specially placed stage lights (usually referred to as lanterns or luminaires in European theatre). However, these lanterns not only reveal the actors and our setting to the audience, they are also an important creative element in their own right.

Until the latter half of the 1950s it was usual for a show to be lit by the director in collaboration with the set designer and the stage electrician. The programme never contained a credit for lighting designer. However, with the development of new techniques and changing attitudes to stage design in general, designers were eventually engaged specifically to create the lighting for a production. The first lighting designer to receive billing in Britain was Michael Northen (1921–2001) when he lit John Gielgud's *King Lear* at Stratford-upon-Avon in 1950. The lighting designer is now one of the set designer's greatest allies. In fact, they are often the same person carrying out both jobs.

Stage lights are not fixed in place. Many theatres incorporate a house-hang, with lanterns hung in the same positions more or less permanently. However, these can usually either be rehung in more favourable positions or supplemented by other lanterns rigged specially for a specific show, or both. Until the early 1960s it was considered important to conceal all on-stage lights from the audience and they were inevitably carefully hidden behind borders or other scenic elements. Little consideration was given to the use of backlighting for extra definition, and most stage lights were generally directed solely from the front. Since then, however, lighting practice has changed considerably and lanterns in full view of the audience have become acceptable, making a much wider range of possibilities available to the lighting designer. Whether to hide or reveal on-stage light sources is now a design decision to be made for each individual production.

The main object of stage lighting is, of course, to reveal the performers to the audience, aiding that process of communication which is the very essence of all theatre. However, it can go much further than this, intensifying mood, creating specific atmospheres and reacting to the events taking place. Light on stage will subtly modulate throughout a performance, often without the audience realizing it. It is possible to change the quality of light in many ways: the focus can be hard or soft, light beams may be wide or narrow. Light may be coloured, diffused or textured by means of gobos. Static or moving images can be projected in a variety of ways. Changes of location or time in an abstract set are often suggested merely by a change in lighting. However, the setting must be designed to allow for the possibility of creative lighting. A set designer who does not consider the needs of the lighting designer is imposing a severe restriction on his own work. Even the latest technological advances will not permit light beams to bend around corners or simply cut off at a specific point. Involve the lighting designer in the creative process at an early stage.

Using Projections

Now that projectors can give reasonably sharp images even under quite strong ambient light, at some stage (often when a production hits budget problems) someone will suggest the use of projected scenery instead of built or painted scenery. The idea is usually discussed, and then abandoned as impracticable. Projections should not be looked upon as merely a cheap alternative to other forms of scenery. They are a useful, but severely limited, design tool, and should not be considered as an end in themselves. Neither are they really economical, for not only do they require specially designed and processed media to project but they are quite useless without appropriate surfaces to accept the images and a set specially designed to make their use technically possible.

To project a clear image on stage you should provide a suitable surface to project upon and sufficient unobstructed space, either in front of it (for front-projection) or behind it (for back-projection) to give the size of image desired. The larger the projected image, the longer the throw that will be required. Consult the lighting designer about this. If it is not possible to place the projector centrally you will find that the image becomes 'key-stoned'. That is, it will be distorted from a rectangular image to a trapezium-shaped image.

This may not be a problem with some textural projections, but could be very noticeable with pictorial images. The lighting designer should be able to provide counter-keystoned slides to compensate for this, but he will need to know exactly where the projector is to be placed in relation to the surface receiving the projected image.

Back-projection is particularly appropriate for stage use since the projector can be set low enough to provide little distortion, without the possibility that the actors will walk into the beam. However, you will need considerable depth to the stage for it to be really effective. A projection beam can sometimes be bounced around a corner by the use of strategically placed mirrors, but the intensity of the final image will always suffer to some extent.

A special vinyl material for back-projection screens is generally available in white, off-white, grey or (most usefully) black. The black rear-projection screen has the remarkable ability to provide a really sharp and clear, coloured, projected image, but if set against a dark background it will become almost invisible when not in use.

Moving projections are ideal for weather and atmospheric effects. Falling rain or snow, various types of drifting cloud, swirling water and many other effects are available, but should always be planned at an early stage in the design process to ensure the best possible technical conditions for them to be really effective.

The Stage Floor

Many theatres have banked or balcony seating, so members of the audience may find that a large percentage of their field of vision is occupied by the stage floor. The treatment of this vitally important element should be an integral part of the design.

The worst kind of stage floor encountered by a designer is the very beautiful and expensive wooden parquet flooring often found in concert halls and school assembly rooms. The managing authority is naturally anxious to preserve its pristine appearance and will allow no nail, screw or spot of paint to approach it. This type of floor is totally intractable and the only solution is to cover it up entirely with sheets of thick plywood or blockboard, or at least a painted floor cloth.

However, most stage floors are only semi-permanent so they can be painted or otherwise treated as required for each individual production, then replaced, completely or in part, when it becomes necessary. Many stages contain traps of various dimensions, and modern theatre buildings often incorporate a stage floor that is specially designed so that any portion of it may be removed completely if needed. This means that you can design steps leading down to the sub-stage area, fit elevators for special effects, set in a pool of real water (use a plastic swimming pool liner) or even plant a garden with real grass (it will need to have special grow-lamps left on over it at night). Most productions will not require such elaborate floors as these, but the surface treatment of the stage floor is as important, if not more so, than any of the other elements in the set.

The simplest method of treating the floor is simply to paint it. This can be remarkably successful on a stage floor, but, since the audience never sees the paintwork from directly in front but always at a sharply oblique angle, much fine detail will be lost. However, contrasts in texture become more apparent for the same reason. A high gloss surface will be even more reflective from the auditorium and contrasting textures will be clearly differentiated. Floors painted to look like marble or polished wood can be particularly effective when the painted surface has been given several coats of emulsion glaze to achieve a high gloss finish.

The treatment of the stage floor will often bring about a subliminal quality that can greatly enhance the set. A conventional box set suddenly becomes a room when rugs and carpets are laid, and fitted carpets, if affordable, can make an amazing difference to a modern room set. Rough floorboards may be laid where appropriate or the floor may be covered with sand for a beach scene. Even stone paving-slabs can be used on stage. It is often possible to borrow them from your Local Authority, but beware, because they are extremely heavy, and check that the floor is strong enough to support them. The sound quality produced by these types of floor surface is often an added bonus: the harsh sound of studded boots can be very effective on stone, even producing the occasional spark in a dramatic scuffle. On the other hand, muffled footsteps on fitted carpets create a subliminal sense of luxury.

Most of the floor was lifted for this studio theatre production of Oedipus Rex *at Theatr Clwyd. The floor of the suspended platform was made from expanded metal and the rest of the floor was covered with stone paving slabs. Directed by George Roman. Lighting by Pat Nelder.* Photo: Barry Hamilton

Actors performing on a mud-covered stage floor in a production of A Light Shining in Buckinghamshire, *in a set designed by Roger Schultz at the Timms Centre for the Arts in Edmonton, Canada. Directed by Conrad Alexandrowicz. Lighting by Cat Mudryk.* Photo: Ellis Bros

The set for *Under Milk Wood* illustrated in Chapter 8 contained three different types of floor surface: the centre of the stage was covered with a neutral-coloured carpet, the surrounding areas were built from rough timber and the area at the front of the stage was dressed with real stone slabs. The actors' footwear was selected for its sound-producing quality, creating a subtle soundscape of contrasting footsteps for this highly poetic piece.

Creative Masking

The discussion of sightlines in Chapter 3 demonstrated the method of estimating which parts of the stage are in view of the audience and which parts obscured either by the architecture of the theatre or by temporary scenic elements. It is usually considered desirable to hide off-stage areas so that stage crews may have concealed access to the wings and actors can make effective entrances and exits to and from the performance area. It is also usually necessary to hide the inevitable off-stage clutter of scenery, prop tables, sound and lighting equipment.

The simplest and most conventional form of masking is by the use of lengths of black fabric hung at the sides of the stage (legs) or in horizontal strips above the stage (borders). The best type of fabric for this purpose is usually considered to be black cotton velour or black wool serge to provide a densely black, non-reflective surface. The tops of black legs, tied by tapes to a flown bar, would be visible to most of the audience, so it is usual to hang a black border on a set of lines immediately in front of them to mask these. The border can also hide, or partially hide, lighting bars if desired. Note that it is usually necessary to leave at least one unused set of flying lines immediately upstage and downstage of the lighting bars because the lanterns take up a considerable amount of space. Avoid the risk of fire by keeping all drapes well away from lights. This typical arrangement of border, legs and lighting bar is shown in the cutaway diagram of a proscenium stage in Chapter 3.

Many theatres have semi-permanent, solid black masking pieces for use immediately upstage of the proscenium so that the width and height may be adjusted to a certain extent. These are referred to as 'tormentors' (vertical side masking) and 'teasers' (horizontal top masking). The teaser usually also serves to hide a downstage lighting bar.

If the back wall of the stage is not completely hidden by the set, the designer needs to consider what is to be used to back his scenery. Black velour or serge curtains (tabs) are usually a standard part of stage equipment and these can be hung to provide a black background, the tops of the tabs hidden by a black border. If care is taken to avoid spill from stage lights spreading on to these blacks, a good void can be created to surround a standing set. But a black void, although usually flattering to any scenery set within it, may not be suitable in all cases. Perhaps the scene is supposed to suggest a bright exterior location or a black background may be considered too sombre for a comic piece. In such cases, the designer may consider a cyclorama (usually abbreviated to 'cyc'). This is simply a large, flat, neutral-coloured sheet of light-absorbent fabric that can be lit either to suggest a sky or in any colour desired. A heavy, tightly woven, mesh fabric referred to as 'filled gauze' is a popular material for cycloramas, but some theatres incorporate a permanent, built cyclorama consisting of a smoothly plastered wall, often curved slightly to enclose the performance area. Sometimes a simple, flat, painted backcloth can be used as a substitute cyclorama or 'sky cloth'. Do not be tempted to paint the sky blue, use a pale, neutral grey and let the lighting designer provide any colour needed with appropriately coloured lights for a much more adaptable effect.

Whatever the cyclorama consists of, it cannot be really effective unless proper provision is made to light it efficiently. Consult with the lighting designer over this, but it is usually necessary to leave about 2.5 to 3m (8 to 10ft) clear in front of it for an even spread of light across its surface, often supplemented by a row of lanterns on the stage floor to light the bottom part of the sky or tint it for a dawn or sunset effect. This lighting groundrow may be hidden behind a built scenic groundrow, either simply straight and painted to match the floor or finished in some manner appropriate to the set. It is possible to design a profiled top for a scenic

groundrow and paint it to suggest features such as distant mountains, trees or houses, for instance, if desired.

Some cycloramas are made from PVC similar to back projection screens and may be lit either from the front or the back. A backlit cyclorama has the great advantage of avoiding the possibility of shadows being cast from the actors or scenery standing close to it. However, it requires a good deal of space behind it for effective lighting, just as the more conventional cyclorama needs in front.

If enough space is available, a cyclorama can provide an excellent surface for projections. These may consist of anything from projected photographic images covering the whole area or smaller images such as a moon, to weather effects such as clouds or visible sunrays.

Often it will be found that a set provides much of its own masking, particularly at the sides, where any tall structure (such as side walls in a room set) may perform a creative function as a scenic element and the additional technical function of masking off-stage areas at the same time. Check the sightlines, as described in Chapter 3, to work out whether any supplementary masking will be required.

A musical, needing several scene changes, will often benefit from a series of semi-permanent portals bridging the stage, consisting of built top and side masking joined together to provide consistent masking for all scenes. A special portal situated near the front of the stage is often referred to as a 'false proscenium' and is a particularly useful device in pantomime to mask the top and sides of painted cloths. Make sure that there is sufficient space between portals to allow any large props or scenery to pass between them.

It may be a creative decision to avoid any visible masking devices altogether and perform on a completely open stage. However, as concealed off-stage areas will inevitably be required, you should be prepared to make some appropriate provision for this.

Curtains and Tracks
Curtains have been used on stages as a means of concealment since the days of the court masques,

when the play often began with the dropping of a curtain, rather than raising it. Large stage curtains are always referred to as 'tabs' (an abbreviation of tableaux curtains) in backstage jargon. Thus we hear of 'house tabs' for the front curtain or 'black tabs' or simply 'blacks' for the frequently used black curtains. Stage curtains are usually made from velvet or velour, but also from a wide variety of other fabrics. Wool serge gives a good light-absorbent surface often used for black tabs, and a fabric known as Dimout made by interweaving a layer of black fabric behind a layer of coloured fabric is comparatively lightweight, inexpensive, available in a wide range of colours and designed to prevent light behind it from leaking through the weave. Suppliers of stage fabrics can usually provide useful swatch-books containing samples of their range. Remember that all stage fabrics must be adequately fireproofed.

Tabs may be tied to a bar and flown as any other scenic item, but are often hung on a special heavy-duty curtain track (or tab track), with a small overlap at the centre so that they may be opened or closed horizontally, operated from off-stage either by hand or winch.

Stage drapes can also be arranged to open and close in a decorative manner rather than just being drawn to the sides. Often seen in theatre illustrations and still encountered in old-style proscenium theatres is the swagged style of curtain operated by cords running through rings

sewn in a diagonal line at the back of each curtain. Note that this type of draped effect can only be achieved if the curtains are suitably proportioned: a careful consideration of the accompanying illustration will show that the height of the curtain must be sufficient to cover over half the total width of the opening. This highly theatrical style cannot work successfully with a stage opening of 'letterbox' proportions.

Curtains do not necessarily have to open at the centre. A wide, single curtain is often used in a mid-stage position, either flown or sometimes hung on a single tab track to be drawn off to one side of the stage, in which case it is referred to as a 'wipe' or 'traveller'. It can be surprisingly effective to reveal scenes in this way, and, indeed, it is the technique traditionally adopted by the Japanese kabuki theatre.

Tab tracks may also be used to move scenic elements across the stage. Thus screens or flat painted pieces, for example, may be arranged to move from side to side in addition to being raised or lowered by the flying system. Remember that any tracked item obviously cannot move beyond the limit of the track, so to move off-stage and completely out of view of the audience, the track must be considerably longer than one normally used for on-stage curtains.

Other techniques are also in use for operating stage drapes. Most commonly encountered are 'profile tabs' and the 'reefer curtain' or 'Austrian

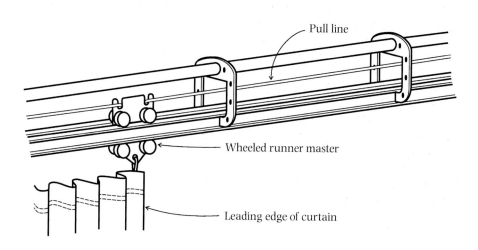

Pull line

Wheeled runner master

Leading edge of curtain

A tab track.

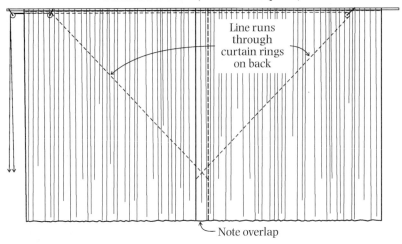

Curtains tied to bar (no runners required)

Line runs through curtain rings on back

Note overlap

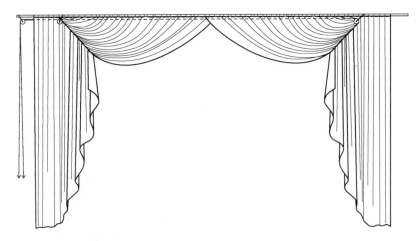

Swagged curtains.

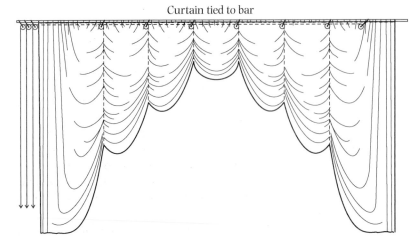

Curtain tied to bar

Profile or contour tabs.

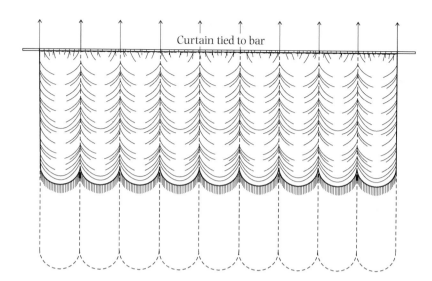

Curtain tied to bar

Reefer curtain or Austrian drape.

drape', both of which are curtains rigged to be raised and lowered in a series of decorative swags by means of lines running through rings attached in vertical rows at the back.

Designing Sets to Tour

Generally, a set designed for a specific location will not be able to tour to other locations without a considerable amount of adaptation, so, if a show is expected to tour, it should be designed and built with this in mind from the beginning. Sometimes when a production has been very successful, it is decided to take it to another theatre or even to several, then the production manager usually has to explain patiently that the set has been built for its specific location, often a different type of stage than one that might be encountered elsewhere, and frequently built *in situ* in a way that makes it impossible to dismantle and load into a lorry. This is not carelessness but a sensible use of resources. If a set is built to tour it will need to be of a more solid construction, designed to be taken apart and reassembled as quickly as possible. This means employing different techniques and different (and more expensive) materials, and a method of construction that demands considerably more time and effort.

Much of the burden of constructing a set to tour will fall to the builder, but it also needs to be

designed with this in mind. You should first acquire plans and sections of any theatres known to be on the tour list. You will probably be depressed to discover that the stages vary considerably in dimensions and facilities; this may mean that you must design a set that can be compressed or extended in as many directions as possible. However, the real problem is not merely fitting your set on to a variety of stages, but ensuring that the sightlines also work. That is, that the important elements can be seen clearly on every stage and that concealed, off-stage areas are appropriately hidden at all venues.

You should endeavour to discover at an early stage:

- Whether any of the venues lack any major facilities you require (such as a flying system)?
- Are any of the flying systems un-counterweighted?
- What type of lorry will be used for the tour? What are its internal dimensions?
- Will the tour encounter any difficult get-ins? That is, can the scenery easily be unloaded from the lorry to the stage? It is not unheard of for scenery to have to be manhandled up a winding staircase, in which case, large pieces can present a serious problem.
- How much time will be available for setting

up? This is most important: will public perform-ances start on Monday nights? Is it intended to erect the set on the Sunday? This could be expensive. It might be decided to start the get-in (unloading from the lorry) early on the Monday morning, rig lights, erect the scenery, light the show, set sound levels, dress rehearse and play the opening performance on the same evening. This allows no possibility of including any elements that are difficult to rig or assemble.

If you are lucky, the set will be erected on Sunday, lit on Sunday night, leaving Monday for rehearsals and any necessary final adjustments. If it is decided to open on Tuesday nights, leaving Mondays completely 'dark' for rehearsals or tech-nical work, then you are extremely fortunate. You may even have time to eat. This schedule leading up to the opening performance depends to a large extent upon the nature of the show: a musical may be using a local orchestra and will need to have time to rehearse with the new musicians, or sometimes extras are recruited locally and have to be incorporated into the production. Scene changes may have to be rehearsed with the local stage crew. On the other hand, a small cast show with a single standing set might be comparatively simple to open on the same night as the get-in.

As designer, you will not be expected to tour with the show, but you should certainly be at the first venue to see the show in and oversee the build, dressing and lighting of your set. You should be paid all your expenses for this, including travel, hotel and meals and, or, as an alternative, an agreed daily subsistence allowance. Minimum rates and conditions have been established by British Actors' Equity, so, if you are working professionally, you should certainly join to enjoy the benefits offered by the Union and make your own contribution to any future negotiations. Keep all receipts to reclaim expenses either from the management or the Inland Revenue at a later date.

Some Legal and Financial Matters

The copyright of the set design automatically belongs to the designer. You do not have to register it nor claim it in any formal way. This means that no one can legally reproduce your design without your permission, and a professional designer should expect a payment for any performances for which he has not been contracted initially. He will sometimes be offered the choice between a fixed weekly amount (a royalty) and a percentage of the net box office takings. It will not be large, less than 1 per cent is normal, but this may amount to quite a large sum if the show is successful. You will need to weigh carefully which you think would be the more beneficial; if the show is not a big attraction, you may be grateful for a low fixed amount, but if you expect the show to play to packed houses at every venue, a percentage might be much more profitable. If you are to receive a percentage, you can expect to be sent a copy of the box office receipts.

You may need to discuss billing to establish exactly how your name is to appear on publicity material. It is usual for the designer's name to appear wherever the director's name appears, usually in the same size of typeface. Do not be embarrassed about asking for this, even if you are working on a semi-professional or amateur production it is a good idea to establish this principle. If things have gone disastrously wrong and you do not wish to have your name associated with the production, you have the right to ask for your name to be removed from all publicity material, including the programme. However, this should not affect any payments due to you and it does not mean that you have resigned your copyright.

Read your contract carefully and do not make any assumptions. Once you have signed it everything in it is legally binding and anything not in it carries no weight at all. Dates for the delivery of the designs and the model should be clearly specified, and you must meet these deadlines, even if you feel that they are unnecessary. If you are made an offer over the telephone, ask for it to be repeated to a partner or any friend who happens to be with you. A verbal contract can be legally binding. Fees are usually paid in three instalments: one third of the total amount on signing the contract, one third on the approval of the designs and the final third on opening night.

Sometimes a successful show will be revived at a later date. Remember that, although the actual scenery belongs to the management, the copyright of the set belongs to you. You must be approached for your permission for the reuse of your design. Expect to be offered a percentage of your original fee and, or alternatively, a further royalty or percentage of the profits. You may also be asked to carry out some additional design work at this stage, and this would mean an additional fee, of course. Your designs, the actual sheets of paper with your original renderings on them, and the set model belong to you and should be returned to you, unless you have agreed to sell them or give them away. Your permission should be asked if they are to be reproduced in publicity material or otherwise exhibited, but do not expect any payment for this.

You may occasionally be given the opportunity to sell the copyright of your set outright. In this case you would be resigning all interest in it and the management may carry out any alterations or use it in any way it wishes.

If you are working professionally you may be able to use the services of a theatrical agent who can sometimes be a great help in finding work by putting you in touch with managements or directors who might be interested in employing you. Your agent will also draw up contracts for you and should be able to give you good advice about your career in general. Your fees will probably be paid directly to your agent on your behalf, who will forward them to you after deducting an agreed percentage. Sometimes your agent will be willing to advance you money if you need it before your fees are paid.

Beware of agents who offer to find you work in return for a fee paid in advance. It is rarely a good idea to enter into this type of arrangement. Indeed, it is sometimes merely a dishonest way of making money from young and inexperienced designers. If you are a theatre design student, you could be approached by someone claiming to be an agent making you this type of offer at your graduation show. You have been warned! There is absolutely no guarantee that you will ever be offered a job. Stick with someone who has reputable credentials: ask for a web site address and see what other clients are on the agent's lists. Too many designers could mean that you may be last in line for any available jobs, but, on the other hand, no designers at all might mean that the agent is inexperienced in this particular field.

Remember that as a self-employed, freelance designer you will be responsible for paying your own income tax and National Insurance contributions. Get into the habit of saving all receipts and travel tickets, however insignificant, to reclaim as expenses against tax. Do not forget items such as magazines, photographs, tips, theatre seats, subscriptions to professional organizations, a proportion of your telephone bill, the cost of heating your workplace, work clothes (if you paint your scenery) and smart clothes to wear to first nights and similar occasions. The Society of British Theatre Designers has a leaflet offering advice about these matters, and you might like to consider employing an accountant.

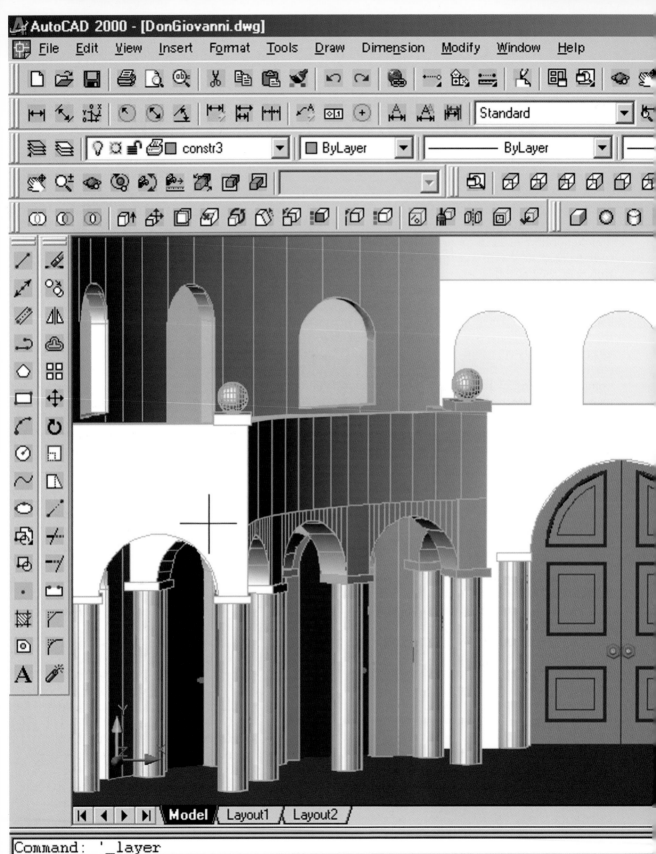

File   Edit   View   Insert   Format   Tools   Draw   Dimension   Modify   Window   Help

constr3   ByLayer   ByLayer

Standard

Model   Layout1   Layout2

Command: '_layer
Command:

16'-5 1/16", 12'-9 3/16" , 0'-0"   SNAP   GRID   ORTHO   POLAR   OSNAP   OTRACK   LWT   MOD

7 COMPUTER TECHNIQUES

You do not have to use a computer – set designers have worked happily for centuries without one. However, they do offer us a range of tools that opens up a host of such exciting possibilities that a designer would be foolish to ignore them completely.

BASIC COMPUTER GRAPHICS

Computer-generated images are now commonplace, but a distinction should be made between two basic types of computer graphic: bit-mapped and vector-based. The computer can display a picture by looking at it as a series of closely aligned, little dots. The dots may be of any colour (the computer can display more colours than can be recognized by the human eye) and very small indeed, perhaps 2,400 dots per inch (dpi), though it is rarely necessary to work at such a high resolution. The little dots are referred to as picture elements, commonly abbreviated to 'pixels' and displayed as 'bits', which are the tiniest amounts of information the computer can handle. A picture composed in this way is referred to as 'bit-mapped'. It is an excellent method for displaying complicated pictures such as photographs, but, if the image is enlarged, the rectangular pixel blocks rapidly become apparent, creating an unfortunate, blocky effect.

In using this method the computer must remember huge amounts of information for each image, so files can become so large that special compression techniques have to be used to reduce

the image file to a more manageable size. One of the most popular formats is the JPEG or JPG (originally developed by the Joint Photographers' Guild, and pronounced 'jay-peg'). This format is able to compress the vast amounts of picture information into very small files. However, it achieves this by slightly degrading the image each time it is saved to a file. This type of format is referred to as 'lossy'. Thus reloading and saving a JPEG image several times for reworking can result in a noticeable degradation equivalent to continually making photocopies from photocopies. It is better to complete work on a picture in a non-lossy format (such as TIFF) and compress as a JPEG only when all work on it is complete. Most graphics software will allow you to do this quite easily.

Vector-based graphic formats store information in a completely different way. Instead of seeing the image as a sequence of coloured dots, this format views an image as a series of geometrical shapes and remembers the formulae required to reproduce them. Thus a straight line is seen as joining position *A* to position *B* with a line of the appropriate width and colour. Rectangles, ellipses, polygons and so on are remembered by the computer in the same way, together with the colour, texture or pattern to fill the shapes if required. The great advantage of this format is that the image may be enlarged or reduced indefinitely without losing integrity and breaking up into obvious pixel blocks. Vector graphics are therefore particularly suitable for technical drawings, and this is the technique used by all drafting programs.

The computer, together with its various adjuncts such as printer, scanner and digital camera, has now become an indispensable tool for the set designer, and it would be difficult to contemplate working without the many

*OPPOSITE: **Part of a computer monitor screen with a three-dimensional digital set model created in AutoCAD.***

advantages it has to offer, in spite of the fact that only a few of its possibilities are yet exploited by set designers in general.

COMPUTER DRAFTING

Most designers now use computer-aided design (CAD) software to produce stage plans and other technical drawings, although the traditional 'hand-drafted' techniques have by no means been abandoned. Many designers find that drawing by hand is more suited to creative thought than drafting on a computer, one great advantage of the drawing board being that it is possible to view a large drawing in its entirety rather than in the piecemeal style offered by a relatively small monitor screen. However, CAD does make it possible to work to a high degree of accuracy, and, once the necessary techniques have been mastered, stylish and detailed sheets of technical drawings can be produced with speed and comparative ease.

The industry standard drafting software is now AutoCAD, by Autodesk Inc. This excellent program offers many techniques that are quite impossible to achieve by traditional means. There is no need to work to scale when using AutoCAD since all objects are drawn initially at full scale, reducing or expanding any part of the drawing to a convenient size as you work. Scale becomes a consideration only when you plot your drawing to hard copy and select a paper size for the print. For this reason, it is unwise to make a definite statement of scale on the drawing, as is good practice in hand drafting, until you know what the scale of the hard copy will be. A clearly dimensioned rule drawn on the page is a more convenient guide to scale in CAD work since this will remain correct whatever the scale of the printout may be. Needless to say, to add text and dimension lines, which are particularly tedious when working by hand, is a much simpler matter when working with CAD.

However, perhaps its greatest advantages are achieved when working in three dimensions. Advanced AutoCAD users can produce a digital 3D model of a complete set and stage, or even an entire theatre, which may then be viewed on screen from

virtually any angle. AutoCAD then allows you to create layouts quickly showing plans, elevations, sections and perspective renderings that can be printed out to scale, all from the one digital model. It is even possible to apply colour and digital textures to the model, establish appropriate light sources and produce a near photo-realistic image of the finished set.

One serious disadvantage of AutoCAD is the high cost of the software. It is very expensive; a reduced version, called AutoCAD LT, is available at a much lower cost, containing most of the same tools but lacking the facilities for 3D modelling. Students can usually obtain software on licence from their college or university or at least at an educational discount.

AutoCAD is not the only drafting program available; TurboCAD from IMSA does not have all the spectacular facilities offered by AutoCAD, but is a first rate program, available in several different versions, at a low cost. CorelDRAW also has some excellent drafting tools alongside a remarkable range of tools for graphic design in general.

Whatever software you buy, do not expect to sit down at your computer and instantly use all the facilities it offers. Some software is much more user-friendly than others, but to make the best use of a complex program such as AutoCAD you will need to spend many hours learning how to use it. The best way to learn is to attend a course: reading the manual alone will not give you the necessary exercises you will need to gain familiarity with the techniques, and feedback from an experienced teacher can be extremely valuable. However, if this is not possible, some good instructional books are available, containing a series of gradated tutorials and exercises, such as the *One Step at a Time* books by Timothy Sean Sykes (see the Bibliography); the *Basic* and the *Advanced* course are published separately. You will need the Advanced version if you have the full version of AutoCAD and wish to experiment with 3D modelling.

David Ripley offers good, inexpensive, distant-learning courses in AutoCAD for theatre from his web site CAD4THEATRE at www.cad4theatre.org.uk, and also the freely down-loadable official *CAD Standards for Theatre*

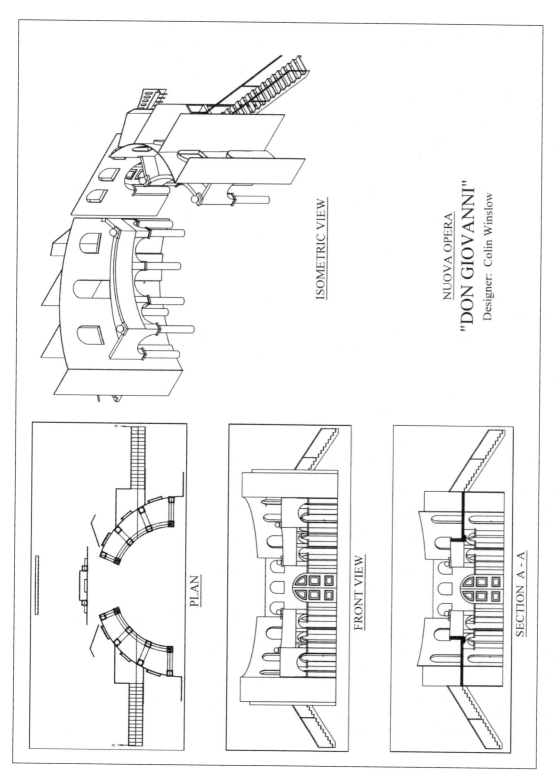

ISOMETRIC VIEW

NUOVA OPERA
"DON GIOVANNI"
Designer: Colin Winslow

PLAN

FRONT VIEW

SECTION A - A

AutoCAD can produce multiple views of the same model.

117

document from the same site, which attempts to standardize drafting conventions such as the use of layers, line-weights and dimensioning styles.

OTHER SOFTWARE

Adobe's Photoshop is probably the most popular bit-mapped graphics program available. It contains a wide range of tools and special effects for manipulating images, and its comparatively user-friendly interface means that even a beginner can quickly come to terms with it. A cut-down version of the program is frequently packaged with new computers, so that you may find that you have it already installed on your system.

Rather more useful to the set designer is the CorelDRAW graphics suite, consisting of several interrelated programs, the main ones being CorelDRAW, a vector-orientated program that can be used to produce technical drawings, and Corel PHOTO-PAINT, a bit-mapped program that offers excellent tools for manipulating photographic images. It is easy to switch between programs and elements can be easily imported and exported from one to the other. The extraordinary wealth

of techniques offered by this complete package means that it may take some time to become familiar with everything that may be of use, but a few hours spent working through some good tutorials will rapidly be repaid. If budgetary considerations limit you to only one software package, this would probably be the one to choose.

For the designer who finds it difficult to come to terms with using a mouse instead of a pencil or a brush, a graphics tablet and stylus may prove invaluable. This comparatively inexpensive piece of hardware offers a drawing surface that is sensitive to a pen-type stylus. You can use it with either hand (a big advantage for left-handers) and it has the feel of a brush or a pencil. The graphics tablet may be used as an input device with most good software packages, including Photoshop and Corel PHOTO-PAINT, but dedicated software such as the very user-friendly Painter program (originally from MetaCreations, but now handled by Corel) is worth consideration.

The Poser software from Curious Labs is a program you can use to create fully poseable, photo-realistic, three-dimensional characters that

Photograph of part of a set model with digital figure created in Poser Pro software, superimposed to give scale.

you can then export to other programs and use to people your set designs, incorporating them in full colour into photographs of the model or rendering them simply in outline to add a human scale to technical drawings. The interface is non-standard, but fairly simple to grasp.

VR Worx from VR Toolbox Inc. is a program designed to produce the interactive 360-degree panoramic views seen on some web sites. However, it may also be used to convert photographs of your set models into a format that can be revolved on screen by using the mouse to be looked at from any angle. It is particularly effective for viewing sets for theatre-in-the-round. You will need a digital camera (see below) to take the photographs and a small turntable to revolve the model in reasonably accurate increments is a great help, for you will need at least thirty-six pictures of the model, taken at about every 10 degrees as it is rotated. The computer identifies any elements in each picture that relate to similar elements in the next picture in the sequence and welds them all together into a continuous, digital loop, any part of which can be viewed on screen, steering around the resulting panorama with the mouse or keyboard. It is also possible to zoom in and out of the image to some extent.

A scene change can be animated from the set model in the same way by carefully photographing the change in small, individual steps (not rotating the model in this instance), then running the resulting series of pictures through the software to produce an interactive animation of the sequence that can be controlled with a mouse in the same manner as the revolving panoramas.

ADDITIONAL HARDWARE

A colour printer to produce hard copy of your designs is indispensable. Fortunately, printers are now extremely inexpensive to buy and even the cheapest can produce surprisingly good results. However, bear in mind that the manufacturers realize that you are going to need a constant supply of ink cartridges, and this is how they make their profits. The cartridges vary considerably in price and the amount of ink they contain; some contain the actual printing head, which is replaced with each new cartridge. These generally give the best results, but are more expensive to replace.

To print out large-scale drawings you will need access to a commercial-size plotter. These are very expensive to buy and take up a considerable amount of space, but if the theatre you are working for does not own one, most good commercial copy bureaux have them. The plotters can produce high quality prints up to about 150cm (5ft) wide and of virtually any length. Check carefully what format is preferred. By preparing your drawings properly in advance so that they can be printed out without any further adjustment you can often save both time and money. You may find it is possible to connect your computer direct to a remote plotter by an Internet link so that you can send your work to it at the touch of a key, just as you would to your own desktop printer.

Second to a printer, there is little doubt that the piece of hardware most useful to a set designer is a scanner. Again, this need not be an expensive piece of equipment, but it provides a way of putting any hard copy image into your computer for subsequent manipulation. Make sure that you buy one with a lid that lifts high enough to allow images to be scanned from thick reference books. Not only will you be able to scan pictures, but small three-dimensional objects such as model furniture can often be effectively scanned too. This gives you the opportunity to incorporate it into a photograph of the set model, even if the actual model is already in use in the workshops or rehearsal hall. Beware of scanning at an over-high resolution, you will only rarely need to scan at higher than about 150 dpi, and generally 75 dpi works well (remember that the World Wide Web cannot display any picture at a higher resolution than 72 dpi).

It is perfectly possible to scan photographs or artwork at a high enough resolution to be printed out in full colour on a large-scale plotter and applied to a hard surface for use on stage, so your set for *The Merchant of Venice*, for example, could incorporate your own large-scale photographs taken on the actual Rialto. Used imaginatively, rather than merely in an attempt to provide a

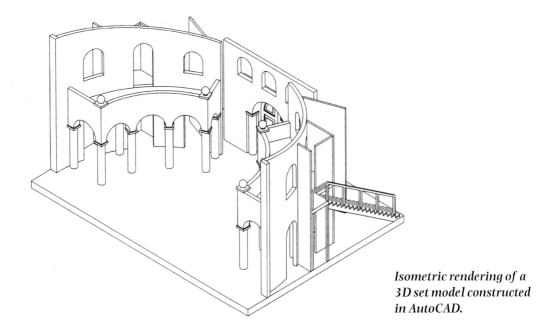

Isometric rendering of a 3D set model constructed in AutoCAD.

photographically realistic background, this technique can produce some effective results. The resolution you use will depend on the size of the final image, so in this instance it may need to be very high. Be sure to use a matte print to prevent glare from reflected lights; avoid wrinkles forming in the paper by using double-sided tape or a spray adhesive to attach the prints to the scenery (paste or glue will inevitably stretch and distort the paper with disastrous results); and take care to avoid infringement of copyright if you use any images other than your own.

Digital cameras are rapidly becoming the photographic standard and replacing the type that uses film. For the designer, they have the great advantage of producing immediate results which can be easily downloaded to a computer for manipulation in a multitude of ways. The set designer will find it to be a really useful creative tool, as well as a means of keeping a pictorial record of his work. The camera has an obvious use in taking photographs of research material and can be used to photograph props and furniture to show to the director for approval without having to go to the inconvenience of actually transporting unwieldy objects to a rehearsal room, which might

then be immediately rejected. However, the inventive designer will soon discover many other, less obvious uses.

If you have made a rough sketch model as described in Chapter 4 it can be touched up on the computer with a bit-map graphic program such as Photoshop or Corel PHOTO-PAINT, concealing or correcting the inevitable inadequacies, adding colour and texture and even drawing on furniture and dressings. The picture might be completed by adding an appropriate Poser figure to give a sense of scale, and you have on your monitor screen a good, speedily produced representation of the finished set, even before you begin the lengthy process of building the final presentation model.

Having created a detailed digital model of a stage set with a program such as AutoCAD, one cannot help wishing that it were possible just to hit a print button on the computer to produce a real tangible model and avoid the hours of work which a model normally takes to build. This possibility has become reality because 3D printers are now available. The printers are very expensive to buy, but you may find that a commercial company or an educational establishment near you uses one and will allow you to have access to it.

The digital model must be fed to the 3D printer in a format it can understand. The most common format is STL (stereolithograph) and many 3D modelling programs (including AutoCAD) will allow you to export to this format. The process is simple, once you have acquired the knack of orientating the model so the dimensions from the point of origin produce no negative numbers. If your computer has an Internet link to the printer, it is then merely a matter of hitting the print button to dispatch the data and, later, collecting the model. The process can be a lengthy one. The model for *Don Giovanni* was produced by a Zcorp Z400 3D printer in about eight hours, and cost a good deal less than the materials alone would cost to build it as a conventional model.

The machine works by 'printing' cross-sections of the model on to a very thin layer of plaster dust,

RIGHT: Set model as produced in one piece by the Zcorp Z400 3D printer.

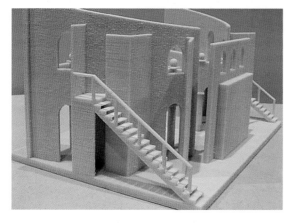

Rear of printed model showing backings and get-off steps.

The Zcorp Z400 3D printer. The actual printer is at the right, the unit in the centre is for airbrushing and the unit on the left is for wax-coating the output from the printer.

121

using an inkjet printer head with a sugar-water binding agent instead of ink. Wherever the binding agent touches the plaster the dust hardens, creating a solid cross-section of the digital model. The printer continues adding and hardening layers of plaster until the model is complete. The model is then excavated from its bed of plaster dust and cleaned off with an air brush. The completed model is already durable enough to be held and passed around but may then be coated with wax for a more polished look and extra durability. The models are remarkably detailed and the method of production completely avoids the problem of undercuts that plagues conventional casting techniques. In fact, models may even be printed out with built-in moving parts if needed. A coat of gesso provides a suitable base for painting in the usual way.

The actual hardware is surprisingly unspectacular and, although cost places it far beyond the reach of most of us, it is not so many years ago that even a conventional colour printer was far too expensive to be considered seriously for home use. It cannot be long before 3D printers become available at a reasonable price and are able to produce models for us in full colour too.

Once familiar with the modelling techniques involved, the set designer will find many uses for a 3D printer. At the moment, there is a size limitation of about 25cm × 20cm × 20cm (10in × 8in × 8in) on most printers, but printing out a model in sections rather than in one piece becomes a positive advantage when it comes to painting it. Furniture can be printed out from a digital library of models on your hard drive, to any scale and in any quantity, at a very reasonable cost, thus saving hours of finicky work.

It can be an exciting experience to explore your digital set model in a virtual reality immersion environment (or 'VizRoom') if you have access to the technology. The VizRoom is a cubicle about 3m (10ft) square, with walls made of back-projection

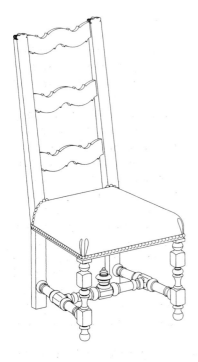

Isometric rendering of a Jacobean chair modelled in AutoCAD.

1:25-scale furniture produced by the 3D printer and painted with gouache (the Jacobean chair is in the top photograph).

Wearing a stereoscopic visor and steering with a joystick, the show's lighting designer Lee Livingstone explores the computer model of the set in the Viz Room. Unfortunately, a photograph can give only an inadequate impression of the remarkably convincing 3D experience.

screens. Behind these walls, large, angled mirrors redirect projectors towards the screens. Wearing a special stereoscopic visor, you stand inside the cubicle as the digital model is projected on to the walls. The effect of reality is startling, the image appears at full size (much larger than the VizRoom itself) and is sharp and convincingly three-dimensional, although, if you reach out, your hand will pass through the apparently solid structures of your set. You can navigate through the environment by means of a joystick, passing through doors to the back of the set or drifting up steps to higher levels.

Techniques such as these are still in their infancy and are, unfortunately, not yet available to most of us. However, computer-based technology advances exponentially and it is inevitable that these, and even more remarkable techniques, will soon become commonplace. I am most grateful to Dr Pierre Boulanger of the Department of Computing Science at the University of Alberta for granting me this experience. More information about the University's VizRoom may be found at www.cs.ualberta.ca/~pierreb/VEDP1.htm

USING THE INTERNET

The Internet has been used as a research tool for years, often, unfortunately, to the exclusion of books or original sources, but there is no denying its value. However, for the set designer it is also an extremely valuable communication tool. Many designers now own their own web site and domain name and have discovered the advantages of having a portfolio of their work and a CV available on-line. However, there are other ways in which the Internet can be used by set designers. For instance, it is not difficult to set up a temporary web site that can be accessed by the director or any other member of the production team who can then see pictures of the model or relevant reference material, download plans and other technical drawings, check on schedules, send emails to other members of the team and even see the progress of a set as it is built and painted in the workshops or set up on stage.

Some Internet service providers (ISPs) will offer free web space to their customers, but if you would like to have a professional-sounding domain name

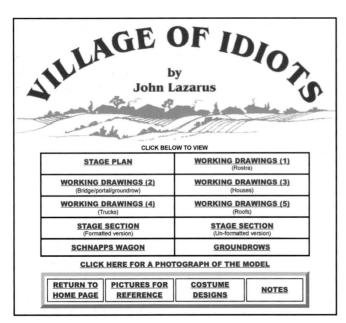

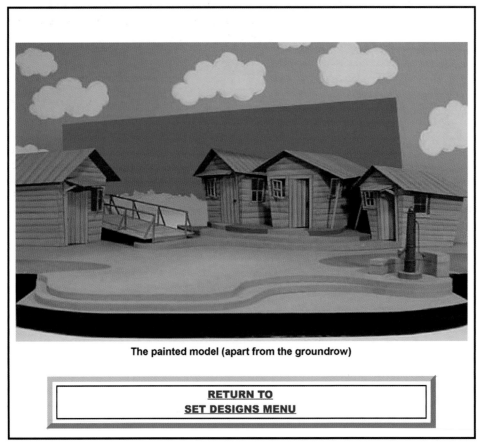

LEFT: Page of a temporary website set up for a production of Village of Idiots *at Red Deer College in Canada. Directed by Lynda Adams.*

BELOW: Photograph of set model from the Village of Idiots *website.*

for your site, such as www.myname.com, you will need to rent the space and register the name. It is not difficult to do. Many companies offer a comprehensive package and will help you through the set-up process.

All web pages need to be written in a special language that all computers can understand. The commonest is called HTML (hyper-text mark-up language). If you would like to see what it looks like click with your right mouse button on any web page and look for 'View source' in the pop-up menu that appears. The odd-looking text that you then see on screen is the actual code used to create the page. Many programs are available that will help you to convert your page designs to HTML (Macromedia's Dreamweaver is one of the most popular), but it is not difficult to learn HTML and you then need no special software to set up your own site. Elizabeth Castro's book *HTML for the World Wide Web (A Visual Quickstart Guide)* is an excellent tutorial.

The illustrations show two pages from a web site created for a production of *Village of Idiots*. The home page (not shown here) contains a list of the entire production team, with links to their email addresses for ease of contact. Everyone was contacted immediately the site was set up and given the address so that it could be checked regularly for developments. The first designs to appear on it were rough sketches following the first discussions with the director. Reference material resulting from research was added shortly afterwards. Rough designs appeared next, followed later by photographs of a sketch model. Eventually plans and working drawings were uploaded to the site, and a photograph of the final model.

Your web site could also include the type of interactive view of the model described above or short video clips demonstrating scene changes. It is also possible, of course, to set up a web-cam in the workshops so that anyone can see the set being constructed at any time merely by logging on to it from the web site. However, the technicians may not welcome being filmed as they work, so make sure they are quite happy about this before proceeding.

Not many members of the team will have dedicated CAD software installed on their computers, so it is a good idea to include drawings in several different formats. Adobe's PDF (Portable Document Format) is useful in this respect since it may be read by any computer with the freely downloadable Adobe Reader software. It is a good idea to date pages as you update them so that it is obvious at a glance if a drawing has been changed since it was last viewed.

Setting up a dedicated web site for an individual show may seem like an unnecessary luxury. However, having made the effort of doing it once, adapting the code and content to another show is a simple matter, and the ease of constant communication between all departments is a great advantage. For the designer, it makes working on more than one show at a time a much more practicable idea because he can always stay in close contact with the progress of a production, uploading new designs or revisions to the old ones, even during any periods of necessary absence from base.

8   MOVING SCENERY

The sets we design are often not expected to remain static throughout the entire performance. They may be required to change or modulate in many ways to indicate a change of location or to suggest some psychological or stylistic change of emphasis for artistic reasons.

A CHANGE OF LOCATION

Many classic plays, such as those by Bernard Shaw, Ibsen or Oscar Wilde, frequently demand changes in location from scene to scene. Sometimes the script will contain detailed descriptions of what the playwright expects the locations to look like. Shaw is notorious for his long set descriptions. In the last act of *Pygmalion* he even describes the pictures hanging on the walls of Mrs Higgins's house in Chelsea. You should always pay attention to what the playwright has to say, but the set descriptions are often written for a theatre of a different period and of a very different nature from the theatre of today. In Edwardian London playgoers were content to wait for fifteen or twenty minutes between scenes for a scene change to occur. Now, in less leisurely times, we feel that a lengthy wait breaks the flow of the performance and loses the audience's concentration, so we demand that scene changes take place in as little time as possible.

We should first consider whether it is really necessary to change the set at all. Victorians enjoyed productions of Shakespeare by the great

OPPOSITE: Not a real empty stage and not real technicians, but actors performing on a set representing the stage of a dilapidated theatre in Louis Nowra's play Cosi. *Photo: Ellis Bros*

actor-manager Sir Henry Irving that took place within a sequence of lavishly designed sets. However, this was certainly not Shakespeare's intentions and today we generally use a much more stylistic type of staging that allows the playwright to speak in a more direct manner to the audience without the encumbrance of elaborate scenic effects. A series of simple arches might be all that is needed to suggest Venice in *The Merchant of Venice*, for example, with any necessary change of location suggested merely by the addition of a drape, a door, a window or some entirely abstract element. We now tend to concentrate upon creating a stage environment within which the play may be performed, rather than representing a series of specific locations. Edward Gordon Craig wrote that he preferred the word 'place' to 'scene': '... it is a place if it seems real – it is a scene if it seems false.'

CREATIVE SCENE CHANGES

This type of scene change may not indicate any specific change of location and may not even be considered essential to the performance, but it can often bring an added dimension to a production by suggesting some kind of poetic, artistic or psychological insight, clarifying the ideas expressed or subtly affecting mood or atmosphere in many different ways.

It is now quite usual for stage lighting to modulate subtly during a scene, even though there may be no obvious logical reason (such as a dawn-break or someone's switching on a lamp or lighting a fire) triggering the change. Similarly, it is sometimes possible for some physical change in the set to perform the same type of artistic function. The accompanying pictures show a setting for a

127

The Blasted Oak and *The Monkey's Paw*

On the Shropshire farm where I was born and brought up, there stood a huge oak tree. One night it was blown down in a great gale and lay for a long time on its side, the spacious hollow trunk exposed and branches sticking out at odd angles. It quickly became a wonderful natural adventure playground for the children in the village: it could be a castle or a pirate ship with no more preparation than a mere statement of the fact, 'I'm Blackbeard, and I'm on the deck of my pirate ship, see.' The trunk instantly became the ship's hull, the branches became masts and the hollow trunk provided a 'below decks' area for prisoners taken in battle. Of course, it did not really look like a pirate ship at all, and after the passage of many years I find that I can only vaguely recall the precise form of that old tree lying on its side. However, today I still have clear mental images of the pirate ship, the cowboys' fort, the crusaders' castle or the space ship that it became in our games.

Similarly, our stage sets need not literally represent the physical locations of scenes. It is often more important to provide the facilities required, leaving the rest to the audience's imagination. Never underestimate the power of the imagination in the theatre. Audiences are surprisingly willing to supplement our work with their own imaginations. There is a well-known theatrical tale of a production of *The Monkey's Paw*, a famous ghost story by W.W. Jacobs: at the end of the play a wife opens the door to the ghost of her son who has been killed in a hideous industrial accident. After one performance a lady in the audience complained that she had been extremely distressed by the overly realistic mangled corpse that was revealed by the opening door. In fact, the director had decided to show nothing at all – her imagination had supplied its own ghost. Let us design our scenery to stimulate the imagination, not to confine it.

production of Dylan Thomas's play *Under Milk Wood*, a poetical play describing a day in the life of a Welsh fishing village. The play begins in darkness, but, as dawn breaks, the black background slowly revealed a small patch of illuminated sky that opened up almost imperceptibly slowly, like the iris of a camera until it reached its maximum extent by the end of Act 1. The motion was reversed during Act 2, until night fell once more by the end of the play. The set itself was extremely simple and all the props were mimed by the actors, giving full rein to Thomas's poetry.

In the production described above, the setting expanded the ideas presented in the play in a poetic and artistically satisfying way. However, there are inherent dangers in this type of design. It is easy for a production to be completely swamped by an over-designed set. The designer needs to be on his guard against this and should always be willing to sacrifice a concept when it becomes merely self-indulgent.

PLANNING SCENE CHANGES

Having decided that scene changes are desirable, they will need to be carefully planned. Here is a list of things to check on initially.

- Establish whether scene changes are to occur during a scene break, with the audience remaining seated, or whether they are to happen during an Interval, when much more time is available. Often, as in the plays of Shakespeare, for example, the script does not indicate where intervals are expected to occur and the decision is left to the director. Usually the second part of a show is shorter than the first and sometimes the director will decide upon two intervals or none at all. This needs to be firmly settled before any scene changes can be planned.
- What technical facilities are available? Is there an adequate flying system? An important

feature to check is the amount of off-stage space available; if a lot of scenery is to be moved on and off stage, it must be stored somewhere in the wings. If there is a workshop or loading dock adjoining the stage this might provide a useful storage area, but you will need to check that it will be available for use during all performances.

• What stage crew will be available to operate scene changes? Bear in mind that members of the stage management, electricians and sound technicians will probably have their own jobs to do during a change and will not be able to assist in moving scenery, so a special crew will need to be brought in if the changes are elaborate. Remember that someone working in the fly gallery will usually be unable to perform any tasks on the stage floor. Noise is often an issue and any moves involving dragging or banging should be avoided. It is generally a good idea to have the crew working in pairs, each operating towards one side of the stage only. This should be worked out in discussions with the production manager, but remember that even a comparatively simple scene change will often require a surprisingly large stage crew to carry it out smoothly in the time available. The

Under Milk Wood *at the Timms Centre for the Arts in Edmonton, Canada. As day breaks, a small area of sky is revealed behind a simple set. Directed by Thomas Peacocke. Lighting by Lee Livingstone.* Photo: Ellis Bros

Approaching noon in **Under Milk Wood.** *The sky window is open to almost its fullest extent. During the second half of the play the opening closes until, as night falls, the background is once again completely black.* Photo: Ellis Bros

Victorian actor-manager Sir Henry Irving, who mounted many spectacular productions at the Lyceum Theatre in London, engaged a crew of eighty carpenters, fifty property men and thirty 'gasmen' for each performance. Now we are lucky if a crew of six is available.

• Is the scene change to occur hidden behind the house tabs or in view of the audience? If it is to happen in view, what kind of lighting may be expected? Frequently scene changes are carried out in low-level lighting or under a blue light. Any operation taking place in view of the audience needs to be particularly smooth and efficient and to work in a half-light will often force the crew to work more slowly. One major advantage of an exposed scene change is that the audience will tolerate a much longer wait, enjoying the glimpse of back-stage activity. Actors can sometimes be persuaded to assist in these changes, but you should bear in mind that in the professional theatre actors carrying out this type of work can demand 'push and pull' payments in compensation for replacing a member of a stage crew. The actor is not simply being difficult, this is an Equity regulation.

WAYS TO MOVE SCENERY

Handling Flats

If scenery is to be moved, it must be designed for this to be possible. The most obvious method is simply for stagehands to manhandle it. Until recently, flats were usually canvas-covered and, although unwieldy, even large ones could be moved (or 'run') by a stagehand working alone. Now, if we require flats they are usually made from plywood on a 3 × 1 frame, often attached to each other by means of pin hinges. However, this method has the disadvantage of taking some time to manipulate the pins into position and is not generally suitable for use in scene changes. For many years flats were traditionally fastened together by cleat and line and this method is still an effective way to provide a good temporary fixing.

Experienced stagehands will often take a pride in the ability to flick the line over the top cleat of a tall flat with great accuracy. For the less skilful,

a monkey-stick will help; the stick remains hanging from the line at the back of the flat when not in use. Today, of course, scenery will only rarely consist of joined-together flats, so many other techniques are utilized, depending on the nature of the scenery.

Using the Flying System

If a theatre is equipped with a well-designed flying system it can be used in a wide variety of ways. Any painted cloths or flat pieces of scenery may be attached to the bar on a set of flying lines and easily raised into the fly tower above the stage and out of view of the audience. With simple flying the movement is swift and graceful, and, as the operators are entirely out of sight, the move is often permitted to take place in full view of the audience. This is the traditional method of moving from scene to scene in a pantomime. The action is usually designed to alternate between full-stage and frontcloth scenes. Thus, after a scene such as a market square, composed of cloths, wings and built pieces occupying most of the acting area, a painted cloth is lowered in front, hiding the entire set and leaving just enough space downstage of it for the action of the next scene. The next full-stage scene can then be erected behind it, ready to be revealed when the frontcloth is flown out again. This means that a succession of colourful scenes can be presented without a break.

Flats and built pieces may also be flown. Whole sections of built walls, even with elaborate architectural features such as doors, windows and mouldings, can be easily flown on a counter-weighted flying system. However, remember to check carefully the size of any projections since they can easily obstruct objects flown on adjacent sets of lines, especially bars of lighting equipment which take up far more space than a flat piece of scenery. Note that it is particularly important to make sure that any opening doors are firmly fixed in the closed position before such a piece is flown out. A door swinging open when it is hanging high above the stage may have disastrous results.

Individual items such as chandeliers may be flown on a specially rigged single line from a temporary pulley in the grid known as a 'spot line',

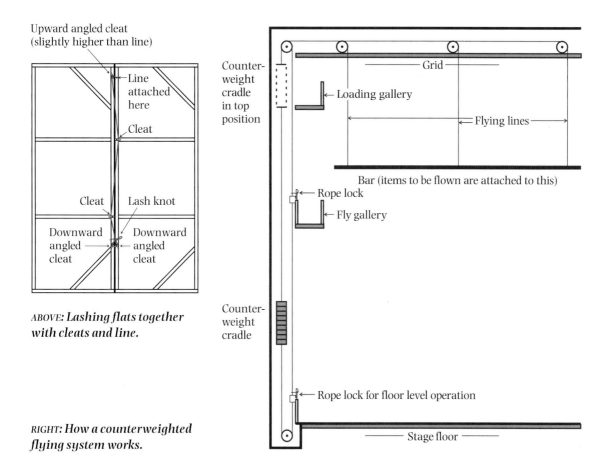

Upward angled cleat (slightly higher than line)

Line attached here

Cleat

Cleat

Lash knot

Downward angled cleat

Downward angled cleat

ABOVE: **Lashing flats together with cleats and line.**

Counter-weight cradle in top position

Grid

Loading gallery

Flying lines

Bar (items to be flown are attached to this)

Rope lock

Fly gallery

Counter-weight cradle

Rope lock for floor level operation

RIGHT: **How a counterweighted flying system works.**

Stage floor

enabling this type of object to be precisely positioned. It is sometimes possible to fly very large, built objects by raising them on two or more sets of lines operated together, but remember that this will usually prevent the use of any sets of lines between those you are using to fly the object. Needless to say, whatever scenery is flown must be designed and built to be stable when suspended above the stage. Anything falling from the flies, even quite small objects, could cause a serious accident.

In theatres without a flying system it is often still possible to use painted cloths by rigging them to roll up and down like a roller blind or to be drawn on and off stage on a heavy-duty curtain track (tab track). The track will need to be long enough to allow the cloth to travel completely out of sight to an area where it can be stored without obstructing the movement of other scenery.

In theatres with limited flying space cloths may sometimes be flown out of sight by tumbling. Note that two adjacent sets of lines are needed to do this.

Trucks and Revolves

A truck in theatrical terminology simply means a platform on wheels. It provides an invaluable method of moving scenic units on and off stage, or changing the position of all or part of a set during a performance, but there are some restrictions to bear in mind:

- The base of the truck must be high enough to contain the wheels or castors. It is safe to assume that 15cm (6 in) will be high enough to accommodate the heavy-duty castors normally used, including the thickness of the platform top. The builder will allow a clearance of about

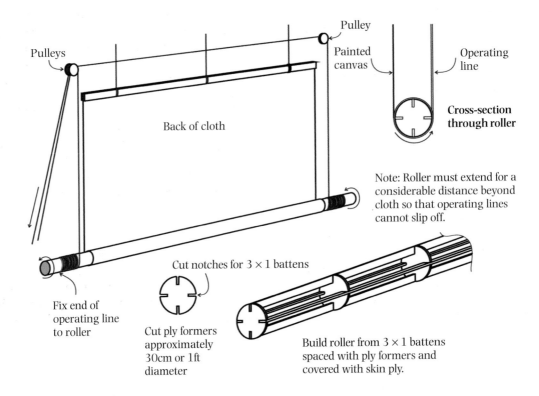

How to construct a roller cloth.

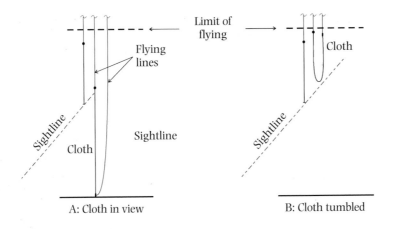

Tumbling a cloth.

1cm (½in) beneath the truck to accommodate any unevenness in the floor and allow wedges to be inserted.

- Scenery designed to travel on a truck must be adequately supported. It may seem somewhat redundant to point this out, but it is a great temptation, for instance, to stand a flat upon a moving platform and imagine that the truck can be revolved to show first one side then the other, without providing any means of supporting that flat. However, trucks can be used far more inventively than this. The accompanying diagrams show an irregularly shaped pivoting truck used to show first a cottage interior scene with furniture and then an exterior view of the same building. The structure is designed to be self-supporting by setting flats at angles to each other. The technical necessity of designing a viable structure has resulted in a visually interesting shape. Note that it is sometimes useful to place the pivot off-centre so that the truck is moved across the stage to a different position as it revolves. Indeed, the pivot point may even be set at some distance away from the truck, connected to the truck's base by a flat metal arm at floor level.

- Always check carefully that there is sufficient stage space to allow pivoting trucks to turn. Do this by cutting pieces of card to represent your trucks to scale and, with pins to act as pivots, try out the moves on a stage plan (see Chapter 10 for detailed descriptions and plans of some actual scene changes involving moving and pivoting trucks).

It is a common misconception that the best equipped stages contain a revolving stage. However, it is actually quite unusual to find a theatre with a built-in revolve, for it is generally far more advantageous to have a revolve built to the

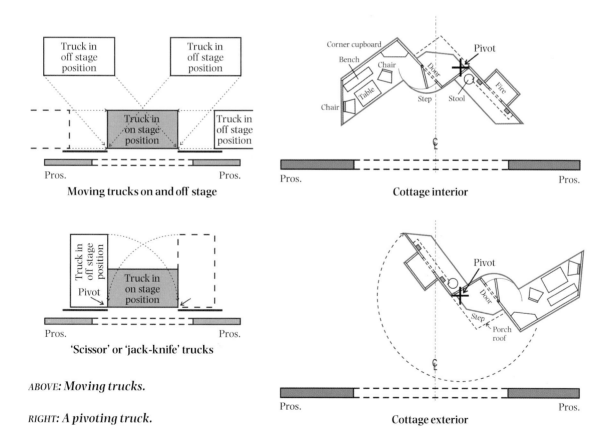

Moving trucks on and off stage

Cottage interior

'Scissor' or 'jack-knife' trucks

ABOVE: Moving trucks.

RIGHT: A pivoting truck.

Cottage exterior

size required and set in just the right position when it is needed for a specific show. A revolving stage is merely a truck with a fixed pivot point. It may or may not be circular in shape; however, it will inevitably be limited by the restrictions pointed out above. If a revolving platform is placed on to a normal stage floor there will be a 15cm (6 in) step all around the edge. This is not always a disadvantage, but, if a completely flat floor is required, it may be necessary to build the rest of the stage floor up to the same height as the revolve. If the show is a particularly elaborate one and you need to move trucks on and off a stage that has been built up to accommodate a revolve, it may be necessary to carry the built-up floor across the entire stage from wall to wall so that the trucks may be operated smoothly without having to negotiate a change in floor level. This was done for the production of *Peter Pan* described below.

The same interior/exterior cottage set shown in previous diagrams has certain advantages when placed on a revolving stage. Now there is no necessity for the step running through the interior; furniture may extend further downstage and carpets could be laid on the floor. The exterior may now include features such as a tree and some garden furniture. An area of artificial grass might also be incorporated.

The accompanying diagram demonstrates a method of using a revolve to contain three built

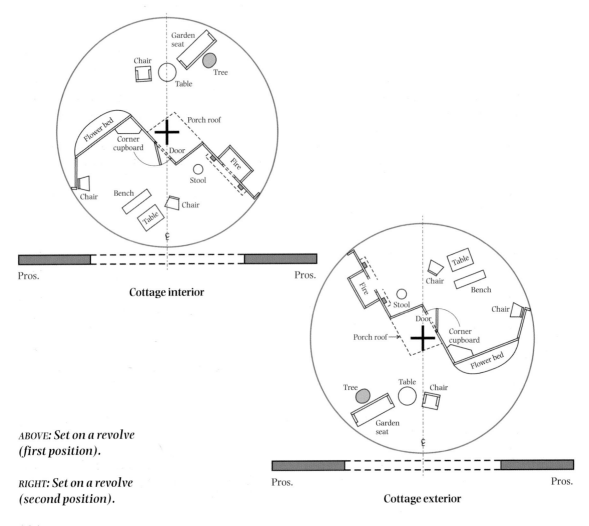

ABOVE: Set on a revolve (first position).

RIGHT: Set on a revolve (second position).

Cottage interior

Cottage exterior

134

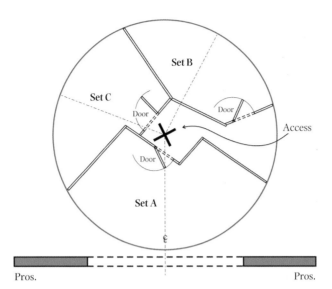

Three sets on a revolve.

Pros.   Pros.

sets. Note that these sets do not completely mask at the sides; this is not necessarily a problem, as black side masking could be provided or a false proscenium or portal bridging the revolve could provide appropriate masking.

The stage plan overleaf is from an actual production of *Peter Pan* at Theatr Clwyd in North Wales. Settings consisted of a series of trucks set on either side of a large revolve. Backcloths were flown in near the centre of the revolve, hiding the upstage part of the revolve so that trucks could

be set in position behind it. Scene changes took place in short blackouts during which the cloth was raised, the revolve turned through 180 degrees and another backcloth was lowered into place. In this case, two portals were used for downstage masking: one for the London scenes and another for all the Neverland scenes. This was a case when the entire stage floor, from wall to wall, had to be built up to the height of the revolve so that large trucks could travel right off stage into the wings.

The Home under the Ground from Peter Pan *at Theatr Clwyd; the model for the scene on the downstage side of the revolve shown in the stage plan overleaf. Note the use of miniaturized costume designs used to make cut-out figures to give scale. Photo: Barry Hamilton*

The Home under the Ground on stage. Directed by Paul Chamberlain. Lighting by Robert Ornbo. Photo: Barry Hamilton

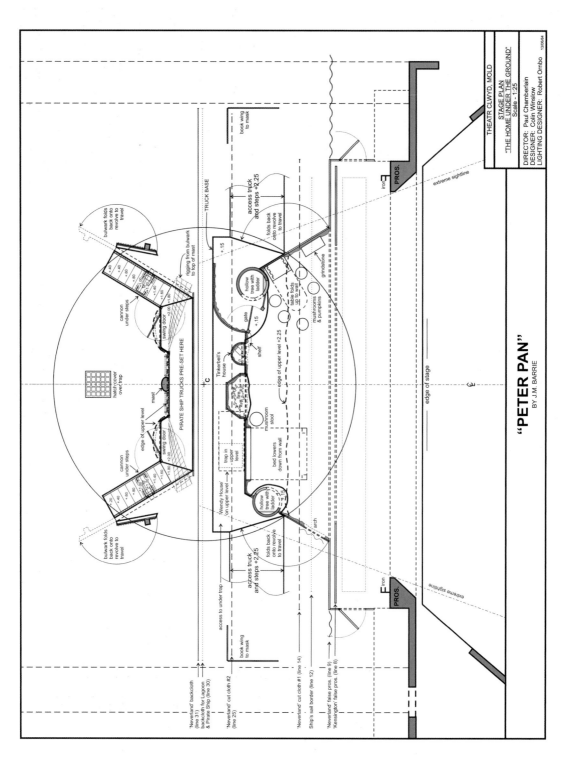

"PETER PAN"
BY J.M. BARRIE

THEATR CLWYD, MOLD
STAGE PLAN
"THE HOME UNDER THE GROUND"
Scale - 1:25

DIRECTOR: Paul Chamberlain
DESIGNER: Colin Winslow
LIGHTING DESIGNER: Robert Ornbo

Stage plan with revolve.

ABOVE: **The pirate ship from Peter Pan at Theatr Clwyd. The model for the scene on the upstage side of the revolve in the stage plan opposite.** *Photo: Barry Hamilton*

RIGHT: **The pirate ship on stage. Directed by Paul Chamberlain. Lighting by Robert Ornbo.** *Photo: Barry Hamilton*

Motive Power

The simplest, and often the best, way to move any scenery built on wheels is simply to push or pull it, and, if a scene change is to take place out of view of the audience, this will probably be the preferred method. Even when scenery is required to travel in full view, operators can often be hidden behind the truck if the scenery it carries is tall enough. However, trucks and revolves may also be operated by a cable and helical winch system, powered by hand, electricity or hydraulics.

If a truck is required to travel along a precise route it will be necessary to provide some kind of guide to prevent it from wandering. A good method is to lay a temporary board floor over the stage with grooves cut into it in appropriate positions, creating tracks for the truck to follow. A metal peg from the truck base can then be dropped into a groove to guide the truck to the desired position. Remote operation is usually achieved by a track and skate system. Here, the groove contains a metal skate attached to a winch-operated cable

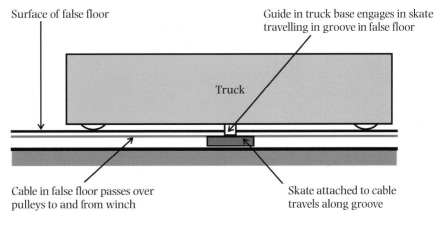

Surface of false floor

Guide in truck base engages in skate travelling in groove in false floor

Truck

Winching a truck.

Cable in false floor passes over pulleys to and from winch

Skate attached to cable travels along groove

travelling in the false floor. A peg from the truck base engages in the skate, thus providing motive power and guidance simultaneously.

Trucks need to be securely fixed into their positions on stage so that they do not shift accidentally when in use. Several types of braking device are available, usually attached to the upstage side of the truck to be operated by a stagehand's foot. However, if conditions permit, often the most secure method is simply to use wooden wedges kicked under the base at one or two strategic points. A bolt fixed to the base of the truck, dropping into a hole drilled into the stage floor, can give a really secure temporary fixing, but this means manoeuvring the truck into exactly the right position for the peg to align with the hole.

It is possible to move trucks on air castors that work like miniature hovercraft. They are capable of lifting heavy trucks and moving them about the stage very smoothly under remote control, gliding on a thin cushion of air. Because the truck is lowered to the stage floor between operations and no wheels are involved, they provide much greater stability than conventional castors. They require an air supply to operate, either from a compressor or from a built-in system such as many theatres now have for operating pneumatic tools and paint sprays. The floor surface must be smooth and level for successful operation. The *Hispaniola* truck described in Chapter 10 was moved using this method.

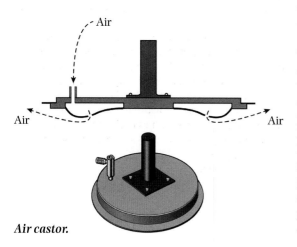

Air castor.

Sinking and Rising

Victorian theatres often contained elaborate machinery to enable either scenery or performers to sink or rise through the stage floor. Typical of these was the 'slote' or 'sloat', an elaborate arrangement of tracks and counterweights that was a standard piece of equipment in large theatres in the middle of the nineteenth century. It is still possible to detect some traces of these machines beneath the stages of one or two of our older theatres. If this type of effect is needed now a special lift is installed for the show, and this can be an acceptable system if the stage floor is one of those constructed with removable sections. The lifts may be operated manually, electrically or by hydraulics. However, few shows now require this type of effect, although it is difficult to imagine a production of *Don Giovanni* without seeing the Don being dragged down to the nether regions on a stage lift at the end of the opera.

Periaktoi

Imagine a prism set on end and you have the basic shape of periaktoi. The base is simply a triangular truck, pivoted at the centre. If three flats are arranged around the sides of the triangle and joined at the corners, the truck may now be turned to reveal each side in turn. In the days when all scenery consisted of painted flats, this was a method often used to change painted wing pieces swiftly and smoothly. Today it can be useful in pantomime where painted scenery still abounds and swift transformations from one scene to another are essential.

A run of periaktoi standing side by side with their corners just touching can sometimes provide an easily changeable back-run, cycling through three different faces or they can be used for changing profiled wing pieces, by designing the profiled edge to extend beyond the triangular base. It is possible to provide more than three changes by hanging additional flats on to the offstage sides, ready to be revolved into view. Used imaginatively, periaktoi can be a valuable scenic device. They may even contain doors or other built elements, provided that no parts extend beyond a circle described by the corners of the triangle.

Periaktoi used for a changeable pictorial background.

Periaktoi used for changeable profiled wings.

Periaktoi

Periaktoi (Greek for 'surrounding the action', singular *periaktos*) have a long and distinguished history that dates back to the theatres of ancient Greece and Rome, although no one can say with certainty exactly what they looked like nor how they were used. They were first mentioned in a treatise on architecture by the Roman writer Marcus Vitruvius (70–15BC) who described *periaktoi* set into spaces in the theatre facade that could be revolved to show different sides painted with backgrounds appropriate to comedy, tragedy or satire. The use of *periaktoi* was elaborately developed during the Renaissance and used by the architect/designers of the seventeenth century, including the great English designer of court masques, Inigo Jones (1573–1632). Complicated machinery underneath the stage floor was sometimes used to make series of them turn or pivot simultaneously at both sides of the stage, so that scenes could be changed in full view of the audience with no stagehands visible.

9 SCENIC TRICKS AND SPECIAL EFFECTS

FALSE PERSPECTIVES

Victorian scene painters were expected to be masters of perspective and we can still sometimes use our knowledge of perspective to advantage today, especially in pantomime, where pictorial painted scenery is still popular.

The two frontcloth designs for *Babes in the Wood* illustrated overleaf contain a number of perspective tricks to give an illusion of distance to physically shallow scenes. Distant objects are painted proportionally smaller in scale and, as is especially apparent in the first example, colours rapidly lose their intensity as they recede into the distance. Note also the value of the small winding path leading to the lake in the foreground to lead the eye away into the picture.

The second example exploits the use of perspective lines converging to a vanishing point. Note particularly the building at the left of the design: roof, windows and the bottom of the upper storey all converge sharply to the same focal point.

Dramatic effects may be obtained by moving the vanishing points to unexpected positions: the painted cloth for the scene above the clouds in *Mother Goose* (see page 143) is drawn in a two-point perspective, with one vanishing point set very low

OPPOSITE: *Simple magic for Benjamin Britten's opera of* A Midsummer Night's Dream *created by paper leaves threaded on black cords, coupled with imaginative lighting by Lee Livingstone. Costumes by Betty Kolodziej.* Photo: Ellis Bros

and another placed high above the top edge of the design. This gives the sense of looking upwards towards the pavilion set in the clouds. Similarly, the giant's castle in *Jack and the Beanstalk* (page 143) has its major vanishing point set high to emphasize the dramatic effect of tall, looming arches, plus a severely restricted colour scheme to create a sinister feeling for a slapstick ghost routine.

The use of perspective tricks is not confined to pantomime: the photograph on page 143 of a production of *Twelfth Night* shows a design entirely dependent upon them for its effectiveness, indeed, there are few right angles in the whole set. The director asked for a romantic, Byronic style, reminiscent of some small Mediterranean island town. The stage at the Pitlochry Festival Theatre was very wide but comparatively shallow, so it was decided to use a false perspective to create an artificial spatial depth. The horizon line is actually visible in this case, as the sea is seen at upstage centre. The vanishing point is set at the precise centre of the horizon line and lines running back from the picture plane of the proscenium all converge towards that point. This includes the edges of roofs, the tops of buildings, lines of stonework and marble floor slabs. The distant buildings beyond the bridge were actually miniatures, less than a metre (3ft) high, on a sloping base. Actors could not, of course, walk here since they would appear to be giants. Instead they exited to right or left immediately after passing under the bridge.

An inherent problem in the use of perspective occurs when we discover that, in order to build a set accurately in perspective, we really need a

Frontcloth design for **Babes in the Wood** *at Bristol Old Vic. Script by Chris Harris and Chris Denys. Directed by Chris Denys.*

Frontcloth design for **Babes in the Wood** *at Bristol Old Vic. Script by Chris Harris and Chris Denys. Directed by Chris Denys.*

sloping floor and all the scenery, including furniture, to be built with sloping bases relative to the floor. This might indeed be possible but is rather impracticable because no piece of furniture could be moved without destroying the illusion, and, unfortunately, actors cannot diminish in size as they move upstage. Consequently, a compromise must be reached, and this is why the type of perspective we use on stage is referred to as 'false'. If the vanishing point is set at a height just above

the actors' heads, and all false perspective is ignored below this level, then we avoid the problem of diminishing actors or perspective furniture. A convenient height would be one level with the top of doors (say 2m or 6ft 6in from the floor), then a possible problem with perspective doors is also avoided. Look again at the photograph of *Twelfth Night* and you will see that, for this reason, the balustrade at stage left does not slope in perspective as one might expect and elements below the level of

*ABOVE: **Backcloth design for** Mother Goose **at Bristol Old Vic. Script by Chris Harris and Chris Denys. Directed by Chris Denys.***

*RIGHT: **Frontcloth design for** Jack and the Beanstalk **at Bristol Old Vic. Script by Chris Harris and Chris Denys. Directed by Chris Denys.***

*Set for **Twelfth Night** at the Pitlochry Festival Theatre. Directed by Joan Knight.*

A skeletal, mono-chrome set for The Orphan Muses *at the Timms Centre for the Arts in Edmonton, Canada. Directed by Kim McCaw. Lighting by Annette Nieukerk.*
Photo: Ellis Bros

LEFT AND BELOW: *Set for a shabby meeting room in the Manitoba Theatre Centre's* An Enemy of the People. *The ceiling is completely flat, built in a false perspective and hangs vertically to enable it to be rapidly flown out in a quick scene change. Directed by John Hirsch. Lighting by Joe Stell.*

the vanishing point, that should logically be built in perspective, have been kept to a minimum.

The set for *The Orphan Muses* is another example of the use of false perspective. The doorways in the angled, skeletal side walls are brought further into sightline by the perspective plan and the detached ceiling is actually only 2.25m (just over 7ft) in depth and flown with the front edge considerably higher than the back to bring it into an apparent logical relationship with the walls. The slightly quirky effect produced was appropriate for this play about dysfunctional siblings, and the design of the ceiling piece made it possible for the lighting designer Annette Nieukerk to light around it with little difficulty.

It may sometimes be effective to cover a perspective ceiling frame, such as the one described above, with sharkstooth gauze. It can then be painted as required and subtle lighting render it either solid or partially transparent, as appropriate.

GAUZES AND TRANSPARENCIES

Gauzes of various types are the means by which some of the most spectacular and versatile stage effects can be obtained. Imagine that you are walking along a town street on a sunny afternoon, you will probably not be able to peer into the rooms of the houses you pass because many people hang net curtains at their windows to prevent this. However, if you walk along the same street as it begins to get dark you will find that many of the occupants have switched on their lights and the net curtains have become transparent. Some will be hardly visible at all if the occupants have not yet drawn their heavier curtains across the windows. Most net window curtains are white, but if, as sometimes happens, there is a pattern printed on them it will disappear together with the curtain. This is the principle of the effect obtained on stage by means of a sharkstooth gauze.

Two main types of gauze are generally in use in the theatre: sharkstooth and scenic. The first is heavier and more closely woven and the second is much lighter in weight with a distinctive honeycomb weave. They are generally available in white, black, grey and, sometimes, pale blue.

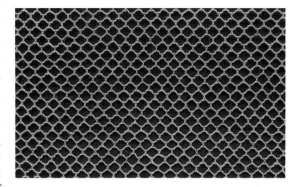

Scenic gauze with distinctive honeycomb weave.

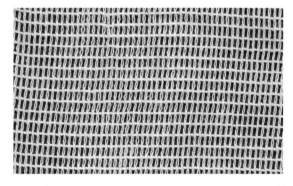

Sharkstooth gauze with heavier rectangular weave, suitable for transformation effects.

If a sharkstooth gauze is hung across the stage and there is no light at all behind it, it will appear to be solid, just like a cloth. If lights are brought up behind the gauze and the light in front is simultaneously diminished (a cross-fade) the gauze will become transparent, and, when there is no light at all in front, it will virtually have disappeared completely. Thus if a design is painted on the gauze, using thin paints or dyes to avoid clogging the tiny gaps in the weave, when lit from the front it will appear as a normal, painted drop, but one which has the ability to more or less disappear with a change of lighting. It may then be flown out fairly unobtrusively if desired.

If the paint is too thick and the mesh becomes clogged in some areas it will become painfully visible when the gauze becomes transparent, to

LEFT: *Painted gauze act-drop for* Mother Goose *at Bristol Old Vic. Script by Chris Harris and Chris Denys. Directed by Chris Denys.*

BELOW: *The gauze drop fades away at the start of the pantomime to reveal the scene set behind it.* Photos: Fat Chance Productions

which the extremely tedious solution is to probe all the clogged interstices with a knitting needle.

Careful lighting is required for the transparency effect to work well. The lighting designer will need to avoid any lights striking the gauze from directly in front and shooting straight through the gauze. Any movement, such as a scene change or actors getting into position, will be seen through the gauze, so it is usual to rig a set of black tabs immediately behind it as a safety precaution. These may be opened or flown out just before the cross-fade is executed and will hardly be noticed by the audience. The effect usually works best if executed very slowly.

Scenic gauze is best used to create a misty or out-of-focus effect. It can add depth to a cyclorama sky and is often a useful adjunct to projected weather effects. Note that complete opacity is never possible when using scenic gauze.

Gauze effects are invaluable for the creation of magical transformations in pantomime. A painted forest can disappear, revealing, perhaps, a scene of fairyland set behind it, or Aladdin's cave can fade away at the genie's behest. The photographs show

a painted sharkstooth gauze used as an act-drop in place of the house tabs in a production of *Mother Goose*, and a gauze treasure map hung as a drape and partially hiding the set as the audience assembles for a production of *Treasure Island*. (If you look closely you can just make out a lighted prop lamp gleaming through the gauze.)

A black sharkstooth gauze can often be used to great effect in combination with a cyclorama: hang the gauze about 3m (9ft) downstage from the cyclorama, with lighting bars immediately upstage of the gauze, and you create the possibility of lighting the cyclorama to create a light back-ground to a set, or alternatively, of removing all cyclorama lighting to allow the gauze to form a black background. In addition to reducing glare from a brightly lit cyclorama, this device can offer a versatile range of possibilities, not only for day-to-night transitions but also to intensify mood by the imaginative use of colour and projections. The set for *The Orphan Muses* illustrated on page 144 uses this technique.

Translucency effects depend upon the use of a lightweight fabric, such as cotton sheeting, that

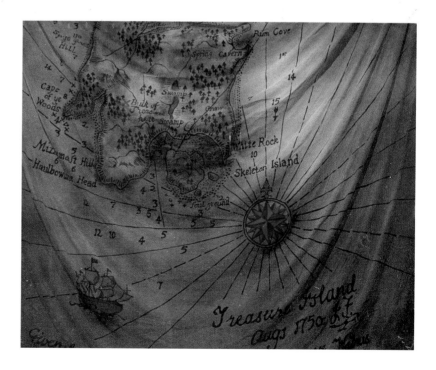

The painted gauze map from Treasure Island *hanging from ropes as a drape in place of house tabs. Photo: Barry Hamilton*

will allow light to pass through it, but not as loosely woven as gauzes, so that it never becomes completely transparent. A backdrop of cotton sheeting, painted with dyes or heavily diluted scene paint, will allow light to pass through it and can be lit from behind or have images, textures or moving effects projected on to it from either the back or the front or both. A great advantage of this type of effect is seen when some parts of the foreground in the design are painted in thick, solidly applied paint and painted black on the back to render those areas completely opaque. Now, when the cloth is backlit, the solid areas will appear in silhouette while other parts are brightly lit. The effect is particularly suited to landscape effects, where details of the foreground landscape are solidly

painted and the sky is painted in translucent colours for backlighting. Sunset and dawn scenes can be remarkably effective, with red light from a groundrow of lights spreading up the sky from behind the silhouetted landscape and the top part of the sky lit with blue light from above. Sunset can fade into night with a slow lighting change, and often the lighting designer will be able to supply stars by flying in pea-bulbs behind the drop, and even a projected moon if needed. Moving projected effects, such as drifting clouds or falling rain, may also be effective here. A grey or black scenic gauze hung at some distance downstage from the translucent drop can enhance this type of effect by adding a slightly hazy one to it.

The scenes on the island in *Treasure Island*

*Backcloth design for the riverbank in **The Wind in the Willows**. Sky painted in heavily diluted, translucent, blue paint, and hills and foreground painted in solid pigments for backlighting. Directed by Steve Richards for Splats Entertainment.*

Hills and foreground painted in solid black paint on back of cloth, omitting river.

ABOVE: A spectacular sunset created by backlighting the cloth in blue with red groundrow lighting at centre. Note effect of the sky reflected in the river.

RIGHT: Cloth lit only from behind in deep blue with projected moon for a night scene.

were produced by a combination of translucency effects. The working drawings (sheets 4 and 5 in Chapter 10) show the designs for this. The drops employed black scenic gauze as a base, with leaves and tree trunks cut from a selection of fabrics having different degrees of translucency and glued to the gauze to form a large, semi-translucent collage of jungle foliage. The effect was most effective when lit from between the drops, suggesting a jungle of apparently considerable depth.

The transparency effects described above are all of a more or less pictorial nature, but the same techniques may be used to produce abstract textures and collage effects that can open up a remarkable range of possibilities to the creative imagination. Gauzes are particularly useful in creating a half-real, dreamlike quality and even when used in a purely abstract way the effect is inevitably romantic to a certain extent. Do not expect them to solve design problems for which they are not suited, and remember that their use is always limited by the technical considerations needed to make them really effective.

Note that any joins or seams in a gauze or translucent cloth will show as a black line when backlit. For this reason fabrics manufactured for

The coronation scene from King's Rhapsody *at the Churchill Theatre, Bromley.*
The backlit rose window was simply painted on cotton sheeting by using dyes, then
glued behind the cutout parts of a plain black backcloth. Directed by Kim Grant.

this type of effect are generally available in a variety of widths up to about 9m (30ft). Seams can sometimes be concealed in the design (along the horizon in a pictorial landscape, for instance), but bear in mind that horizontal seams usually work better than vertical ones since the weight of cloth tends to pull out any puckers.

BLACK LIGHT

Black light is actually ultraviolet (UV) light. The colour violet is seen via the shortest visible wavelength of light. When the frequency is increased, causing the wavelength to become even shorter, the light produced becomes virtually invisible to the human eye. However, special pigments will react to this invisible or 'black' light, glowing very brightly in complete darkness. The effect is popular on the disco dance-floor and is frequently seen in pantomime, typically in haunted house or 'underwater' routines. Since only objects treated with UV pigments are visible to the audience, a performer dressed in black against a dark background becomes completely invisible and is able to operate special UV props such as ghosts or fishes, which then appear to move as if by magic. The range of possible effects is limited only by the imagination: fish can eat other fish, dragons can be cut in half, flowers blossom, caterpillars turn into butterflies and a dancing skeleton, produced by a performer in black tights with UV bones applied to them, can be seen to remove its own head by merely lifting off a UV skull mask. Any flat, UV-painted object can be made to disappear, merely by flipping it over to a plain black-painted reverse side.

A special UV light source is essential. These are usually in the form of a strip light and are not dimmable. A deep violet lighting gel is often suggested in order to avoid the use of these rather inconvenient lamps; however, gels cannot produce a true ultraviolet and the effect is comparatively feeble, with some generally visible, dark purple, ambient light. The effect works best in complete darkness, with no source of light other than UV.

A small amount of ambient light is possible, but the effect is diminished as normal light is increased.

UV-sensitive fabrics can be bought from specialist suppliers to make up into costumes, but remember that faces will disappear completely under UV. Special make-up is available, but the effect is usually crude and mask-like and can look odd and clown-like under normal stage lighting. Any fabric can be made to fluoresce brightly in pale blue by washing it in a biological detergent, which is why tee shirts and jeans glow at a disco. Make sure that any black clothing used for invisibility is washed only in pure soap to avoid its glowing when not required. (Oddly enough, considering its name, Lux soap flakes work well for this.)

The range of UV pigments is rather limited, and they do not lend themselves to colour mixing as with normal pigments. Often the paints do not fluoresce in the same colour as they appear under normal light. A useful range of special UV paints is available that are virtually invisible under normal lighting, making it possible to paint designs that become visible only under UV light.

There are some less obvious ways in which a black light effect can assist the set designer. A Milky Way of stars painted on a sky cloth as tiny dots of invisible UV paint (the little rubber eraser on the end of a pencil is ideal for printing these dots) will not be seen under normal lighting but will gradually appear as the stage lights are dimmed to a night state. Windows of painted houses will light up at the same time if painted with invisible yellow UV paint. UV may also be used as an inexpensive way to suggest neon signs.

The photograph shows UV paint used to produce a glowing version of Vincent Van Gogh's 'Starry Sky' as a pre-set behind a set for Nicholas Wright's play *Vincent in Brixton*. A black sharkstooth gauze hanging in front of it allowed it to disappear when the UV lights were turned off and the action of the play started, preventing the effect from becoming too obtrusive. You can see some spectacular examples of UV effects produced by the specialist firm of UV/FX Scenic Productions in California by visiting their web site at www.uvfx.com.

Model of a set for **Vincent in Brixton** *for Theatre Network in Edmonton, Canada, showing a UV version of Van Gogh's 'Starry Night' backing a selectively realistic set. Directed by Jim DeFelice.*

FOG, SMOKE, MIST AND PYROTECHNICS

Fog and smoke can be produced on stage from a range of special devices, often referred to as smoke guns, although they are not really guns and do not produce real smoke. The fog is produced from water-based glycol and glycerol. It has been extensively tested and is generally considered non-hazardous. Each machine is designed to produce a specific type of effect, ranging from dense, billowing clouds of smoke to just a misty atmosphere. The compact, box-like machine is loaded with a special fluid and the resulting fog is dispersed into the air, sometimes by means of a pump to maintain a constant pressure; hoses can be attached if necessary, to duct the smoke to where it is required.

A fine, ambient haze can be produced from a machine, usually referred to as a 'cracker', designed to break mineral oil into tiny particles, which it will then disperse as a fine mist. However, concern has been expressed that, in concentrated form, the fog can penetrate the lungs and cause lipid pneumonia. More recently, hazers, operating on water-based glycol have become available to produce a similar effect and no adverse effects have been discovered. Crackers and hazers are both designed to run continuously to give a smoky effect. They will render light beams visible and are therefore popular at pop concerts and the like.

The most spectacular of the smoke and fog effects is produced by the use of dry ice. This is frozen carbon dioxide, which sublimes (changes from a solid to a gas) when immersed in warm water to produce voluminous white clouds. The effect is often seen in the vampire-haunted graveyards of horror films. As the gas is considerably heavier than air, it tends to cling to the floor. It can be ducted to where it is required and be directed to run down slopes or fall from a height. However, a major disadvantage of this effect is often the difficulty of obtaining supplies of dry ice; it can be stored for a day or so in a properly designed, insulated container, but a regular supply will be needed for a lengthy run. It is often used by hospitals, laboratories and ice-cream manu-facturers, who can sometimes be persuaded to cooperate. Remember that frozen carbon dioxide is dangerous. It is extremely cold

An energetic battle scene from The Hobbit *at the Redgrave Theatre, Farnham, enhanced by clouds of stage smoke. Directed by Graham Watkins. Lighting by Peter Edwards.* Photo: Astonleigh Studio, Odiham

(−78°C) and can cause severe cold-burns if it touches the skin, so specially insulated gloves and goggles must always be worn when handling it.

All these smoke and mist effects are, to some degree, unpredictable since they are affected by naturally occurring air currents. It might be necessary to switch off air-conditioning or to use fans to obtain the effect required. However, an additional degree of unpredictability is added in the presence of an audience, for any large group of people produces a certain amount of natural heat and, as hot air rises, a current can be set up which often has surprising results on smoke effects. The production manager will need to check the smoke detectors, which may have to be switched off, and this sometimes means that a fire officer must be in attendance during performances.

An unexpected result from the use of smoke effects on stage can be a severe outbreak of coughing from the audience. This is, in fact, entirely psychological since the products have been carefully developed to avoid this. They have been exhaustively tested and singers are used to performing through them without difficulty. However, if one person starts to cough, others will inevitably follow. For this reason, scented fog-fluids are available in a variety of flavours that are usually effective in discouraging the tendency to cough. Piña colada has been discovered to be the most effective flavour, although you may prefer to choose a scent more appropriate to the production (unfortunately, a haunted graveyard flavour has yet to be developed). Spectacular fire effects can sometimes be obtained by projecting flame effects on to thick clouds of stage smoke.

Smoke can also be produced from pyrotechnic devices. A variety of slow-burning smoke pellets are available that are particularly useful for producing a trail of smoke arising from an imitation fire. If only a small amount of smoke is needed, an incense cone or a smouldering coil of insect repellent may be used. However, remember that extreme precautions must be taken to avoid the possibility of anything catching fire. Take the advice of your local fire officer.

Other pyrotechnic devices produce flashes and explosions. Most common are the flash-with-a-cloud-of-smoke type that we see in pantomime, typically at the entrance of the Demon King. These are electrically detonated and require a flash box device to be hidden somewhere near where the effect is to occur. The pantomime Demon traditionally enters downstage left, on the 'bad' side of the stage and flash boxes can be hidden in the footlights or behind a small, scenic shield placed near the edge of the stage. Pyrotechnic flashes are quite capable of setting fire to scenery or costumes, so make sure that they are well isolated and treated with particular caution. If they are set too close to scenery, the flash may leave an unsightly, grey scorch mark.

A wide variety of pyrotechnic flashes are now available, including some elaborate ones that will explode with a spectacular shower of large, coloured stars. However, if used in a pantomime, and the effect is to be used at every entrance of the Demon King plus a transformation scene, bear in mind that the number of flashes required for the run of the show can add up to a considerable number. Check whether these are to be paid for from the design budget: they can become a sizeable expense.

WATER

It is best to avoid the use of real water on stage whenever possible. Moving effects projectors can simulate rain or moving waves, if used with artistry and skill. A special tubular ripple device housed in a box about 60cm × 25cm × 25cm (24in × 10in × 10in) is excellent for projecting undulat-ing water on to the lower parts of scenery to create a sea or river effect. Watery puddles can sometimes be suggested by placing plastic mirror material beneath irregularly shaped holes cut in a floor cloth. The effect of ripples of light reflected from a watery surface can be created by bouncing light on to scenery from oven-trays of water placed in carefully selected, concealed positions about the stage floor. The slight vibrations from actors' foot-steps will often be sufficient to activate them and create realistic, watery ripples of light on the scenery.

Occasionally there is a need for real water, as in *Singing in the Rain* or the hair-washing scene in *South Pacific*. A practical tap on stage can be rigged to produce real water, or real 'rain' behind a stage window can be produced by running water into a trough pierced with small holes set just above it. If the trough contains an old towel to absorb the water, a realistic dripping effect will occur after the flow of water is turned off and the rainstorm is over. For a wider cover, a pierced water pipe can be flown above the stage.

It is a fairly simple matter to divert water by plastic hoses to places where it is required. If a convenient water source is not available, a supply can be provided on-stage by means of a gravity-feed tank in a fly gallery or some suitable position above the set. The biggest problems are in controlling and retaining it. It is hardly necessary to point out the dangers of bringing water into contact with electricity, so stringent efforts must be made to provide a reliably safe method of containment. A large receptacle, built into a platform or the floor of the stage, can be waterproofed by lining it with plastic sheeting to provide a safe collection tank, or to divert the water to a suitable drain or storage area. The tough plastic liners designed for use in garden pools are useful for this. Always check with your local fire or safety officer, who may be able to offer some helpful suggestions. Remember that he has the authority to close the show completely if he is not satisfied that all the necessary safety precautions have been taken.

Mirrors and Other Reflective Materials

High gloss, reflective floors are often needed, and vinyl floor surfaces, specially designed for dance work, are available in a wide range of colours, with matt or gloss finishes. They are designed to lie flat when rolled out and are excellent for dance shows. However, they are expensive to buy, and a good reflective surface can be produced by merely coating a painted floor with one or more layers of a high gloss varnish. Black or dark colours produce the best reflection.

Large mirrors have become feasible on stage since the introduction of metallized, plastic materials. These are sold in a variety of formats, the cheapest of which is known as shrink-mirror. This is a lightweight, flexible, plastic laminate, available in rolls of different widths, designed to be mounted on a frame and shrunk with an electric heat source to a taut, wrinkle-free surface. The frame must be extremely rigidly constructed, and the plastic mirror should be stretched over the edge and firmly fixed at the back. Stapling it to a normal 3×1 timber frame will not work because the fabric will pull on the staples as it shrinks, producing ugly radiating wrinkles from each staple. Sandwiching the material between the frame and a strip of card has proved effective. It is helpful to use a strip of double-sided, adhesive tape between the frame and the mirror sheet.

Mirror scrim is a material similar to shrink mirror which behaves much like sharkstooth gauze when properly lit. That is, the apparently solid mirror can be rendered transparent, revealing whatever is set behind it, merely by a change of lighting.

Occasionally mirrors and pictures framed in glass used as set dressings will reflect stage lighting into the audience. It can be distracting for anyone sitting in seats where light is reflected into their eyes, so the designer should carefully check for this from all parts of the auditorium at dress rehearsals. Photographers' dulling spray is usually offered as a solution, but the problem can often be eliminated completely merely by tucking a small wedge behind the offending mirror to deflect it slightly away from the light source.

Closely related to the plastic mirrors is a wide range of plastic materials that will shimmer and glitter spectacularly under stage lighting. They are available in a huge range of colours or with a diffraction finish, which reflects light in all the colours of the spectrum. They are popular for use in revue, particularly in the form of a 'slash' curtain, consisting merely of thin, reflective plastic material cut into long strips of about 1cm (½in) wide and hung close together from a bar to form a curtain. Constant motion creates a large amount of shimmer and performers can simply walk

View from the wings at Bristol Old Vic as a fairy takes to the air.
Photo: Fat Chance Productions

through it at any point as required. A black slash curtain can often be particularly effective and less obtrusive than the more usual silver.

The same glittery plastic is also available chopped into small fragments to make a coarse glitter dust for gluing to surfaces in exactly the same manner as a much finer version is sometimes used to decorate old-fashioned Christmas cards and the like. All glitter effects work best when in motion. When glitter is applied to a drape or a backcloth the effect may be enhanced by persuading members of the stage crew to stand just out of sight, holding the edges with one hand. The very slight movement created merely by breathing will double the amount of shimmer.

FLYING

Hoisting performers into the air is dangerous and should never be undertaken without proper safety precautions. If a production requires much flying (*Peter Pan*, for instance) then a specialist firm such as Kirby's (the same family business that flew the very first Peter Pan in 1904) or Flying by Foy

should be employed to advise and install the apparatus. This should ensure not only safety but also a reasonably trouble-free technical period.

Performers will need to wear a special harness beneath their costume. This has points to attach lifting cables, either at the centre of the back or at each hip. The simplest technique is the pendulum method: this is simply a counter-weighted line passing over a pulley in the grid to an operator at the side of the stage, enabling an actor to be lifted into the air. To travel from one part of the stage to another, the actor must begin the flight at a distance from the suspension point which is equal to the distance to the point of landing at the opposite side. When lifted and lowered, he will simply swing to the desired spot. This technique sounds primitive, but, with careful planning and rehearsal, it can be remarkably effective and trouble free. It will also enable Peter Pan to fly through an open window by designing the opening in just the right position and at the right height for the cable to pass through it. More sophisticated methods are now in use, however. Peter Foy (1926–2005) developed a more sophisticated

155

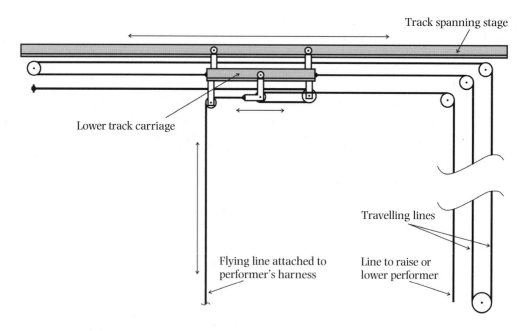

Track on track flying system (patented by Peter Foy).

version of the pendulum system, and a 'track on track' system, in which a tracked carriage containing the pulley for lifting or lowering is used to control height while travelling on a second track spanning the stage.

It is sometimes disconcerting to find that the flying cables are more visible than might be expected, but there are several techniques which can be used to make them less apparent: the use of matte black cables, trying to avoid their being hit direct by light beams, low lighting levels, decorating the set with a busy background containing as many vertical lines as possible and the use of blue as background colour. However, it is sometimes surprising to note that cables can become invisible to a large extent simply as a result of the spectators' desire not to see them. The audience *wants* Peter Pan to fly.

Whatever flying method is used, it should be planned at an early stage in the design process, for not only will a considerable amount of clear space in the grid be required, but the set itself may have to be specially designed to accommodate each individual flight.

SOME OTHER SPECIAL EFFECTS

It is impossible to describe the whole range of special effects now available to the designer, many of which will never be required in a lifetime of work. Some, such as mirror balls, bubble machines and confetti cannons, are effects developed for use on the dance floors of clubs and discos. They should never be used indiscriminately. An inadequate production cannot be saved by these tricks and they could possibly distract from a really good production, but they can be effectively employed where really appropriate.

Some of the most effective theatrical tricks are the ones that have been used on stages for a great many years. Typical of these is a snow bag; this is a simple device to scatter artificial snow or confetti over the stage with a good, general spread and an adjustable speed of fall. It consists of a large sheet of canvas, wide enough to extend across the entire area of stage to be covered by the effect, and about 2.5m (8ft) deep. It is attached to two battens and flown on two sets of lines, so that, whatever is desired to fall is held in the bag thus created. The canvas has long slits cut in it towards one side; this means that, when the side with the slits is lowered, the snow will be scattered through the holes. The fall may be controlled by raising or lowering one side of the snow bag.

Very realistic, artificial snow may now be bought, but torn paper seems to work better from a snow bag, falling with an attractive flutter. However, paper snow should always be fireproofed and care should be taken to sling the bag below the level of nearby lighting bars to avoid the risk that paper might land on hot lanterns and smoulder.

A trick popular in Victorian pantomimes was the 'transformation flat'. It is a fairly simple device, consisting of a painted flat with a weighted canvas flap attached across its centre. The edge of the flap can be raised to the top of the flat, showing a decoratively painted surface, and dropped on cue by a quick-release mechanism so that it falls to the bottom of the flat, revealing different paintwork on

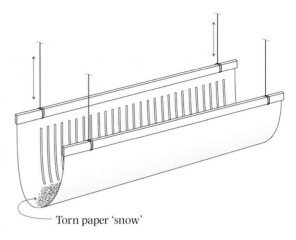

Torn paper 'snow'

A snow bag.

A confetti cannon explodes at the end of a joyously inept amateur operatic performance in Louis Nowra's play Cosi. Directed by Michael Murdoch. Lighting by Annette Nieukerk. Photo: Ellis Bros

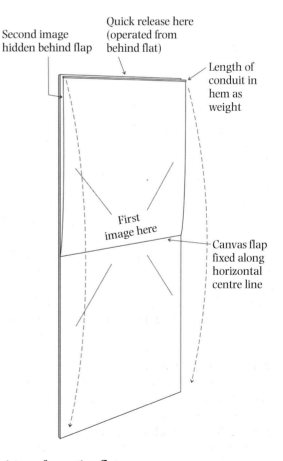

Second image hidden behind flap

Quick release here (operated from behind flat)

Length of conduit in hem as weight

First image here

Canvas flap fixed along horizontal centre line

A transformation flat.

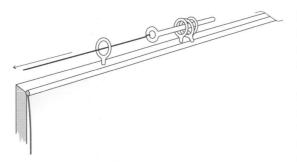

A quick-release device.

the other side. The instantaneous change is surprisingly effective when used imaginatively. If you want to try this effect, stretch out the canvas and paint it before applying it to the flat to avoid a shrinkage problem, and use a double flap of canvas, as shown in the illustration, to avoid the possibility of paint's bleeding through from one side to the other.

Objects are often required to fall on cue, either from the flies or from some part of the set. If it is not possible for a member of the stage crew to be concealed behind scenery, some kind of remote, quick-release device will be needed. The one

A traveller cloth used in the pantomime Dick Whittington *at The Theatre, Chipping Norton. The total width was about 20m (65ft 6in). It was slowly drawn across the stage as Dick 'walked' all the way to London from his home village.*

illustrated is fairly simple to rig, but a more hi-tech method is to hold the object in place with an electromagnet and release it by merely switching off the current.

A scenic delight in spectacular productions of the Victorian and the Edwardian theatre was the moving panorama, in which a long painted cloth was drawn across the stage from one side to the other, providing a spectacular, moving background for a horse race or a speeding train. A simplified version can be used effectively in pantomime in scenes such as Sinbad's ship travelling from country to country. On a small stage it is sometimes possible to feed a single curtain track right across the stage and along the side walls, so that a very wide backcloth can be drawn across and stored out of the way at one side of the stage. The picture shows such a cloth designed to accompany Dick Whittington's walk to London at the tiny theatre in Chipping Norton. The lack of available height was used to advantage here, for the cloth could simply be moved by hand from the back by the use of rods hooked to the runners at convenient intervals, rather like those used on tall, domestic window curtains.

A useful device for this type of effect, rarely found in theatres now but still available from suppliers, is known as a 'banjo' tab track. This is a double track formed into a loop at each end, roughly in the shape of a banjo, that enables painted cloths to be drawn off stage and stored around the loop or drawn across the stage on the other track to reveal another design at the back. In

addition to providing a good travelling effect, such as that described above, it would be possible to use this type of track to cycle through a sequence of several painted cloths in theatres where full flying facilities are not available.

CREATING MAGIC

Special effects of any kind need to be precisely planned and carefully rehearsed. The set designer will probably be greatly involved in the design of any large-scale effects, but their success will depend upon skilful teamwork from all technical departments, the performers and the director too. Any spectacular effect on stage, from the helicopter in *Miss Saigon* to the most basic trans-formation scene in a village hall pantomime, will inevitably encompass changes in scenery, lighting, sound, props and often costume too. Careful timing is vitally important for the full impact. Do not make the mistake of trying to make everything happen simultaneously and in the twinkling of an eye. Usually, with any effect of this kind the spoken dialogue prepares the audience before the actual event. The anticipation can be built to breaking point by the skilful construction of the scene leading up to a theatrical effect.

A good example of this is the event described by the director Sir Tyrone Guthrie (1900–71) as 'the greatest moment in all theatre', the moment when Peter Pan flies in through the nursery window in the first scene of the play. The entrance is prepared early in the scene. A face has been seen at the

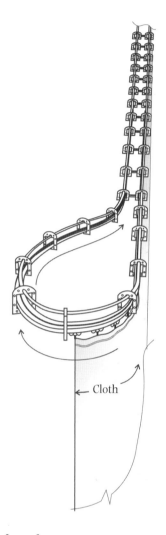

← Cloth

A banjo tab track.

window ... When Mrs Darling puts her three children to bed, she explains that no harm can come to them as long as the nightlights she has lit beside each bed are burning ... The room lights are switched off, and all is quiet. A nightlight begins to flicker and then goes out. The same thing happens to each nightlight in turn. We are on the edge of our seats, when the window is flung open and Peter flies up into the room, landing at the front of the stage. We hardly have a moment to catch our breaths, before he is off again, flying all over the room.

This is a good example of the importance of careful timing. The extinguishing of the three nightlights is a slow, gradual process. Tension builds as each one goes out, and the precise moment when the window bursts open for the swift, seemingly jet-propelled, flying entrance of Peter, is crucial for the maximum effect.

Wendy wakes up. Peter is nervous and hides behind the window curtains. Wendy switches on the lights and Peter emerges to tell her about his home in the Neverland. Now the stage is brightly lit again, and Peter has had his flying cable removed while he was hiding behind the curtains. All is quite logically back to normal for Peter's conversation with Wendy. Everyone in the audience knows that Peter is just an actor hanging precariously from a wire attached to his back, but the structure of the scene and the build-up to his first entrance work a magic far greater than the comparatively simple technology used to lift him into the air.

Later in the same scene, Peter promises to teach the children to fly. They try jumping off their beds, but fail miserably. At that moment the family dog is heard barking off-stage. Someone is coming, and Wendy quickly switches off the lights, telling the children to hide. The door opens and the maid reprimands the dog for barking, remarking that they must be safe because she can hear them breathing. Now the stage lights have been lowered again, rendering the flying cables less visible, and there has been just enough time for the children to have their wires attached while in their individual hiding places. They quickly learn to fly and are soon all flying away out of the window with Peter.

It is a shrewdly written scene that can create a stunning piece of theatrical magic.

We are often told that, 'it's all done by wires', but this is nowhere near the truth, for wires alone are not nearly enough. The real magic in this first scene of *Peter Pan* is created by skillful writing, timing and direction. These are elements that are available for use in any production, wherever it may take place, they are not dependent upon an elaborately equipped stage or a huge budget. They can be present in both a primary school play and a production at the National Theatre.

Transformation scenes in pantomime are an opportunity for the set designer to show off. If the audience leaving a performance of a play by Harold Pinter or Caryl Churchill is talking excitedly about the wonderful set, the designer might consider his work to be a failure, for he has probably not served the production as he should. However, if the audience at *Aladdin* is not talking about the Cave of Jewels over the interval ice creams, then the design is equally a failure.

Here is a sequential checklist to work through when planning any elaborate stage effect:

1. Start by discussing the effect in detail with the director. Try to establish exactly what you are aiming to achieve, and some rough idea of the technicalities involved.
2. Discuss the effect with the production manager, so that safety can be considered, and advice taken from a safety officer if needed.
3. If any work is likely to involve specialists in specific techniques, get in touch with them immediately for an initial discussion, they may offer some invaluable suggestions and advice.
4. Make a working scale model so that you can demonstrate the intended effect as clearly as possible and try to make the operation of the model foolproof, the designer fumbling with little bits of insecure cardboard will not create enthusiasm nor give a clear impression of what is to take place.
5. Describe the effect in detail to everyone concerned, including actors and stage management, no one should be unclear about what is

intended to happen, even if modifications become inevitable later.

6. Test any special devices as they are constructed to get them working as smoothly as possible and always be prepared to adjust and adapt; if you are lucky, you will be working with a group of people with a wide range of individual skills, listen to their advice and suggestions and consider them carefully.

7. Before the complete effect is rehearsed with actors, try to find time to rehearse the technical aspects with the stage crew alone; the actors will have more confidence if they feel that everyone really knows their job and is giving them maximum support.

8. Allow plenty of time for the rehearsal of elaborate effects, they will take longer to get right than you would ever believe possible; remember that often an effect takes a considerable length of time to set up, so two or three attempts can take much longer in preparation time for each run than the actual rehearsal of the effect; never physically help with the execution of a special effect at a rehearsal, unless you intend to be there helping at every performance.

Do not forget to give the stage crew a break after several rehearsals of an effect. You may feel exhilarated when things go right, but the crew may be physically exhausted after several runs and a gradual deterioration due to tiredness can easily set in. Do not forget to say 'thank you' and let them know when they have done well. You will often, quite unfairly, be given all the credit for the work they do. Remember that your designs need the cooperation of the technicians to be effective. If it is possible, allow members of the crew a chance actually to see the effect they are creating, even if only via a video camera. They are often working, quite literally, in the dark and are only rarely able to see the total effect.

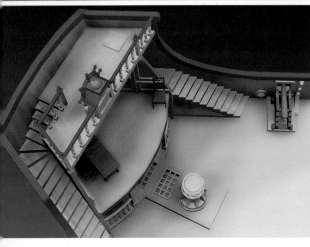
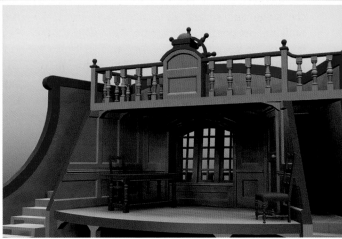

10 A PRODUCTION OF *TREASURE ISLAND*

This chapter contain a complete set of stage plans and working drawings for an actual production of *Treasure Island* at Theatr Clwyd in Mold, North Wales. This is a well-appointed producing house with its own scenery and props workshops and an excellent costume department. The designs indicate that the budget for this spectacular Christmas production was a comparatively large one. The show was not an easy design job, however. Much of the play took place on board ship, but there were also scenes on shore in England and several at various locations about the island. The task was made more difficult by the fact that the production team, including the set designer, were not engaged until a very late stage, so the design work was done under considerable time pressure. It is described here in some detail as an example of heavy technical requirements combining with artistic considerations to produce a visually satisfying production.

Theatr Clwyd has an extensive forestage that can be sunk to form an orchestra pit; however, for this production it was decided to use it as an extension to the stage and thrust the action as close to the audience as possible. Steps were built at the front edge of the stage to permit actors to enter from the auditorium when appropriate. Two-tiered, rough,

timber structures were built at each side of the proscenium for entrances from the 'assembly' areas at each side of the forestage (see stage plans and working drawings, sheet 7). These semi-permanent structures had to be carefully designed to avoid obstructing the safety curtain or blocking sightlines from the end seats.

Although a Christmas show, the production was certainly not a pantomime and was intended to appeal equally to adults and children. The script indicated scenes involving scenery that was to be climbed over, banged against, fallen from and generally treated in a very rough-and-tumble manner. A pantomime style would have been inappropriate. Most scenes took place in exterior locations and a cyclorama seemed to be desirable as a background, but, in order to avoid the usual brightly lit rectangle of sky, a special elliptical masking frame was constructed, covered in black serge with a black sharkstooth gauze immediately in front of it (see working drawings, sheet 7). The cyclorama was hung immediately behind it to be backlit and receive projected cloud effects. This created a versatile background, to be used behind all the scenes.

The many scene changes were designed to be carried out in full view of the audience, mainly by the use of trucked and pivoting units. Some of these trucks were very big, and workshop space adjoining the stage at stage right had to be used as an additional storage area. Many important scenes took place on board *The Hispaniola*, so it was decided to build a sizeable cross-section of the ship showing the main deck, captain's cabin and poop deck. This became the biggest truck by far, contain-ing three distinct levels with interconnecting stairs.

OPPOSITE: Set models for **Treasure Island***:* **The Admiral Benbow Inn, The Stockade** *and three views of* **The Hispaniola** *truck. Not physical models this time, but digital versions modelled in 3D, lit and rendered in AutoCAD. The resulting screen-captures were imported in Corel PHOTO-PAINT for colour adjustment and final rendering.*

163

Establishing the precise dimensions of this truck and how it was to be manoeuvred into a number of positions about the stage were tricky but crucially important tasks upon which all other scene changes depended. The overall dimensions of the Hispaniola truck were about 10.5m × 6m × 5m high (or 34ft 6in × 19ft 6in × 16ft high). This was clearly a case for air-castors. A small additional truck could be attached to the back which was designed to perform the additional function of representing the exterior of The Spyglass Inn in Bristol Docks (see stage plan and working drawings, sheet 2).

Instead of the house tabs, the audience was greeted by a map of the island, showing the position of the buried treasure. This map, painted on to sharkstooth gauze, was simply slung from two ropes and hung partly draped at the front of the stage. The painted map, considerably smaller than the proscenium opening, hid only the centre part of the set, another sizeable truck representing both the interior and the exterior of The Admiral Benbow Inn

(see stage plan and working drawings, sheet 1). The play began with a slow lighting change, during which the gauze map became transparent, revealing a sleeping figure in the chair by the fire. It was then flown out as the action began.

All the trucks were moved by stage crew hidden behind them. At the end of the first scene the Benbow Inn truck was moved off to stage right as a large stone archway was flown in downstage. The *Hispaniola* truck had been preset at stage left, with The Spyglass Inn truck attached, and hidden by the tall flats at the stage left side of the Benbow Inn truck. It was then pushed into position and the next scene was set.

During the Bristol Docks scene, a metal pivot was dropped into a hole in the stage from the upstage corner of the *Hispaniola* truck (see stage plan) and additional smaller trucks were added to the off-stage side of the main truck.

The Bristol Docks scene ended with the decision to set sail, and the down-stage arch was flown out as

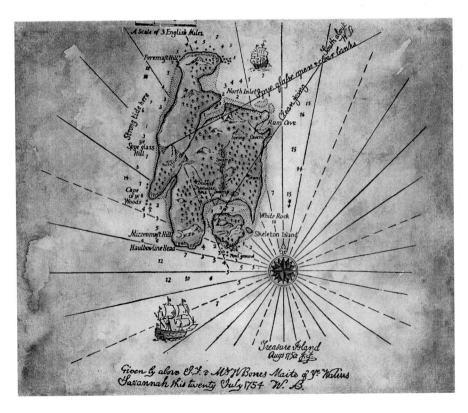

Design for the
Treasure Island
map painted on
sharkstooth gauze.

The Admiral Benbow Inn in Treasure Island *at Theatr Clwyd. Photo: Barry Hamilton*

the huge *Hispaniola* truck revolved slowly on to the stage, the extra trucks at each side opening out to complete the set. An exciting *coup de théâtre* was presented as the ship appeared 'fully manned' on all levels, the sailors loading bales into the hold and making preparations for the journey.

The second half of the play consisted of scenes on-board ship and at various locations about the island. This meant that during the interval the large metal shutters between the stage and workshops had to be raised so that 'dead' trucks could be moved completely off the stage and the island trucks brought in from the storage area. The island scenes initially presented a design problem since, up to now, all the scenes had taken place in built structures such as inns and the ship, but here the settings became organic, mainly in jungle locations. It was decided to use appliquéd gauzes; pieces of thick scene canvas, thin cotton sheeting and flimsy muslin were painted and spattered in various shades of green and yellow, then cut into an assortment of leaf shapes in a wide range of sizes. These shapes

were then glued, overlapping each other, to stretched panels of black scenic gauze, creating a jungle-like collage. These translucent drops hung at intervals over the entire depth of the stage, with strong shafts of light, provided by the lighting designer Pat Nelder, streaking between them, created a surprisingly effective forest. Some foliage panels were hung on tab tracks so that they could be regrouped to suggest different parts of the forest, or part to reveal the trucks that were used to provide the specific elements required by the script, such as a hidden skeleton, a hole for treasure (an open stage trap behind a low truck) or a hill top (see stage plan and working drawings, sheets 4 and 5).

The stockade consisted of three trucks, carrying rough timber structures, the largest of which was the 'cabin' (see stage plan and working drawings, sheet 6). Originally it had been planned to build the cabin and the stockade from real logs, however, these turned out to be extremely expensive and dangerously heavy, so eventually the entire structure was clad in lightweight, vacuum-formed

The Hispaniola *prepares to weigh anchor. Photo: Barry Hamilton*

logs provided by Peter Evans Studios at very short notice in response to a panic call.

The director Roger Haines made inventive use of the opportunities offered by all the sets. However, one of the most effective scenes was one that had not been originally planned but added at quite a late stage in the rehearsal process. Haines realized that the set offered the possibility of showing the outside of *The Hispaniola* truck for a scene in which Jim escapes from the island in a coracle. The scene took place under moonlit night lighting, with the high side of the ship looming darkly at *stage right*. The actor rowed the little coracle across the stage from the left, through a misty sea created by low-lying, dry ice fog. He threw a rope ladder over the side of the ship, and, as he clambered up the side and over the bulwark at the highest level, the ship was slowly pivoted back to its main full-stage position, revealing a pirate hiding in the captain's cabin, who was bravely tackled by Jim, who, by then, had climbed down the ladder from the trap door in the floor of the top level.

Unpainted, vacuum-formed logs for the stockade scene in **Treasure Island.**

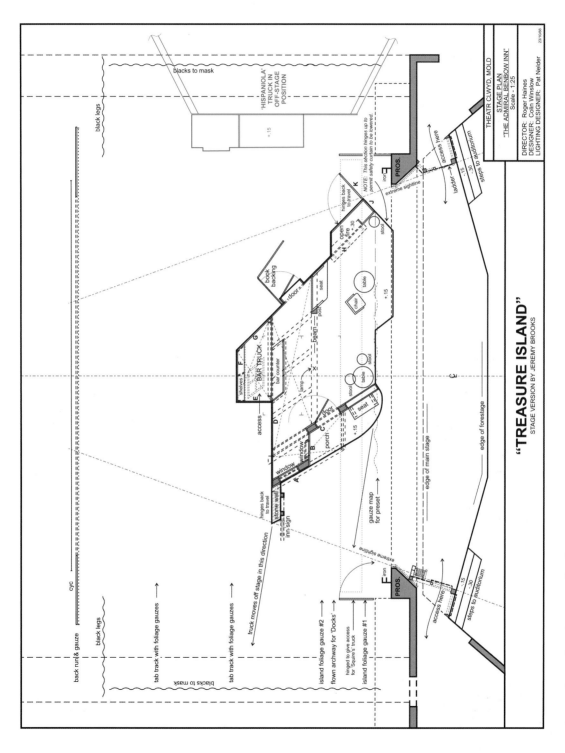

The labels visible within the stage plan include:

blacks to mask

'HISPANIOLA' TRUCK IN OFF-STAGE POSITION

+15

black legs

THEATR CLWYD, MOLD
STAGE PLAN
"THE ADMIRAL BENBOW INN"
Scale - 1:25

DIRECTOR: Roger Haines
DESIGNER: Colin Winslow
LIGHTING DESIGNER: Pat Nelder

23/10/98

NOTE: *This section hinges up to permit safety curtain to be lowered.*

access here

-15 -30 steps to auditorium

ladder

iron

PROS.

extreme sightline

hinges back to travel

K

J

open fire +30

stool

stool

H

book backing

door

seat

post

beam

table

chair

+15

G

F

BAR TRUCK

shelves

bar counter

E

access

D

lamp

X

stool

stool

table

C

door

window

B

porch

seat

+15

window

hinges back to travel

stone wall

inn-sign

"TREASURE ISLAND"
STAGE VERSION BY JEREMY BROOKS

A

gauze map for preset

extreme sightline

edge of main stage

edge of forestage

truck moves off stage in this direction

back runl& gauze

cyc

black legs

tab track with foliage gauzes

tab track with foliage gauzes

blacks to mask

island foliage gauze #2

flown archway for 'Docks'

hinged to give access for 'Squire's truck

island foliage gauze #1

PROS.

iron

access here

-15 -30 steps to auditorium

Stage plan 1 for Treasure Island.

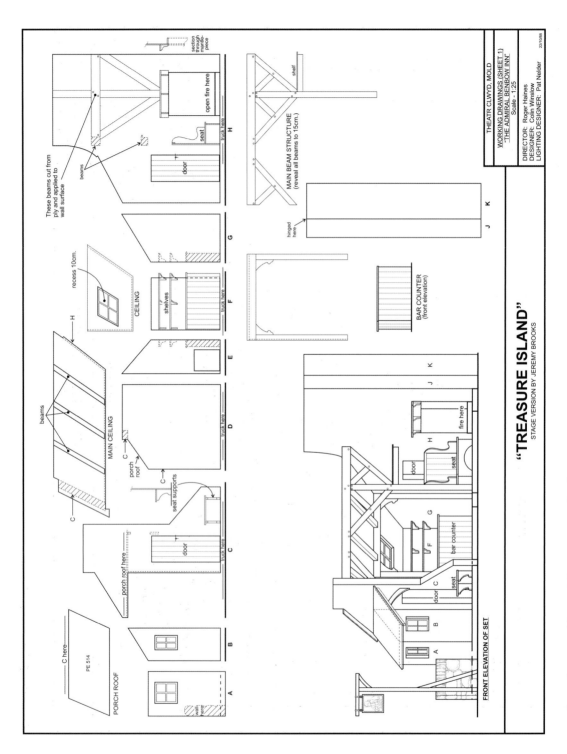

Working drawing (sheet 1) for Treasure Island.

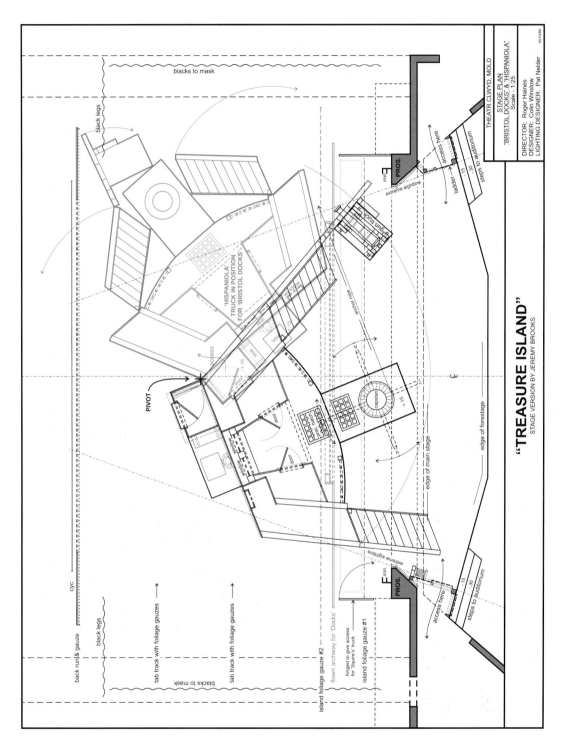

Stage plan 2 for Treasure Island.

169

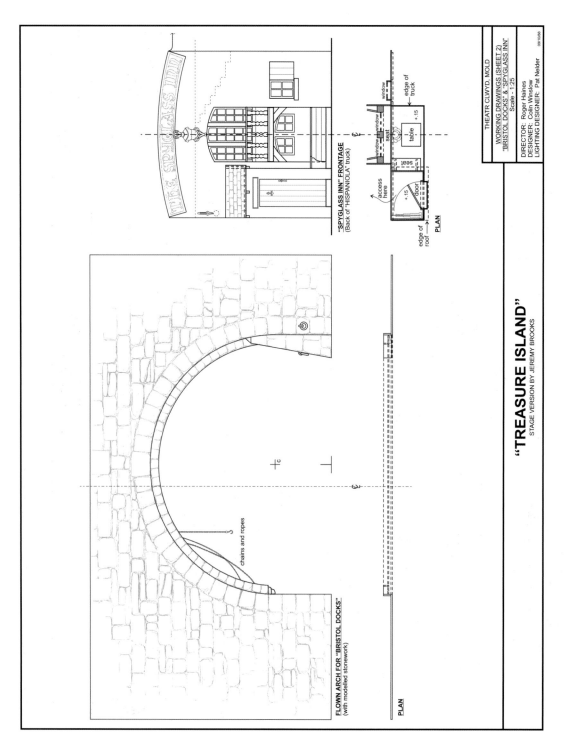

Working drawings (sheet 2) for Treasure Island.

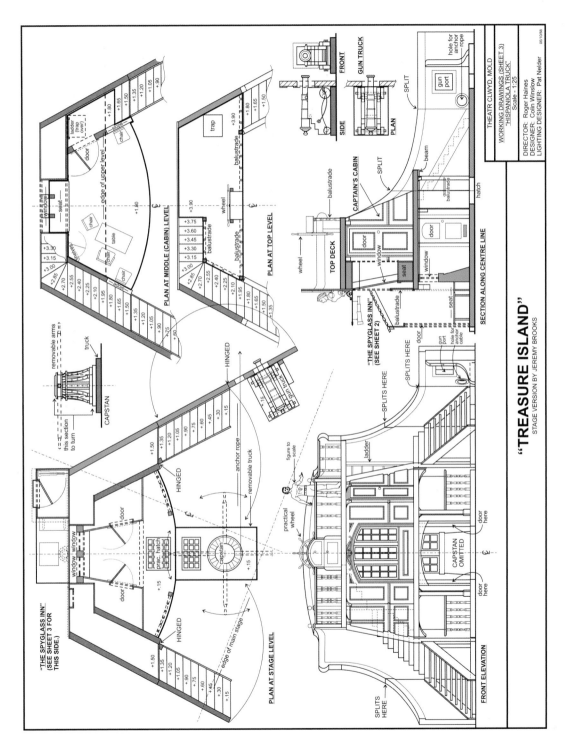

Working drawings (sheet 3) for Treasure Island.

171

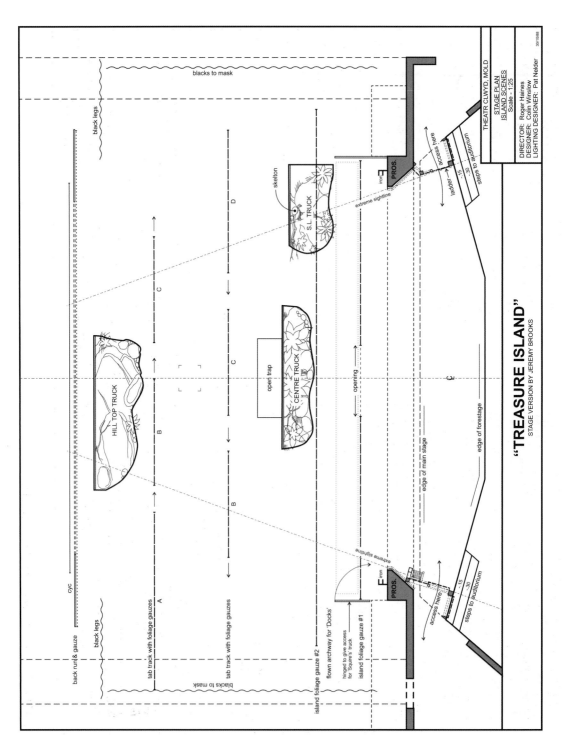

Stage plan 3 for Treasure Island.

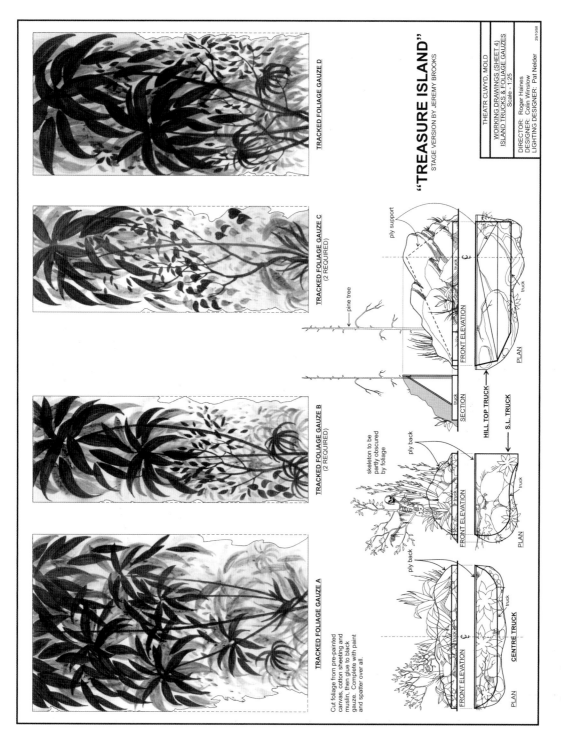

TRACKED FOLIAGE GAUZE D

TRACKED FOLIAGE GAUZE C
(2 REQUIRED)

TRACKED FOLIAGE GAUZE B
(2 REQUIRED)

TRACKED FOLIAGE GAUZE A

Cut foliage from pre-painted
canvas, cotton sheeting and
muslin, then glue to black
gauze. Complete with paint
and spatter over all.

← pine tree

ply support

SECTION

FRONT ELEVATION

PLAN

truck

truck

HILL TOP TRUCK

S.L. TRUCK

skeleton to be
partly obscured
by foliage

ply back

FRONT ELEVATION

PLAN

truck

ply back

FRONT ELEVATION

CENTRE TRUCK

PLAN

truck

"TREASURE ISLAND"
STAGE VERSION BY JEREMY BROOKS

THEATR CLWYD, MOLD

WORKING DRAWINGS (SHEET 4)
ISLAND TRUCKS & FOLIAGE GAUZES
Scale - 1:25

DIRECTOR: Roger Haines
DESIGNER: Colin Winslow
LIGHTING DESIGNER: Pat Nelder

29/10/88

Working drawings (sheet 4) for Treasure Island.

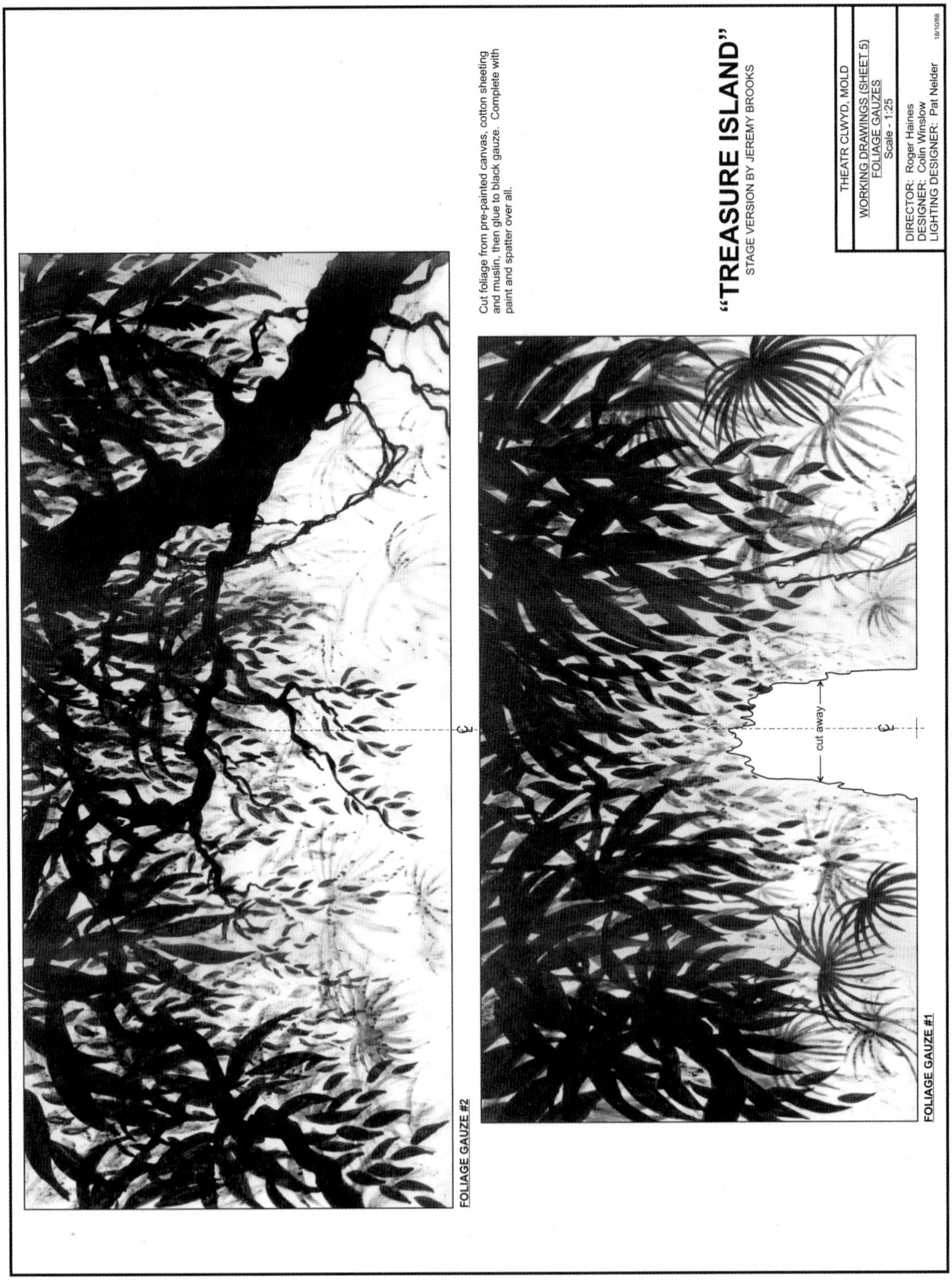

Cut foliage from pre-painted canvas, cotton sheeting and muslin, then glue to black gauze. Complete with paint and spatter over all.

"TREASURE ISLAND"
STAGE VERSION BY JEREMY BROOKS

THEATR CLWYD, MOLD
WORKING DRAWINGS (SHEET 5)
FOLIAGE GAUZES
Scale - 1:25

DIRECTOR: Roger Haines
DESIGNER: Colin Winslow
LIGHTING DESIGNER: Pat Nelder

FOLIAGE GAUZE #2

FOLIAGE GAUZE #1

cut away

Working drawings (sheet 5) for Treasure Island.

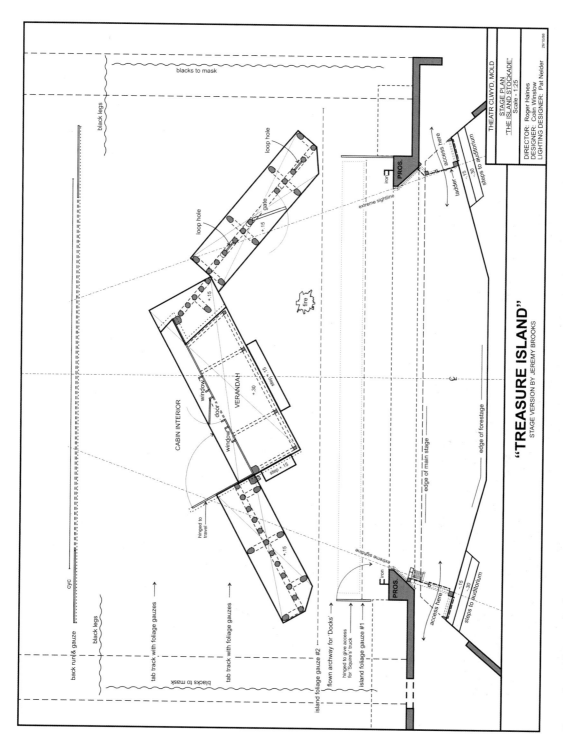

Stage plan 4 for Treasure Island.

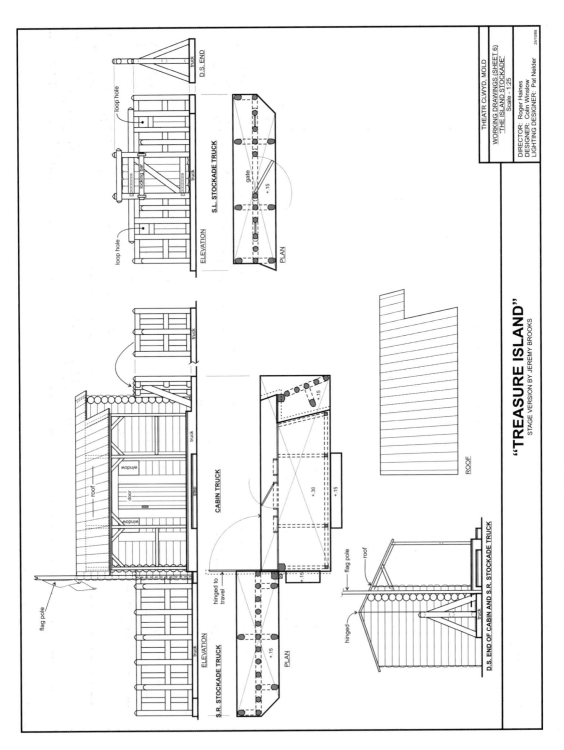

Working drawings (sheet 6) for Treasure Island.

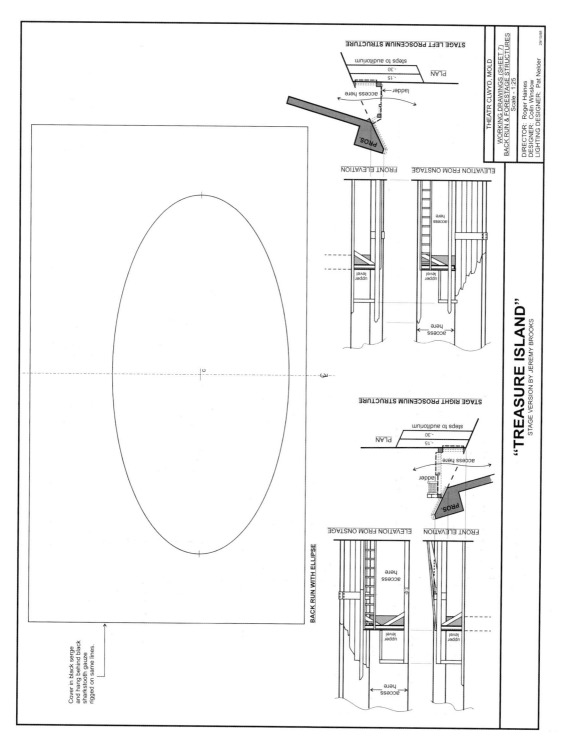

Working drawings (sheet 7) for Treasure Island.

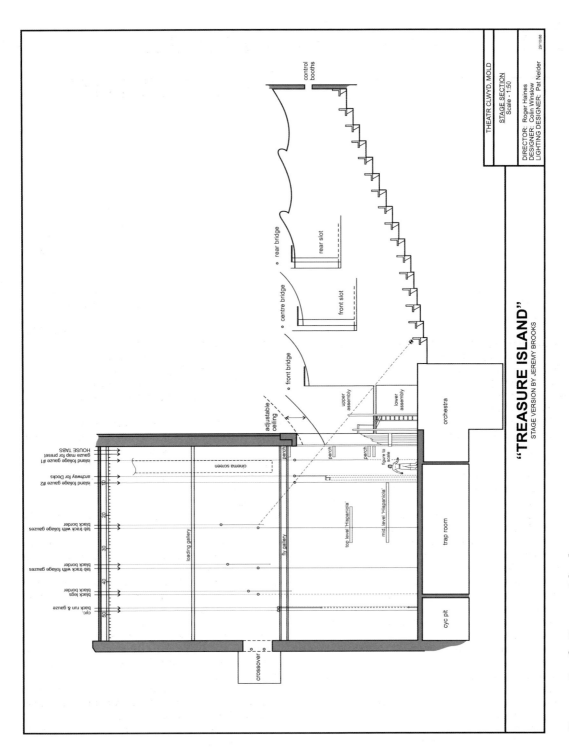

Stage section for Treasure Island.

GLOSSARY OF TECHNICAL THEATRE TERMS AND JARGON

[Note: words in *italics* refer to definitions elsewhere in the Glossary]

above situated *upstage* of another object or performer.

act drop painted *cloth* or curtain sometimes lowered instead of *house tabs* at the end of each act.

acting area that part of the stage on which any action or performance takes place.

apron extension of the stage floor projecting into the *auditorium*.

arena (theatre) stage entirely surrounded by the audience.

A.S.M. assistant stage manager.

auditorium that part of the theatre occupied by the audience during a performance.

Austrian drape *see* reefer curtain.

backcloth *see* cloth.

backdrop *see* cloth.

backing an appropriate scenic element placed behind an opening in a set (such as a window or a door) to hide *offstage* areas.

back projection screen *see* B.P. screen.

backstage areas of the theatre surrounding the stage and not generally open to the public containing dressing rooms and workshops, for example.

banjo (or **banjo track**) continuous double *tab track* with a loop at each end, so that a painted *cloth* or curtain may be drawn across the stage or reversed to show a second design on the back.

bar (or **barrel**) horizontal metal pipe, suspended from the *flies*, used for hanging scenery or lighting equipment.

Bauprobe (German) a trial build; a set may sometimes be assembled temporarily before completion to check its appearance or practicality.

below situated *downstage* of an object or performer.

black light *see* UV.

blacks plain black stage *drapes*, usually made from *velour* or *serge*.

black tat waste black fabric, useful to fasten behind scenery to hide gaps and *light leaks*.

blackwrap thin, matte, black, metal foil used to prevent light spills from *lanterns* or to trim the beam.

bleachers retractable, stepped, seating units.

bleed (through) 1 as through a *gauze*; gradually to reduce the lighting in front of a *sharkstooth gauze*, at the same time as increasing the light behind so that the gauze slowly becomes transparent, revealing whatever is set behind it.

bleed (through) 2 term applied to certain paint pigments that are difficult to cover completely with subsequent layers.

blind describes a piece of scenery on stage in a position where it is unseen by the audience.

board short for lighting or sound control board.

book (the) the specially prepared *prompt copy* of a script used by the *stage manager* running the show.

book backing free-standing *backing* consisting of a pair of *flats* hinged together like a book.

book ceiling scenic ceiling piece constructed as two hinged *flats* and *flown* vertically by the hinged edges so that it folds face to face and takes up less space in the *flies* when not in use.

book flat (or **booked flats**) two *flats* hinged together to open like a book.

book wings *see* wing flats.

boom vertical scaffolding pole to support *lanterns*, typically used for side lighting.

border horizontal top *masking* hung above the stage, usually made from fabric or painted cloth (*soft border*) but sometimes built as a solid unit (*hard border*).

box 1 a small, partitioned off, semi-private section of *auditorium* seating generally situated at the sides of an old-style auditorium.

box 2 short for *lighting box* or *sound box*.

box set a realistic room set, often complete with ceiling.

B.P. screen (or **B.P.S.**) back-projection screen made of special translucent material suitable for rear projection (*cf.* R.P. screen).

brace 1 adjustable support for *flats*; the top of the brace hooks into a screw eye on the back of the flat, and the foot is held in place with a *stage weight* or *stage screw*.

brace 2 a diagonal length of timber forming part of the framework of a *flat*.

brail to divert a *flown* piece by means of a length of rope or sash cord rigged to one of the *flying lines* or the end of the *bar* (*cf.* breast).

breakaway describes any *prop* or piece of scenery designed to fall apart or break on *cue*.

break down to make a *prop*, costume or scenic element appear old, worn or dirty.

breast to divert a *flown* piece by means of a separate line slung across the *flies* to deflect all the *flying lines* supporting the piece in the desired direction (*cf.* brail).

bridge 1 (**lighting bridge**) narrow platform bridging the stage or *auditorium* to provide access to lighting equipment.

bridge 2 (**paint bridge**) platform often installed in scenic workshops that may be raised or lowered to provide access for painting tall scenery.

bridge 3 a transverse section of the stage floor that may be raised or lowered mechanically.

bubble machine electrically-operated device to produce soap bubbles for decorative effect by passing a wheel of wire loops through a soap solution.

business (abbr. **biz**) sequence of moves or actions on stage centred upon a specific *prop* or props.

call 1 notification of a working session for performers or technicians (e.g., *rehearsal call*).

call 2 a request over the *backstage* speaker system for performers or technicians to come to the stage.

call 3 acknowledgement of applause (*curtain call*).

call 4 one of four warnings at timed intervals that a performance is about to begin (*see* half).

cans headset, usually with microphone attached, for communication between technicians during performances or rehearsals.

casual (or **cazzie**) part-time worker, especially one engaged to help with technical work during a *set up* or *get out* period or to help with scene changes during performances.

centre line imaginary line indicated on the *stage plan* and marked *CL*, bisecting the stage from front to back.

centre stage the most favourable position from which a performer may dominate the stage, not necessarily the geometrical centre.

chalk line *see* snap line.

chippy a carpenter.

circle (the) upper level of *auditorium* seating, where the most expensive seats are usually located.

cleat and line traditional method of fastening together adjacent pieces of scenery by lashing with sash cord passed over a series of hooks at the back.

cloth 1 (or **drop**) large, painted canvas hanging vertically as a decorative background.

cloth 2 a backcloth (or backdrop) large painted canvas completing the rear of a scene.

cloth 3 a *cut-cloth* painted canvas with areas cut out of it to reveal scenery set behind.

cloth 4 a *frontcloth* painted canvas hung near the front of the stage, backing a scene played in front of it.

Commedia dell'Arte form of popular theatre flourishing in Italy from the sixteenth to the eighteenth century.

contour tabs *see* reefer tabs.

counterweight(ed) (flying) system method of flying scenery in which the weight of a *flown* piece is balanced by heavy weights (counterweights) in a *cradle* for easier operation.

cracked oil (abbr. **cracker**) special unit to produce a fine mist effect by forcing air bubbles through a reservoir of highly refined mineral oil and fine filters; the resulting haze renders light beams visible, accentuating the decorative effect of *spotlights*; however, due to serious health concerns, these machines are not recommended for use in enclosed spaces, where a *hazer* will produce a similar and less hazardous effect.

cradle suspended metal housing carrying the weights in a *counterweighted flying system*.

crossfade to fade out a lighting *state* at the same time as another state is faded up on *cue*.

cue lights small lights, usually in pairs of red (for *stand by*) and green (for *go*), to give *cues* to actors or technicians.

cue 1 (for actors) line of dialogue that triggers a response, such as another line of dialogue or an action.

cue 2 (for technicians) any on-stage action or line of dialogue that signals some technical event, such as a change of lighting, sound effect or a scene change.

cue to cue (often written as **Q to Q**) technique of cutting dialogue during a *technical rehearsal* so that actors perform only those sections containing cues for technical effects.

curtain round burst of applause at the rise of the *house curtain*, usually intended to compliment the set designer.

curtain speech address to the audience at the end of a performance by an actor, usually the leading man or lady, speaking out of character.

curtain up start of a performance.

cut-cloth *see* cloth.

cyclorama (abbr. **cyc**) plain background to a set, often curved, capable of being lit to represent a sky.

dark describes a theatre at a period when no performance is taking place.

dayman member of the *stage crew* employed full time, as opposed to those working only during performances (*cf.* showman).

D.B.O. dead black out, sudden extinguishing of all lights during a performance.

dead 1 predetermined level for a *flown piece* or *lighting bar* (*see* in dead *and* out dead).

dead 2 any object associated with a production that is no longer in use.

dead line a single *line* from the *flying system* set at a fixed height and not required to move during the performance.

décor continental term for scenery, sometimes rather pretentiously used in Britain.

Dexion angled metal strips pre-drilled with holes for bolting together; useful for rapid construction of framework for *rostra*, seating units, etc.

D.F.R. durably flame retardant, applied to drapes or other fabrics used for scenery construction that will withstand a number of cleanings without losing their flame-retardant properties. (*cf.* N.D.F.R. *and* I.F.R.)

dimmer device to modulate the brightness of *lanterns*.

dimout double-woven fabric for stage curtains, coloured on the front and black at the back for greater opacity.

dips small trap doors in the stage floor providing access to electrical sockets beneath.

dock area used for storing scenery, on or adjacent to the stage.

double purchase *counterweighted flying system* in which the lines are passed over extra pulleys to provide *mechanical advantage*.

downstage towards the front of the stage (*see* below).

drapes stage curtains of any kind.

draw tabs stage curtains hanging on a *track* rigged to open and close.

drencher special sprinkler pipe to spray the back of the *safety curtain* with water in the event of fire (*see* sparge pipe).

dressing decorative items added to a stage *setting* to provide verisimilitude or suggest atmosphere, style or period.

dress rehearsal (abbr. **the dress**) *rehearsal* with full scenery, lighting and costumes as at a performance.

drift distance between a *flown* piece and the *bar* on which it is *flown*; a flown piece may not be attached to the bar direct, but hung from it by lengths of cable, to allow the bar to remain out of sight when the flown piece is lowered into position.

drift line the cable referred to above.

drop alternative term for a painted scenic *cloth* (*see* act drop).

dry ice frozen carbon dioxide used in a special device to produce a heavy, white, low-lying fog.

D.S.M. deputy stage manager.

Dutch border border rigged to run up and down stage beyond the ends of the across-stage borders, to complete top *masking*.

Dutchman (or **Dutching**) American equivalent of *stripping*.

Dutch metal inexpensive substitute for gold leaf.

Dutch pink dull, yellowish, natural pigment used in scene painting.

elevation technical drawing showing a front, side or back view drawn to scale.

end-stage stage with seating directly in front, but without a *proscenium arch*.

extras performers without speaking roles appearing solely to add numbers to crowd scenes, etc.

false proscenium (abbr. **false pros**) temporary *proscenium* set at some distance *upstage* of the actual *proscenium arch*.

filled gauze special closely woven *sharkstooth gauze* providing a good light-absorbent, crease-resistant surface, intended to be used for cycloramas.

flash box small metal box containing an electrically-detonated device to ignite *pyrotechnics* producing an explosive flash and/or a cloud of smoke on cue.

flat scenic element consisting of a rectangular timber frame, covered with canvas and/or plywood.

flies (or **flys**) area above the stage into which scenery can be hoisted.

floor cloth *see* stage cloth.

floor plan *see* stage plan.

floor pockets North American term for *dips*.

flown suspended on *lines* from the *grid*.

fly floor (or **fly gallery**) high working platform at the side of the stage for operating the *flying system*.

flying harness close-fitting structure of leather or woven straps with a device for attaching cables either at the back or on the hips; worn by an actor beneath his costume when required to be *flown*.

flying space amount of space available above the stage for use by the *flying system*.

flying system method of suspending scenery or lighting equipment on pulleys above the stage.

fly line (or **flying line**) a rope or cable used to suspend scenery from the *grid*.

flyman technician who operates the scenery suspension system.

flys *see* flies.

F.O.H. *see* front of house.

follow spot *spotlight* which may be moved by an operator during a performance, usually to 'follow' a performer.

footlights series of *lanterns* set in a row along the front edge of the stage floor.

forestage *see* apron.

fourth wall imaginary wall assumed to be between actors and audience, typically in a *box set*.

French brace wooden support in the form of a right-angled triangle, fixed to the back of a *flat*.

French flat (or **Frenchman**) large *flat* or series of flats battened together and *flown* as one piece, typically forming the rear wall of a set.

frontcloth *see* cloth.

front of house (abbr. **F.O.H.**) any areas open to the public apart from the *auditorium*.

fun factory popular slang for a theatre or other place of entertainment.

FX abbr. for (special) effects.

gaffer tape wide, heavy duty, canvas backed adhesive tape intended for fixing trailing cables to the floor, but with innumerable other uses (including, it is said, curing warts).

gallery highest level of *auditorium* seating, and usually the cheapest seats, in an old-style theatre.

gate leg (rostrum) collapsible *rostrum* with removable top and folding supporting framework.

gauze fine mesh *cloth* which, when lit from the front appears to be opaque or semi-opaque, but becomes transparent when scenery or performers are lit behind it (*see* sharkstooth and scenic gauze; *cf.* scrim).

gel special coloured medium placed in *lanterns* to colour the light.

Germans North American term for sets of *fly lines* running up and down stage beyond the limits of the usual across-stage sets usually carrying side masking or *Dutch borders*.

get in 1 process of installing scenery, *props*, costumes, etc. for a specific production into a theatre.

get in 2 the loading dock or whatever facilities are provided for unloading scenery, *props*, etc. from a lorry into the theatre.

get off *off-stage* steps, usually hidden from the audience, providing access to a *rostrum* or upper level of a *set*.

get out 1 removal from the theatre of all scenery, *props*, costumes, etc. connected with a production.

get out 2 minimum amount of money needed to be taken each week in ticket sales to cover production expenses.

gobo small plate of thin metal with a design cut into it which, when placed into the gate of a spotlight, projects the design onto the stage; typically used to create the effect of light striking through foliage or a window frame.

go up to start the show, as in, 'What time do we go up?'

grave trap *trap* near the centre of the stage, usually about 1m × 2m (3ft × 6ft 6in), often used to suggest a grave when required.

green room *backstage* area used by actors awaiting cues, or for relaxing between performances.

grid 1 abbr. for *gridiron*, strong steel or timber framework just below the stage roof, supporting and providing access to the *flying system* pulleys.

grid 2 (vb.) to raise a *flown* piece as high as the *flying system* will allow.

ground plan *see* stage plan.

groundrow 1 long, low piece of scenery, typically *profiled* and painted as distant hills, rooftops etc. (scenic groundrow).

groundrow 2 series of *lanterns* placed in a row on the stage floor to light the bottom part of *cloths* and/or scenic groundrows.

half (the) warning call given to actors in their dressing rooms, either personally or via the intercom system, at half an hour before they will be called to the stage to begin a performance, that is, 35min before the advertised starting time; subsequent calls are the *quarter* at 20min, *five minutes* at 10min and *beginners* at 5 min.

hard masking *masking* consisting of *flats*, as opposed to *drapes* (*cf.* soft masking).

hazer device to disperse a fine, non-toxic water-based, glycol mist into the air for decorative effect (*cf.* cracker).

header a *flat* either *flown* or supported by other flats, typically to form the top section of a wide archway or portal; a header does not touch the stage floor.

hemp house (or **rope house**) theatre with a rope and pulley *flying system*, as opposed to a *counterweight system*, using wire cables.

house used to refer either to the *auditorium* or the audience.

house curtain *see* house tabs.

houselights *auditorium* lighting.

house manager (or **front of house manager**) one responsible for organizing all those parts of the theatre to which the audience is admitted.

house seats small number of good seats set aside at each performance for use by members of the theatre's staff or special guests.

house tabs (or **house curtain**) semi-permanent curtains hanging just behind the *proscenium arch*, traditionally opened (or raised) at the start of a performance and closed (or lowered) at the end.

I.F.R. inherently flame retardant; applied to fabrics with a high percentage of fibres of a flame-retardant chemical make-up and thus more durably flameproof than *D.F.R.* (*see also* N.D.F.R.)

in-dead predetermined level for any *flown* item when lowered into its position on-stage.

inset (noun) small scene set within a larger one.

instrument North American term for a *lantern*.

iron fire-resistant safety curtain immediately behind the *proscenium arch*, and in front of the *house tabs* legally required to be lowered and raised in the presence of the audience at every performance.

isora *cyclorama* made from a translucent plastic material for lighting from behind.

I.W.B. internally-wired *barrel* to hang *lanterns* on.

Juliet balcony small opening or balcony at an upper level just *downstage* of the *proscenium arch*.

keystone effect an image projected on to a surface not directly in front of the projector will inevitably produce a trapezoidally-distorted image or 'keystone' shape; slides can be specially processed to compensate for this.

lamp tramp lighting technician

lantern (or **luminaire**, **lamp**) individual item of stage lighting equipment.

leaf border *see* tree border.

legs lengths of curtain fabric hanging vertically to mask the sides of the stage.

light curtain low-voltage, downward-pointing lighting units hung in a row above the stage to creating the effect of a curtain of visible light beams; developed by the Czech designer Josef Svoboda (1920–2002).

lighting bar *see* bar.

lighting box (or **booth**) lighting control room, usually situated at the rear of the *auditorium*, with a clear view of the stage.

lighting designer one responsible for designing the lighting scheme for a production.

lighting rig *see* rig.

lighting state predetermined arrangement of light levels.

light leak light seeping through a join between two *flats* or through thin canvas; usually rectified by stapling surplus black fabric to the back.

line 1 short piece of spoken dialogue.

line 2 cable or rope used on stage, typically as part of the *flying system*.

lining stick length of wooden lath, with a bevelled edge and a handle, used by scene painters for ruling straight lines with a paintbrush.

Linnebach cyc type of *cyclorama*, suspended from a curved *track* so that it can be drawn around the back of the stage to be stored in a vertical roll at one side; named after its inventor Adolf Linnebach.

Linnebach projector device used to project shadow images from a painted slide on to scenery (typically a *cyclorama*), developed by Linnebach in 1900.

loading gallery (or **loading floor**) high platform against a side wall of the stage, above the *fly floor*, for loading counterweights into the *cradle* (see counterweight system).

louvred ceiling scenic false ceiling made in long sections running across stage and hung so that the *downstage* edge of each section is higher than the *upstage* edge to permit lighting through the gaps.

luminaire European term for any kind of lighting instrument (*see also* lantern *and* instrument).

Marie Tempest improvised device made from a cord and a weight rigged to the top of a stage door to ensure that it will remain either open or closed as desired.

mark small piece of coloured adhesive tape or paint on the stage floor to indicate the correct position of a piece of scenery, furniture, etc.

maroon electrically-detonated, explosive device to produce an *off-stage* explosion; designed to be used in a special bomb tank with appropriate safety precautions.

mask to hide *off-stage* areas, *lanterns*, etc. from view of the audience.

masking 1 scenic elements that primarily perform the function of hiding *off-stage* areas, *lanterns*, etc. from view of the audience.

masking 2 an actor blocking the audience's view of another actor.

Matcham, Frank (1854–1920) the great Victorian theatre architect; he created over 200 theatres and *music halls* throughout Britain, some of which are still in use.

M.D. musical director.

mirror ball revolving sphere covered with small pieces of mirror; when *spotlights* are directed at it, a decorative effect of small, swiftly moving dots of light is created.

mirror scrim flexible plastic mirror, similar to *shrink mirror*, but may be used for transparency effects in the same manner as *sharkstooth gauze*.

model box 1 simplified scale model of a theatre stage containing the designer's *set model* to place it in its architectural context.

model box 2 proprietary computer-aided design system used to visualize stage *settings* three-dimensionally in different venues.

monkey stick length of thin dowel attached near the top of a *cleat line* to enable it to be looped over a high cleat hook with comparative ease.

multiple set stage set containing several different locations all visible at the same time.

NATTKE National Association of Theatrical, Television and Kine Employees; trade union for theatre technicians.

naturalism performance presented as realistically as possible, with little apparent artifice (*cf.* realism).

N.D.F.R. non-durably flame-retardant; applied to materials used on stage treated with water-soluble, flame-proofing solution, requiring eventual retreatment (*cf. D.F.R. and I.F.R.*).

NODA The National Operatic and Dramatic Association; largest theatrical institution in Britain, with a membership of over 2,300 companies; provides a network of services for amateur theatre and operatic societies.

noise boys sound technicians.

off-stage any position out of view of the audience.

OISTAT Organisation Internationale de Scénographes, Techniciens et Architectes de Théâtre (International Organization of Scenographers, Theatre Technicians and Architects), international body of theatre professionals.

on-stage any position within the *acting area*.

on the book *see* book.

O.P. opposite prompt; stage right from an actor's viewpoint when facing the audience (*cf.* P.S.).

open dress (rehearsal) *dress rehearsal* taking place before an invited audience.

orchestra pit sunken area immediately in front of the stage for musicians, often partly recessed beneath the stage.

orchestra stalls *auditorium* seating at the front of the *stalls*.

out-dead predetermined level for a *flown* piece when raised to its 'rest' position.

pack pile of *flats* stacked in the *wings* or *scene dock* ready for use.

paint bridge platform running the width of the *paint frame*, usually designed to be raised or lowered by a hand or electric winch so that painters may reach all parts of scenery attached to the frame.

paint frame large, vertical framework to which scenery is nailed for painting, sometimes raised or lowered through a long slot in the floor so that painters may reach all parts of scenery attached to it.

PAL precision automated lights; remotely controlled *lanterns* with programmable movement, colour change and shape of beam.

pantomime (abbr. **panto**) somewhat bizarre traditional British Christmas entertainment, loosely based upon a well-known fairy tale.

paper to provide free seats to increase the size of the audience, as in 'to paper the *house*'.

paper rope smooth, decorative type of rope made from crushed paper and available in a wide range of thicknesses; not suitable for use as conventional rope.

parcan *lantern* holding a *par lamp*.

par lamp lamp containing its own optical system, producing a virtually parallel beam.

pass door door providing access between the *auditorium* and the stage.

peasouper *dry ice machine*.

penny plain, twopence coloured small printed sheets of scenery and characters intended to be cut out and used in toy theatres, popular in the nineteenth century; reprints are still sold today (*see* Pollock's).

Pepper's ghost rather cumbersome Victorian stage trick whereby a hidden performer is reflected in a large sheet of glass set at an angle across the stage and thus appears to be transparent and ghost-like.

perch 1 position for hanging *lanterns*, situated above head height at the sides of the stage.

perch 2 vertical opening in a side wall of the *auditorium* in which *lanterns* may be positioned.

periaktoi three *flats* set in the form of vertical prisms on revolving bases, so that they may be revolved to display any side.

photo call session arranged to take publicity photographs of a production.

pillar brakes/stops foot-operated brakes commonly used on scenic *trucks*.

pin hinge flap hinge with a removable pin so that the two halves may be separated; useful for providing a temporary connection between pieces of scenery.

pipe North American term for a *bar* in the *flying system*.

pit 1 abbr. for *orchestra pit*.

pit 2 area of *auditorium* seating in the centre of the lowest level.

playbill theatre poster.

pocket open-ended hem at the bottom of a *cloth, gauze* or *cyclorama* through which a length of chain or steel conduit pipe is inserted to weight the cloth and prevent distortion; a deeper pocket may accommodate a wooden batten.

Pollock's shop, now in Covent Garden, London selling reprints of Victorian toy theatre sheets (*see* penny plain, twopence coloured).

portal unit of semi-permanent *masking* consisting of built *wings* and *header* fastened together.

preset 1 special *lighting state* necessary where *house tabs* are not used, to light a stage *setting* in an appropriate manner before the performance begins.

preset 2 to place *props* or scenic items in precise positions before a performance.

priming preparatory coat of paint when painting scenery.

producer one who mounts a production, selects actors, designers and leading technicians and raises financial backing.

producing house theatre that mounts its own shows.

production desk temporary desk with adjustable lights, lighting control monitors and headsets, placed in the centre of the *auditorium* to be used by the *director, lighting designer*, etc. during technical and *dress rehearsals*.

production manager (abbr. **p.m.**) one with overall responsibility for the technical organization and budget control of a production.

profile or **profiling** plywood extension to the edge of a *flat*, cut to a decorative shape as required by the design.

profile tabs (or **contour tabs**) stage curtains raised by vertical lines in the manner of a *reefer curtain* but to varying levels, to create a decorative framing effect.

profit share production in which participants work unpaid in return for a share of any profits; the actual profits are usually little or nil.

promenade performance performance with no audience seating; the audience moves from one location to another, following the action.

prompt 1 to suggest the next *line* to an actor suffering a memory lapse.

prompt 2 the *prompt side* of the stage.

prompt book (or **prompt copy**) master copy of the script containing all actors' moves and technical *cues*, prepared and used by a *stage manager* when controlling the performance (*see* book).

prompt corner *stage manager's* control point at the side of the stage, traditionally *stage left*, not necessarily used by a *prompter*.

prompt desk special unit, containing a dimmable light, a shelf for the *prompt copy*, a small *switchboard* for operating *cue lights* and various other communication systems used by the *stage manager* to control the show.

prompter one who follows a performance from a script and assists actors suffering memory lapses.

prompt side *see* P.S.

props (abbr. for **properties**) furniture and other objects used by actors *on-stage* during a performance.

prop table *off-stage* table on which *hand props* are *set* in precise positions to be used by actors in performance.

proscenium (abbr. **pros**) dividing wall between the stage and the *auditorium*, containing the *proscenium arch*.

proscenium arch architectural frame surrounding the opening in the *proscenium* wall, whether it is actually 'arched' or not.

proscenium doors doors in the *proscenium* used by performers entering on to a *forestage*; common in eighteenth-century theatres.

P.S. prompt side; *stage left*, from an actor's point viewpoint when facing the audience (*cf.* O.P.).

push and pull special payments made to actors required to move scenery or furniture instead of a stage hand during a performance.

pyrotechnics (abbr. **pyros**) special effects involving fireworks, such as explosions, flashes or smoke.

Q abbr. for *cue*.

Q to Q *see* cue to cue.

quarter (the) *see* half.

quick change room small, usually makeshift, 'room' at the side of the stage, used by actors for quick costume changes when there is no time to return to the dressing room.

rag *see* house tabs.

rake slight upward slope of the stage floor from front to back, often found in older theatres.

ramp *rostrum* with a sloping top (*see also* rake).

rat stands lightweight metal music stands for orchestral use, especially those made by R.A.T. Manufacturing Ltd.

razzle dazzle glitter, energy and style calculated to impress the audience and disguise a possible lack of genuine talent.

read through first *rehearsal*, at which the play is read aloud by the cast with the *director*, and when designer(s) usually present their work.

realism style of staging using theatrical devices to produce the effect of reality (*cf.* naturalism).

rear projection screen *see* R.P. screen.

receiving house theatre functioning as a venue for touring shows rather than mounting its own productions.

reefer curtain (or **Austrian drape**) stage curtain rigged with vertical cables running through rows of curtain rings set at regular intervals along the back, enabling it to be raised in a series of decorative 'scoops' or swags.

rehearsal any practice session for actors and/or technicians.

rehearsal props substitute *props* for use in *rehearsal*.

rep *see* repertory.

repertoire production system in which two or more productions are rotated in the course of a season.

repertory (abbr. **rep**) production system usually employing a permanent group of actors mounting a sequence of plays, each one for a limited *run*.

resin box tray of resin placed in the *wings* for dancers to apply to their shoes for added grip.

return narrow *flat* fixed at a right-angle to a wider one, appearing to be part of the same structure.

reveal narrow *flat* or piece of timber fixed at an angle behind the edges of an opening in a *set*, such as a doorway or a window, to give an illusion of thickness and solidity to the surrounding wall.

revolve (or **revolving stage**) circular platform, that may be revolved by means of a winch, operated either electrically or manually.

rig 1 to hang lights and scenery in preparation for a performance.

rig 2 specific physical arrangement of lights for a performance.

rig 3 to prepare a *prop* or piece of scenery in some special way for a particular effect.

ripple effect special lighting effect that projects watery-looking ripples by rotating *gobos* or a *tubular ripple* effect.

riser vertical part of a step.

roller cloth *cloth* fixed to a long roller in such a way that it can be raised by wrapping itself around the roller, rather like a roller-blind.

ropelight small light bulbs set inside flexible, translucent PVC tubing used for decorative effect.

rostra plural of *rostrum*, although 'rostrums' is more frequently heard.

rostrum platform of any shape providing a raised section of stage floor.

royalty percentage of profits or an agreed sum of money paid to a writer, *director*, composer or designer in return for the right to perform, reproduce or reuse his work.

R.P. screen rear projection screen, term for *back projection screen* more commonly encountered in North America than in Britain.

run 1 series of performances of the same production.

run 2 several *flats* set in a straight line.

run 3 (vb.) to rehearse whole or part of a show without stopping.

run 4 (as in 'to run a flat') to hold a *flat* upright, with both hands at one edge, and move it smoothly across the stage.

runners 1 pair of *tabs* rigged to open by parting horizontally from the centre.

runners 2 strips of carpet fixed to the stage floor in the *wings* to deaden the footsteps of *stage crew* and actors moving around *off-stage*.

safety chain short length of chain with a spring hook at each end; must be used as a safety device wherever *lanterns* are hung overhead.

safety curtain not a curtain as such, but a large, fireproof shutter, usually metal, immediately behind the *proscenium arch*, lowered in the event of fire to seal off the stage area completely from the auditorium.

Samoiloff effect trick lighting technique developed by Adrian Samoiloff in 1922 for special scenic effects, based on the principle that a green object appears black under red light and vice versa.

sandbag sturdy canvas bag of sand, with a metal ring at the top, used to weight unused *flying lines* and prevent them from running back over the pulleys in the *grid*.

sandwich batten double wooden batten supporting or weighting a *cloth* at top and/or bottom; the fabric is trapped between the two battens.

S.B.T.D. Society of British Theatre Designers, professional organization for set, costume, lighting and sound designers.

scatter accidental spread of light outside the main beam.

scene dock storage area for scenery adjacent to the stage.

scene shifter one who assists with scene changes during a performance.

scenic gauze fine net of small hexagonal mesh used for special atmospheric effects (*see* gauze *and cf.* sharkstooth gauze).

scenographer academic term for a scenery designer.

Scottish play (the) Shakespeare's *Macbeth*, euphemism used to avoid bad luck supposedly brought about by quoting it or mentioning it by name.

scrim 1 a loosely woven fabric.

scrim 2 to cover *props* or scenery with glued scrim or other suitable fabric, for protection and to provide a surface suitable for painting.

scrim 3 (American) *gauze*.

scumble scene painting technique of applying painted texture using short strokes in all directions with a nearly dry brush.

section (or **cross section**) accurate scale drawing showing a structure as if sliced through in order to demonstrate construction.

serge (black) thick wool fabric with a black, non-reflective surface, used for *masking*.

set 1 (or **setting**) scenery for whole or part of a production.

set 2 to place *props* or scenery in pre-established positions.

set 3 (**set of flying lines**) group of lines, usually three but sometimes five or seven on very wide stages, spaced horizontally across the stage and operated together to fly a single item.

set model accurate, coloured scale model of a stage *setting* produced by the designer to demonstrate his design scheme.

set round burst of applause in appreciation of the stage *setting*, occurring usually at *curtain up*.

setting line line on the stage floor, either physical or imaginary, parallel to the front edge of the stage, from which measurements are taken when *setting up* scenery.

set up 1 *see* fit up.

set up 2 to prepare *props*, etc. for a performance.

SFX abbr. for special effects.

sharkstooth (gauze) special fabric of fine rectangular mesh, suitable to be painted for special transparency effects obtained by changing light levels, revealing a scene or objects set behind.

shimmer curtain stage curtain made of, or containing, materials designed to glitter under stage lighting.

shin blaster/buster *lantern* set close to the floor at the sides of the stage, mainly used in dance shows and ballet.

shot bag similar to a *sand bag* but smaller and filled with lead shot; often sewn into the hem of stage curtains to improve the hang.

show floor special vinyl flooring, available in several colours, providing a good surface for dance shows; designed to lie flat without being fixed.

showman member of the *stage crew* employed to work during performances only (*cf.* dayman).

show report written record made by the *company manager* after each performance, containing details of running times, audience reaction and comments on any mistakes or unusual events; usually circulated only to the *producer*, *director* and *theatre manager*.

shrink mirror thin, flexible, reflective plastic material which may be stretched over a frame, then shrunk to remove wrinkles by applying heat to produce a convincing but lightweight mirror.

shutters adjustable pieces of metal in a *spotlight* for trimming or changing the shape of the light beam.

side elevation *see* elevation.

sightline imaginary line, drawn on *stage plans* to indicate the limit of vision from a specific point in the *auditorium*.

sill iron strip of flat metal fastened across the bottom of an opening in a piece of scenery, such as a doorway, to sit flat to the floor and provide support across the width of the opening.

Sitzprobe (German) first rehearsal with full orchestra in opera, the singers usually seated.

size animal glue available in granular form to be dissolved in hot water before use; traditional ingredient used for fixing scene paint when using powder colours.

skip large, heavy duty, travelling hamper for *props* or costumes.

sky border *border* painted to look like open sky.

sky cloth *backcloth* painted and lit to look like open sky.

S.L. written abbreviation for *sightline* used on *stage plans*, etc.

slapstick 1 very broad, knockabout farce, often involving messy routines with materials such as water, flour and custard pies (*see* slosh).

slapstick 2 pair of thin wooden laths lashed together at the end by which they are held, producing the noise of a loud slap when struck against an object, traditionally carried by the *Commedia dell'Arte* character Harlequin.

slash stage curtain made of long thin strips of reflective, plastic material hanging loose, so that performers may pass through it at any point (*see* shimmer curtain).

slave truck *truck* used to carry another truck or other wheeled object on to the stage to a *rostrum* of the same height, so that the truck it is carrying may run off it directly on to the rostrum without having to be man-handled over the step.

slips seats at the extreme ends of the upper tiers in a traditional horseshoe-shaped *auditorium*, usually with a severely restricted view of the stage.

sloat (or **slote**) long, horizontal *trap* cut in the stage floor though which pieces of scenery or performers can be raised from below; in use during the nineteenth century but now generally obsolete.

slosh any harmless, easily removed substitute for paste, cake-mix, etc. used in *slapstick* scenes.

slosh cloth large piece of *stage cloth* laid to protect the stage floor during *slapstick* scenes.

slot horizontal opening in the *auditorium* ceiling in which *lanterns* may be hung.

S.M. stage manager.

smoke gun (or **smoke machine**) device for producing artificial smoke or mist (*cf.* dry ice/cracked oil/hazer).

smoke pellet small pellet that smoulders when ignited, producing quantities of smoke.

smoke powder ignited in a *flash box* to produce smoke; slow-burning versions are available for prolonged effects.

snap line (or **chalk line**) chalked length of thin cord stretched between two points and 'twanged' to mark a long straight line; available in a special container to coat it with chalk powder as it is drawn out.

snow bag slashed canvas bag rigged from the *flies* for sprinkling imitation snow.

soffit narrow *flat* or length of timber attached to the underside of a *hard border* or *header*.

soft masking large *drapes* used as *stage masking*.

somersault harness *flying harness* with two cables attached at the performer's hips instead of one line attached at the centre of the back.

song sheet 1 banner, usually flown, painted with the words of a song for community singing.

song sheet 2 traditional scene in a *pantomime*, in which the audience is encouraged to join in competitive community singing.

sound box sound control room, usually situated at the rear of the *auditorium*.

sparge pipe the *safety curtain*'s drencher pipe for emergency use (*see* sprinkler).

sparks *electrics* department or a electrical technician.

spatter scene painting technique of flicking paint from a brush to achieve a fine, speckled texture.

special *lantern* positioned for a specific effect only.

spirit gum special adhesive for sticking hairpieces, etc. to the face.

spot bar *bar* above the stage or *auditorium* on which *lanterns* are hung.

spotlight *lantern* with a focusable beam.

spot line single *line* specially rigged from the *grid*, used for hanging on-stage chandeliers, etc. or for special effects.

sprinkler device to drench the *safety curtain* with water in the event of an emergency.

stage box one of the *auditorium* boxes nearest to the stage.

stage brace adjustable support for scenery, designed to be hooked to the back and held in place with a *stage weight* or *stage screw*.

stage cloth canvas floor covering, usually painted as part of the scenery.

stage crew team of *stagehands* working a show.

stage director one in overall charge of stage staff and any activity taking place on the stage.

stagehand member of the *stage crew*.

stagehouse part of the theatre building containing the stage and *flies*.

stage left left-hand side of the stage from the actor's point of view.

stage manager (abbr. **S.M.**) one assisting in organizing and running rehearsals and/or performances on-stage.

stage plan (or **ground plan** or **floor plan**) scale plan of the stage showing positions of scenery and furniture.

stage screw fixing for the foot of a *stage brace* designed to be screwed into the stage floor by hand.

stage weight heavy, cast-iron weight designed to hold the foot of a *stage brace* in place.

stagger through an early attempt to *run* a show in rehearsal.

stalls main *auditorium* seating at the lowest level.

star trap small hexagonal or octagonal trapdoor containing six or eight triangular flaps hinged around the perimeter to permit a performer to be propelled upwards through the stage floor by means of special lifting machinery below; typically used for entrances of demons in Victorian *pantomime* but now generally obsolete.

state predetermined arrangement of light or sound levels.

straight play play without songs or music.

strike 1 to remove a *setting* or a *prop* from the stage.

strike 2 to dismantle and remove an entire production from the theatre at the end of a *run*.

stripping disguising a join in scenery by gluing a strip of muslin or thin canvas over it and painting to match surrounding paintwork.

studio theatre informal performing space used for small-scale or experimental works.

sugar glass imitation glass made from hardened sugar solution, used to make window panes, bottles, etc. to be broken harmlessly during a performance.

surprise pink lighting *gel* of a mauve/pink colour, popular for its glamorous and generally flattering effect.

swag curtain rigged to be opened by raising it in a curved drape to either side.

swivel arm metal arm pivoted at its centre beneath a *tab track* or *bar* so that *soft masking* tied to it may be set at any angle desired.

S.W.R. steel wire rope.

tab line imaginary line, usually marked on a *stage plan*, indicating where *tabs* fall when lowered to the stage.

tabs pair of stage curtains, rigged either to part horizontally from the centre, or to be *flown* (*see* house tabs).

tab track heavy duty curtain track on which *tabs* are hung so that they may be opened or closed horizontally.

tab warmers lights set specially to enhance the *house tabs* before the start of a performance or during an intermission.

teaser 1 black *border* used for top *masking*.

teaser 2 (American) framed *border* used for top *masking*.

technical director one with overall responsibility for technical aspects of the stage.

technical rehearsal (abbr. **tech**) rehearsal intended primarily for technical aspects of a production, rather than the actors' performances.

theatre-in-the-round performance in which the *acting area* is completely surrounded by the audience.

three-fold three *flats* hinged together, often used to form a self supporting and free-standing *backing*.

throw distance from a *lantern* to the object lit.

throw a line to throw a thin rope over a hook at the top of a *flat* for lashing together in a *cleat and line* system.

thrust stage stage jutting forwards into the audience with seats on three sides.

thunder sheet large hanging sheet of metal, which, when shaken by one corner, produces the sound of a clap of thunder.

T.I.E. Theatre in Education, theatre company performing specifically to school children.

top and tail method of speeding up a *technical rehearsal* by omitting any lengthy dialogue passages that contain no technical events (*see* cue to cue).

top hat black metal cylinder to fit in front of a *lantern* to reduce *scatter*.

tormentor plain black *masking flat* set at either side of the stage, immediately *upstage* of the *proscenium*.

track 1 stage curtain track

track 2 any kind of rail or guiding system used on-stage.

transformation scene popular effect in *pantomime* in which a scene 'magically' changes to another in view of the audience.

transparency *cloth* or part of a cloth painted in dyes or thin paint and lit from behind for special effect.

trap removable section of the stage floor.

trap room area underneath the stage accessed by *traps*.

traveller (or **traverse curtain** or **wipe**) stage curtain, which may be drawn across the stage from one side to the other instead of opening in the centre.

traverse curtain *see* traveller.

traverse stage long *acting area* with audience seated at either side.

treads 1 steps.

treads 2 flat, horizontal parts of a flight of steps.

tree border (or **leaf border**) canvas *border* to painted to suggest overhead foliage.

trim precise adjustment of a *flown* piece so that it hangs straight and parallel to the stage floor.

tripe electric cable connecting *lanterns* on *bars* to outlets at the side of the stage.

truck platform on castors carrying all or part of a *set*.

truss sturdy metal framework across the *acting area* or *auditorium* to support *lanterns*, etc.

tubular ripple lighting device projecting the effect of horizontal water ripples by passing light through a revolving cylinder with irregular wavy slits cut into the sides of the cylinder.

tumble to *fly* a *cloth* on two *sets* of *lines* by attaching a second set to the bottom of the *cloth*, thus causing it to fold in half when *flown*; useful on stages with limited height.

upstage area of the stage furthest from the audience.

UV (or **black light**) ultra violet radiation, normally invisible but causing special pigments to fluoresce in a black-out.

vandyke crystals strong brown stain in the form of water-soluble crystals, useful for *breaking down*, graining, etc.

velour heavy, short-piled fabric that hangs well and looks luxurious when lit, commonly used for stage curtains.

vision gauze gauze used for a special effect such as a magical 'vision' or *transformation scene*.

vomitory (abbr. **vom**) access to the *acting area* from the *auditorium*, usually by means of a passage beneath the seating, particularly in *theatre-in-the-round* and *thrust stages*.

walk to move about the stage under the direction of the *lighting designer* so that light designed to hit the actors can be checked in various positions.

walk down final scene of a *pantomime* or musical revue in which the whole cast enters to acknowledge applause, usually descending a decorative flight of steps.

walk up (as in '**to walk up a flat**') to raise a *flat* from the floor by wedging the bottom of it against a wall or someone's foot, then lifting it to a vertical position by moving hand over hand along the underside.

wardrobe master/mistress/supervisor one in overall charge of the costume department.

ways electrical channels in a stage lighting control system.

wind machine wooden drum with slats around the sides and a handle to revolve it against a strip of taut canvas, in imitation of the sound of whistling wind.

wing flats vertical scenic elements at the sides of the stage, decorative and/or to provide side *masking* (see book wings).

wings 1 areas at the sides of the stage beyond the *acting area*.

wings 2 vertical pieces of scenery or fabric (*legs*) used as decorative elements or to provide side *masking*.

wipe (track) single *tab track* usually crossing the full width of the stage, so that a *cloth* or *drapes* may be drawn right across the stage from one side to the other (see traveller).

workers (abbr. for **working lights**) lights used to illuminate the stage for *rehearsals* or technical work.

working drawings scale drawings of scenery or *props* for construction.

wrangler one responsible for supervising animals (or sometimes, by extension, children) appearing on stage.

wrap-around cyc(lorama) *cyclorama* that extends down each side of the stage as well as along the back, thus virtually enclosing the *acting area* on three sides.

XF written abbreviation for *crossfade*.

yo-yo (effect) device to move a *gobo* up and down, often over another static gobo, to provide a moving projection.

BIBLIOGRAPHY

Bablet, D., *The Theatre of Edward Gordon Craig* (Eyre Methuen, 1966)

Bay, H., *Stage Design* (Drama Book Specialists, 1974)

Bibiena, G.G., *Architectural and Perspective Designs* (Dover Publications, 1964)

Brook, P., *The Empty Space* (McGibbon & Kee, 1968)

Carter, P., *Backstage Handbook, an Illustrated Almanac of Technical Information* (Broadway Press, 1994)

Castle, D., *Sensation Smith of Drury Lane, the Biography of a Scenic Artist Extraordinary, Engineer, and Inventor of Stage 'Disasters'* (Charles Skilton, 1984)

Castro, E., *HTML for the World Wide Web: A Visual Quickstart Guide* (Peachpit Press, 2003)

Ching, F.D.K., *Architectural Graphics* (Van Nostrand Reinhold, 1975)

Ching, F.D.K., *Design Drawing* (John Wiley, 1998)

Craig, E.G., *Scene* (Oxford University Press, 1923)

Gascoigne B., *World Theatre* (Ebury Press, 1968)

Gillette, A.S., *Stage Scenery, Its Construction and Rigging* (Harper & Row, 1972)

Hewitt, B., *The Renaissance Stage – Documents of Serlio, Sabbattini and Furttenbach* (University of Miami Press, 1958)

Jones, R.E., *The Dramatic Imagination* (Theatre Arts Books, 1992)

Juracek, J.A., *Surfaces – Visual Research for Artists, Architects and Designers* (W.W. Norton, 1996)

May, R., *History of the Theater* (Chartwell Books, 1986)

McKinven, J.A., *Stage Flying, from 431BC to Modern Times* (Meyerbooks, 2000)

Meyer, F.S., *Handbook of Ornament* (Dover Publications, 2002)

Parker, W.O. and R.C. Wolf, *Scene Design and Stage Lighting* (Holt, Rinehart & Winston, 1996)

Payne, D.R., *Scenographic Imagination* (Southern Illinois University Press, 1993)

Payne, D.R., *Theory and Craft of the Scenographic Model* (Southern Illinois University Press, 1985)

Pecktal, L., *Designing and Drawing for the Theater* (McGraw-Hill, 1994)

Pritchard, R.E., *Shakespeare's England* (Sutton Publishing, 2000)

Reid, F., *Designing for the Theatre* (A. & C. Black, 1996)

Rosenfeld, S., *Georgian Scene Painters and Scene Painting* (Cambridge University Press, 1981)

Rosenfeld, S., *A Short History of Scene Design in Great Britain* (Blackwell, 1973)

Ruthven Hall, P. and Burnett, K., *Make Space, design for theatre and alternative spaces* (SBTD, 1994)

Ruthven Hall, P. and Burnett, K., *Time + Space, design for performance 1995–1999* (SBTD, 1999)

Ruthven Hall, P. and Burnett, K., *2D > 3D, design for theatre and performance* (SBTD, 2002)

Sabbatini N., *Pratique pour Fabriquer Scènes et Machines de Théâtre* (Editions Ides & Calendes, 1942)

Simonson, L., *The Stage Is Set* (Theatre Arts Books, 1963)

Speltz, A., *The Styles of Ornament* (Dover Publications, 2002)

Sykes, T.S., *AutoCAD 2000 – One Step at a Time (Basic)* (Prentice-Hall, 2000)

Sykes, T.S., *AutoCAD 2000 – One Step at a Time (Advanced)* (Prentice-Hall, 2000)

Walne, G., *Effects for the Theatre* (A. & C. Black, 1995)

Warre, M., *Designing and Making Stage Scenery* (Studio Vista, 1996)

Wickham, G., *A History of the Theatre* (Cambridge University Press, 1992)

Winslow, C., *The Oberon Glossary of Theatrical Terms* (Oberon Books, 1991)

Wood, M., *Shakespeare* (BBC Worldwide, 2003)

WEB SITES

www.cad4theatre.org.uk: CAD for Theatre (offers low-cost, distance-learning courses in AutoCAD for theatre, and contains the ABTT CAD Standards Document)

www.theatredesign.org.uk: The Society of British Theatre Designers (SBTD) (contains many photographs of members' work and up-to-date details of training courses)

www.uvfx.com: UV/FX Scenic Productions in California specializes in producing backdrops and murals incorporating ingenious UV effects; their web site shows some spectacular examples of their work

www.winslow.uk.com: the author's personal web site

INDEX

INDEX